International Multi-Unit Leadership

To my brothers Andrew and Robert

With thanks to Adam Fowle, Tim Clarke and Iain Napier

International Multi-Unit Leadership

Developing Local Leaders in
International Multi-Site Operations

CHRIS EDGER
Birmingham City University, UK

Routledge
Taylor & Francis Group

LONDON AND NEW YORK

First published in paperback 2024

First published 2013 by Gower Publishing

Published 2016 by Routledge
4 Park Square, Milton Park, Abingdon, Oxon OX14 4RN

and by Routledge
605 Third Avenue, New York, NY 10158

Routledge is an imprint of the Taylor & Francis Group, an informa business

Gower Applied Business Research
Our programme provides leaders, practitioners, scholars and researchers with thought
provoking, cutting edge books that combine conceptual insights, interdisciplinary rigour and
practical relevance in key areas of business and management.

British Library Cataloguing in Publication Data
A catalogue record for this book is available from the British Library.

The Library of Congress has cataloged the printed edition as follows:
Edger, Chris.
  International multi-unit leadership : developing local leaders in international multi-site
  operations / by Chris Edger.
    pages cm
  Includes bibliographical references and index.
  ISBN 978-1-4094-6070-1 (hardback: alk. paper)—ISBN 978-1-4094-6071-8 (ebook) —ISBN
  978-1-4094-6072-5 (epub) 1. Leadership. 2. International business enterprises. I. Title.

  HD57.7.E323 2013
  658.4'092—dc23
                                                                              2013018268

  ISBN: 978-1-4094-6070-1 (hbk)
  ISBN: 978-1-03-283745-1 (pbk)
  ISBN: 978-1-315-58947-3 (ebk)

  DOI: 10.4324/9781315589473

Contents

List of Figures

List of Abbreviations

3Cs	Commitment, control and change
3Es	Energy, expertise and EI
3Ss	Systems, standards and sales-led service
B2C	Business to consumer
BHI	Batrus Hollweg International
BOH	Back of house
CEO	Chief executive officer
CLT	Cultural leadership theory
CME	Co-ordinated market economy
COO	Country of origin
CSR	Corporate social responsibility
CV	Curriculum vitae
EBITDA	Earnings before interest, tax and depreciation
EEI	Environmental emotional intelligence
EFQM	European framework for quality management
EHCN	Ex-host country national manager
EI	Emotional intelligence
EPOS	Electronic point of sale
EQ	Emotional quotient
ERP	Enterprise resource planning
FDI	Foreign direct investment
FOH	Front of house
GDP	Gross domestic product
GLOBE	Global leadership and organisational effectiveness
GM	General manager
GSAM	Goldman Sachs asset management
HCN	Host-country national (manager)
HMUL	Host country multi-unit leader
HR	Human resources
HRD	Human resources director
HRM	Human resources management
IQ	Intelligence quotient
IT	Information technology
IHRM	International human resource management
IMPM	International market portfolio management
IMUE	International multi-unit enterprise
ISOM	International services operations management
JV	Joint venture
KPI	Key performance indicators

L&D	Learning and development
LFX	Leader-follower exchange
LME	Liberal market economy
LMX	Leader-member exchange
M&A	Merger and acquisition
MBA	Master of business administration
MCS	Management control systems
MNC	Multi-national corporation
MQ	Moral quotient
MUE	Multi-unit enterprise
MUL	Multi-unit leader
MUM	Multi-unit manager
NBS	National business system
NED	Non-executive director
NPS	Net promoter score
OPE	Operational planning executive
P&L	Profit and loss
PhD	Doctor of philosophy
POSE	Portfolio optimisation through social exchange
PRP	Performance-related pay
PRT	Power resource theory
REVPAR	Revenue per average room
ROCE	Return on capital investment
ROI	Return on investment
RPM	Retail portfolio management
SBU	Strategic business unit
SECI	Socialisation, externalisation, combination, internalisation
SHRM	Strategic human resources management
SME	Small and medium enterprises
SOP	Standard operating procedure
SVP	Senior vice president
T&D	Training and development
TCN	Third country national manager
TQM	Total quality management
VP	Vice president
WVS	World values survey

About the Author

Chris Edger is the author of *Effective Multi-Unit Leadership – Local Leadership in Multi-Site Situations* and holds the chair of Multi-Unit Leadership at Birmingham City Business School (BCBS), Birmingham City University, UK. He also teaches at the University of Birmingham and the Warwick Business School, UK, where he is the winner of several teaching excellence awards on the Warwick MBA Programme.

Chris has over 20 years of senior leisure and retail multi-unit operations, sales and support expertise working for domestic and internationally-owned multi-site companies. During his career he has held Area Management and Regional Operations Director (400+ units) positions. In addition he has held Executive Board positions as Group HRD, Commercial Director and Sales Managing Director in organisations with multi-site interests in China, Eastern Europe and Germany. He has been a member of an Executive Management team that transacted two major cross-border M&A deals that totalled £2.3 billion and $1.7 billion, respectively.

His specialist teaching areas on the MSc in Multi-Unit Leadership and Strategy at BCBS (shortlisted for the CIPD 'Learning and Development' Award in 2011) are Service Leadership and Operational Improvement within retail, hospitality and leisure multi-unit contexts. Chris also provides specialist coaching, training and consultancy advice to a range of multi-unit organisations regarding MUL development and performance. Frequently commentating on issues such as the 'high street, 'leading from the middle' in multi-site organisations and 'multi-site service' issues, Chris has appeared in media outlets such as ITV Central, BBC News On-line, Channel 4 News, the Retail Gazette, InfoDaily, City A.M., Propelinfo, Express and Star etc. He can be contacted at chris@localleaders.co.uk.

Chris has a PhD in Cross-Border M&A (Warwick Business School), MBA and DMS (Nottingham Business School), MSc(econ) with distinction (London School of Economics and Political Science), BSc(hons) with University Prize for academic performance, Brunel University.

Acknowledgements

This book has benefitted from the contributions, insights and advice of many people over the past few years; not least Professor Alicia El-Haj (Keele), Andrew Edger (Finance Director, Osram Russia and Slovakia), Tania Edger (Siemens, Russia), Major Robert Edger (Commandant Gurka Training, British Army), Professor Duncan Angwin (Oxford Brookes), Emeritus Professor Mike Terry (Warwick) and Professor Chris Brewster (Reading). I also am extremely appreciative of the help and guidance provided by Martin West (commissioning editor, Gower) and Jonathan Norman (publisher, Gower).

I would especially like to thank the executive and academic 'panel' that contributed to this book in a variety of ways: Dr Lisa Qixun Siebers (Nottingham Business School, author of Retail Internationalisation in China), Ian Burke (Executive Chairman and CEO, Rank Plc), Reg Sindall (EVP Group Resources, Burberry Plc), Paul Willcock (Managing Director, Genting), Professor Gerald Noone O.B.E. (Leuven and Newcastle), Andy Vaughan (ex-Senior Strategy Director, Sodexo), Nick Wylde (MD, Stanton Chase International), Kevin Todd (President and CEO, Rosinter Restaurants Russia), Andrew Kitching (HRD, Booker Plc), Bryn Thomas (Senior Strategy Director, PSA Peugeot Citroen), Dr Nollaig Heffernan (Ecole Hotelier Lausanne), Bob Dignen (York Associates, author of *Communicating Internationally in English*), David Jones (CEO, Lanner International Plc), James Hyde (Senior Partner, Korn Ferry International), Clive Chesser (ex-Operations Manager, Haagen Dazs International), John Woodward (Global CEO, KUE Singapore), Jeremy Townsend (CFO, Rentokil Initial Plc), Mara Swan (EVP Strategy and Talent, ManpowerGroup), Mike Balfour (Founder, Fitness First) and Professor Paul Turner (BCBS, ex-SVP HR Convergys).

Thanks also to those at BCBS for their forbearance and tolerance during this long project: Professor Chris Prince, Professor Martin Reynolds, Dr Clinton Bantock, Stephen Willson, Debbie Colley and Janet Madden. Congratulations to Lee Moody for presiding over an outstanding 'Leaders in Leisure' programme and the Charity duo (Paul and Jo) for setting up an audacious and successful business!

I am particularly grateful to Adam Fowle (CEO, Tesco Family Dining, Chairman Giraffe Concepts Ltd, and NED Le Bistrot Pierre) for his leadership/advice over the past 20 years. Our 1996 coast-to-coast tour of US casual dining and leisure concepts/products (Cheesecake Factory, Six Flags, Mall of Minneapolis, Disneyland, Foxwoods, Hooters, Chicago Steakhouses, Las Vegas, etc.) was inspirational! Thanks also to Tim Clarke (Senior NED, ABF, NED Timothy Taylor and Hall and Woodhouse) and Iain Napier (Chairman, Imperial Tobacco; NED, McBride, Grants, Molson Coors) for your unstinting and generous support during my commercial career. Thank you to all three for letting me balls it up on occasion!

… the same people who are so strongly held in check by custom, respect, habit, gratitude … they are not much better than uncaged beasts of prey in the world outside where the strange, the foreign, begin …
Nietzsche

1 *Introduction*

In 2000, growth markets – any economy outside of the developed world that is at least 1 per cent of current global GDP (such as China, Russia, Brazil, India, Mexico, Korea, Turkey and Indonesia) – represented 13 per cent of global GDP. This subsequently rose to 25 per cent in 2011, being projected to reach almost 50 per cent by 2050 (GSAM 2012). This is in contrast to nations with developed status whose combined share of global GDP is forecast to reduce from 63 per cent in 2011 (it was 78 per cent in 2000) to 31 per cent in 2050. A major component of growth market, emerging and other market momentum will be the rapid expansion of these nations' service sectors catering for consumptive demand created by urbanisation and 'economic enfranchisement' (ATKearney 2012, Sharma 2012). A vital element of this growth will be the (continued) extension and proliferation of retail, leisure, hospitality and service-based multi-site entities, many of which are owned by internationalising organisations seeking expansion outside of saturated, 'no/ low'-growth developed market terrains.

One of the main challenges – indeed a major inhibiter (Schneider and Barsoux 2003) – for these internationalising organisations is developing and retaining local talent in order to facilitate successful expansion of developed market multi-unit brands internationally into growth and emerging contexts:

> *In a decade examining retail expansion in developing countries, we know that new markets are only as effective as their workforces, and harnessing a local talent pool is crucial to reaching customers. Expatriates deployed from home markets provide much needed support in the early stages, but long-term success hinges on a skilled, reliable, and affordable local workforce. (ATKearney 2012: 22)*

In my previous book, *Effective Multi-Unit Leadership*, I argued that in developed economies one of the most pivotal actors with regards to providing local leadership – delivering operational systems, brand standards and sales-led service within multi-unit organisations – was the multi-unit leader (otherwise known as the area or regional manager responsible for more than two units of the same concept). In this book I extend this thesis by arguing that one of the most important variables in internationalising multi-unit organisation success is what I term the 'host country multi-unit leader' (HMUL). Arguably HMULs fulfil a more complex and ambiguous role than their home country counterparts, being sandwiched between their units and 'two masters': both the owner and subsidiary/partner policy-makers. How do they optimise performance in this cross-national middle-management space bedevilled with cultural and interpretative issues – simultaneously satisfying the needs of their 'two masters', their staff at unit level and, most importantly, their customers? More importantly, given the dearth of local talent within certain markets, how do IMUEs (international multi-unit enterprises) nurture and develop this vital cohort which metaphorically ensures the 'rubber hits the road'?

This book, based on primary research material garnered for this, and the first book, over the period 2007–2013, is an attempt address this question by asking: what are the key activities of HMULs, how do they discharge their responsibilities effectively and what are their most important personal characteristics? To this end the effective MUL framework proposed in the first book (which comprised some HMUL data input) will be used as a starting-point for the analysis, although, as will be demonstrated, significant differences exist, if not in the overall dimensions and make-up of the role, in expediting the role in a more complex international organisational space with, in extremis, major issues created by the dynamics of place and distance. From an academic perspective this book should make a contribution to an area that has hitherto been largely overlooked – most texts and scholarly research on internationalisation to date focusing on expatriate and 'global management' cadres rather than host country national management. For practitioners the book should offer internationalising multi-unit companies some best-practice insights into how they select, develop and retain a critical managerial cohort in their organisations.

1.1 Why 'Host' Country Multi-Unit Leaders (HMULs)?

The questions that arise from the subtitle of this book – continuing the arguments put forward above – are, first, why are HMULs such an important subject of enquiry and, second, why is it important to understand how IMUEs select, train and develop them? In answer to the first question, it is significant that whilst there is a plethora of literature relating to 'international managers' (Lane et al. 2009), there is very little commentary regarding host country managers. This is a mystery given the fact that

> *HCN (Host Country National) managers in a foreign subsidiary can be expected to afford a higher degree of control to the parent MNC than expatriates posted from the parent organisation.* (Volkmar 2003: 93)

Local HCN managers with the appropriate language and leadership skills (that fit with extant national norms, values and behaviours) should, in theory, be expected to translate strategy into action far more effectively than their expatriate counterparts. In addition, given local customs, nuances and idiosyncrasies (specifically in relation to dispersed units and stores), 'being intelligently local (for organisations) should include a greater role for local management' (Quelch and Jocz 2012: 22).

But why does this book focus upon their activities and development? Like the first book, research for this text established that effective HMULs (i.e. 'host' regional managers, store directors, territory managers, city, area and district managers) stood out in comparison to their peers by exercising efficient managerial control and displaying values-based local leadership characteristics. That is to say that in addition to their designated managerial duties (i.e. checking systems and standards conformance) effective HMULs were extremely adept at taking centrally designed/derived frameworks, practices and policies and adapting them, within reason, to local markets. To this extent they required a high degree of tacit knowledge and judgement as to how to meld policy, practice and product to the local market but also how to do this within certain ethical parameters.

However, in the case of HMULs it is their ability not only to apply their tacit and explicit knowledge in local marketplaces that makes them stand out as successful operators, but also – as valuable 'eyes and ears' of the host and owner organisations, respectively – to perform a valuable feedback function, ensuring that their multi-unit product 'fits' and evolves appropriately with regards to positioning, pricing, people and place. Hence the denomination HMULs: a high-performing cohort of 'host country' local leaders that, whatever the cultural or business context, optimise their portfolios by the application of local knowledge-based practices. But how do IMUEs and their subsidiaries identify and develop such a critical managerial cohort given the talent-based constraints they face in many markets? This conundrum forms the central point of enquiry for this book.

1.2 What Is the International Multi-Unit Enterprise?

Olsen et al. (1992) provide a useful definition of generic multi-unit enterprises as organisations that 'compete in an industry with more than one unit of like concept or theme'. The international multi-unit enterprise can be defined as a geographically dispersed organisation built up from standard units such as branches, service centres, hotels, restaurants and stores (franchised or managed), which is aggregated into larger international geographic groupings such as regions, countries, divisions and areas (Garvin and Levesque 2008). Although international multi-unit enterprises may choose different ownership and contract structures in order to grow beyond their original country of origin base (see below and Chapter 2) these organisations now cross many geographic territories and industrial sectors such as retail banking, apparel, accessories, grocery and food retail, hospitality and leisure. Their international economic importance is signified by the fact that in some national contexts foreign-owned multi-unit enterprises can account for a high proportion of annual FDI (foreign direct investment), making a crucial contribution to domestic GDP growth in 'growth' and 'developing' markets.

1.3 History of the International Multi-Unit Enterprise

The growth of the multi-unit enterprise from the late nineteenth century in 'developed' national settings was facilitated by five interrelated factors such as industrialisation/ urbanisation, new technologies aiding the mass production of goods, the rise in economic buying power of a burgeoning middle class, the development of advanced transport infrastructures and increased consumer demand for consistency, affordability and quality (Edger 2012: 8–11). Similar forces have acted as drivers for multi-unit proliferation in 'growth' and 'developing' markets albeit other factors such as commodity wealth, the international flow of capital, growth of smart technologies and ideological repositioning from planned and/or command to liberalising free market economies (certainly in the case of the former Soviet Bloc and China) have had a significant impact upon the upwards trajectory of multi-unit internationalisation over the past 30 years. This section will, first, consider the four main phases of internationalisation and, second, reflect upon both internationalisation successes and failures.

The *first phase* of multi-unit internationalisation followed a so-called 'developed to developed' pattern of expansion (Benson and Ugolini 2003). Here multi-unit enterprises facing saturation in their home markets and/or spotting opportunistic market gaps or avenues for geographic 'roll-up' opportunities, moved into 'developed' foreign markets (clustering in major conurbations first) that were characterised by a strong rule of law, high levels of consumption and solid extant supply chain infrastructures. Early movers in the twentieth century were the 'dime retailers' FW Woolworths expanding into the UK from the US, although it was not until the latter part of the century that fast food retailers (i.e. McDonalds), 'hard grocery discounters' (Aldi and Netto), apparel (i.e. C&A), banking (i.e. Barclays), mid-market grocery (i.e. Ahold and Carrefour), furniture (i.e. IKEA) and home improvements (i.e. B&Q) began a process of international roll-out or 'roll-up' (Bower 2001). It is notable that one multi-unit enterprise form – hotels (i.e. Hilton and Holiday Inn) – extended their reach beyond developed territories from the 1950s, but this was mainly to cater for travellers and tourists from 'developed' economies.

The *second phase* of internationalisation, so-called 'developed' to 'growth' market expansion, which gained real momentum from the 1990s onwards, was caused by the market 'pull' factors elucidated above, but also 'push' factors such as the expense (i.e. cost of land, labour and goods) and harsh competitive environments in 'developed' contexts:

> In the past five years, US-based Walmart, France-based Carrefour, UK-based Tesco and Germany-based Metro Group saw their revenues in developing countries grow 2.5 times faster than revenues in their home markets. (ATKearney 2012: 2)

This phase can be divided into two major waves. First, the aggressive expansion of food retailers into the ex-Soviet Bloc territories (i.e. Tesco, Aldi and Carrefour) and, second, as China liberalised its laws of retail ownership in the early twenty-first century, a huge drive by western multi-unit firms to gain access to the dynamic urban conurbations of the world's most populous, fastest-growing economy. During this period the success of premium goods multi-unit enterprises (i.e. Burberry, Gucci, etc.) in opening up territories in the Middle and Far East was also a significant parallel development. By 2012, some of these markets had been relabelled from 'growth' to 'mature' (i.e. ex-Soviet Bloc countries Poland, Hungary and the Czech Republic) with regards to certain sectors such as grocery retail and home improvements. However, significant growth potential remains in countries such as Turkey, Brazil, Mexico, China and India (particularly following 2011 retail liberalisation), where due to education, technology, demographics and increased productivity, demand for goods and services from standardised multi-unit enterprises is likely to remain high for the foreseeable future (O'Neill 2011).

The *third phase* of international multi-unit expansion, occurring at present, is the push into territories now denominated as 'developing'. Some of these markets – such as Sri Lanka, Malaysia, Philippines, Chile and Peru – have huge potential when assessed in terms of market attractiveness (demographics, education, inflation and debt), country risk (rule of law and political stability) and market saturation (competitive environment).

Multi-unit enterprises that have deployed capital and/or expanded into these markets during 2011–2012 include: Sri Lanka (Benetton, Mango and Levi's), Indonesia (Yum! and IKEA), Malaysia (Debenhams and H&M), Philippines (Topshop, Uniqlo and Quiznos), Peru (Gap, Zara, Brooks Brothers and Yum!) and Chile (Walmart, Gap and Dunkin' Donuts) (ATKearney 2012: 3–26).

In the future there is likely to be a *fourth phase* of multi-unit internationalisation where national 'champions' from today's 'growth' and 'developing' markets seek markets in 'developed' economy environments (Wild 2012). The success of Nando's (a fast-growing international casual dining chain with South African origins) might provide a template as to how they might succeed in developed environments through creative positioning (i.e. universal ethnic appeal) and market-leading operational efficiency (i.e. pre-pay casual dining format). Certainly Middle and Far Eastern investors and conglomerates have started to either take strategic stakes in 'developed' market multi-unit enterprises (i.e. Dubai Investment Authority's stake in Sainsbury's) or purchase or partially own leisure assets (i.e. Malaysian investment in casino groups in the UK).

As will be explored later on in the book, the process of internationalising multi-unit enterprises is fraught with danger. Whilst there have been numerous success stories – including Tesco in the ex-Soviet Bloc, McDonalds worldwide and Yum! in China – the process is littered with set-backs and failures. Notable examples of 'developed' to 'developed' transmission failures include Walmart in Germany, Sainsbury's in the US and (more recently) Tesco in Japan/US and Best Buy in the UK. Also 'developed' to 'growth' expansion can result in serious set-backs. For instance, in China during the period 2011–2012, UK home improvement group B&Q closed two stores, Walmart abandoned a convenience store pilot in Shenzhen and Carrefour was forced to reduce its roll-out ambitions owing to a lack of prime and secondary site opportunities. One major factor in these and other multi-unit enterprise 'road bumps' has been the emergence of strong local competition (i.e. China Resource Vanguard and Yonghui multiple grocers in China that account for more market share than the global entrants) who possess 'local knowledge and savvy management teams (which) allow them to develop rapidly' (ATKearney 2011: 10).

1.4 Challenges of the International Multi-Unit Enterprise

Internationalising a domestic multi-unit enterprise model – whatever its home primacy and/or success – is bedevilled by risk. The section above touched on some of these dangers, but what are dominant challenges facing 'developed' internationalising organisations in 'growth' and 'developing' markets at this present time? Broadly speaking they can be subdivided into two categories: macro and micro. External macro challenges encompass three main factors: *home market disruption*, *local market competition* and *smart technologies* which threaten the viability of the internationalising multi-unit form which, by its very nature, requires huge levels of capital investment during all phases of its life cycle. Internal micro challenges include issues such as: whether to *standardise or localise*, leveraging *local human capital*, *parent versus subsidiary tensions*, ensuring *consistency of standards* given time, space and distance and, finally, dealing with the complexities of *format, channel and contract proliferation*. These will be considered in turn.

1.4.1 MACRO CHALLENGES

1.4.1.1 Home market disruption

One of the principal reasons why multi-unit firms internationalise is that they have created a domestic platform that has given them a degree of ascendancy in their home market (consequently there are limitations to their growth potential unless they seek foreign challenges) and/or they are in possession of what they believe is an inimitable product or business model that is capable of 'conquering' foreign markets (Rugman and Hodgetts 2003). Often the home country bases of these enterprises serve as the 'cash engines' for growth with profits and collateral (i.e. borrowing raised against existing assets) being deployed abroad. This model is fine as long as their foreign 'excursions' start making speedy financial returns, mitigating the upfront risk.

However, as discussed in my previous book (Edger 2012: 11–18), multi-unit enterprises operating within 'developed' terrains have faced formidable economic, consumer and technological forces since the 2007 economic downturn. The reasons for this major economic correction will not be reprised here; suffice it to say that the banking, sovereign debt and eurozone crises over the period 2007–2013 have had profound effects on 'developed' market consumer behaviour as labour markets have contracted, real wage levels have stalled and discretionary spend levels have fallen. Coupled with this, major developments in smart technology have altered the way in which people shop, with consumers being far more price conscious and savvy about where the best deals lie. Multi-unit enterprises that have been unable (or unwilling) to adapt their business models to this new multi-channel paradigm have either gone bust or suffered catastrophic market share losses/dips in profit performance.

What have been the effects of this 'developed' disruptive holy trinity – economic, consumer and technological – upon internationalising multi-unit enterprises? First, many firms have had to rein in their foreign ambitions due to restrictions on available funds. Responding to acute investor pressure, international companies such as Tesco, Walmart and Carrefour have been forced to seriously appraise their international ambitions, ending ventures that appear to have been a significant drain on financial and human resources (Hawkes 2013). For instance, in May 2012 Tesco sold off its operation in Japan, announcing the following year that its Fresh and Easy chain of convenience stores in the US – which up to that point had failed to reach breakeven, having cost the company over £1 billion in direct investment – was 'up for sale'. Turning around poorly performing subsidiaries is not deemed by the investment community to be an effective use of management time, particularly when their flagship domestic organisations are haemorrhaging profit, cash and/or market share. Second – due to restrictions in cash flow – some firms have been forced to find more efficient (i.e. less expensive) ways to pursue international expansion (i.e. JVs rather than M&A – where IP and know-how is traded for funds by a local co-investor). In June 2012 Burger King announced a major expansion plan in 'growth' and 'emerging' markets, saying that this would be achieved through JVs and partnerships in Russia and Asia.

1.4.1.2 Local market competition

When internationalising companies select new markets for expansion they are looking for two main things: lack of competition and favourable forward demand patterns. In the early days of expansion into 'undeveloped markets' foreign entrants might have found it easy as they encountered weak, fragmented local competition (usually characterised by a large 'independent' sector). What has happened in many of the territories that international multi-unit firms have 'colonised' over the past 20 years is that strong local 'multiple' or 'chain' competition has emerged to challenge them (especially in China). Why?

First, isomorphism has occurred. Local 'chains' have sprung up and learnt quickly from foreign entrants, mimicking many of their best-practice approaches (i.e. product quality, sourcing and supply chain, positioning, pricing, promotions, operational systems, standards and service, etc.). In many cases they have poached HCN 'first wave' managerial recruits from these international entrants into their own operations to provide them with the explicit and tacit knowledge to erode the competitive advantage of, and in some cases defeat, foreign competition. Second, because local companies have superior 'intuitive knowledge' about their own markets and do not report - or pay franchise fees - to an international parent where decision-making processes can be slow and cumbersome, they are more nimble when adjusting their offer to local preferences, customs and tastes. As Kentucky Fried Chicken has found in Indonesia;

> ... KFC is fighting for market share ... facing growing competition ... [from] aggressive local rivals ... such as Hoka Hoka Bento, which serves up Japanese-style fast food, and Es Teler 77, which offers noodles and other simple Indonesian dishes ... 'We are very scared of the local brands that are eating up our market share,' says Mr Ledres [General Manager of Fast Food Indonesia; operator of Indonesia's 440 franchised KFC outlets], noting that they 'have low marketing costs and no royalty payments to the brand owner, like us'. While KFC runs costly television and billboard advertisements, local brands use cheaper promotional channels such as social media, word-of-mouth and – in the case of Wong Solo, a grilled chicken chain with 160 outlets – Islamic prayer meetings ... (Bland 2013)

They are also more cognisant of important factors such as local laws and regulations (especially with regard to labour and planning) and have, in all probability, better formal and informal links with local officials who are more disposed to the needs of 'local champions'. Third, as the cost of land for prime sites (i.e. malls and out-of-town shopping centres) in many 'growth' and 'developing' nations has – in response to increased commercial demand – exponentially increased, local operators have proved far more adept at adapting their formats and efficiently expanding their estates into cheaper secondary and tertiary locations than their foreign competitors. Portfolio management for foreign entrants has become far more complicated as markets have become more crowded and saturated; there is far more risk in these aforementioned circumstances that location choices will misfire (Pelle 2007, Marr and Reynard 2010).

What are the consequences of the emergence of strong local resistance to internationalising multi-unit firms? In some cases (as previously stated) organisations have abandoned markets, either closing their store networks or selling off their assets to local competitors (usually for a knock-down price, taking a large non-cash write-down on their balance sheets). In other instances organisations have fought back through means such as rationalising their estates, devolving more autonomy to their subsidiary (with regards to product, positioning, people, price and place; see Chapter 2) and/or consolidating with local competition.

1.4.1.3 Smart technology

One major threat posed to internationalising multi-unit enterprises is the same as the one currently challenging their 'developed' nation land-based models – that of game-changing web-enabling technology (such as smart phones, tablets and personal computers), which has opened an instant window on the retail world (enabling instant product and price comparisons) for the consumer. In 'developed' markets online retail spend has accelerated, reaching 11 per cent and 6 per cent of retail sales in the UK and US, respectively, by 2012. Over 40 per cent of web-based enquiries in the UK in 2012 related to 'retail searches', a high proportion of which were price comparison sites – a trend forecast to accelerate dramatically over the next decade (Butler 2011). As a result certain product categories have been commoditised: outlets selling books, music, value clothing, cards, video games, electrical and white goods have been most affected. Indeed, supermarket retail firms that had significantly increased their 'non-food' space in the 1990s and 2000s in order to sell these product categories are currently reviewing their 'race for scale and space' approach (Wallop and Ruddick 2012). Also, many multi-unit operators have gone 'multi/omni channel' (combining 'click and brick'), setting up online 'order and deliver' and 'click and collect' services, or have opted to vacate the high street and move to a totally web-based model.

It has not been all bad news for retailers; many firms that have embraced the multi-channel challenge have benefitted. First, through using the web as a 'virtual i-Street' shop window, certain organisations who have invested in search engine applications are able to route browsers to higher-margin product areas. Second, it has helped companies utilise their physical assets more effectively through driving volume via 'click and collect', customised promotions and direct marketing. Third, in the leisure sector in particular, firms have been able to increase throughputs in non-peak periods through a combination of revised product formulation (offsetting margin erosion) and aggressive price promotion through couponing sites (such as vouchercloud.com). To this extent the web has proved extremely successful in smoothing demand, decreasing operator reliance on peak sales to recover lost overhead. Fourth, the emergence of cloud-enabled 'wallet apps' and pre-payment capabilities on 'smart' mobile or tablet devices offers firms the opportunity to reduce their transaction costs, principally through decreased labour. Indeed, innovation relating to means and speed of payment such as 'wave and pay' could herald the third major speed of transaction revolution (behind self-service and barcode scanning) in little under a century, rendering many transaction-based till-based operatives redundant.

Internationalising multi-unit enterprises have been confronted with the same pressures and opportunities when addressing 'growth' and 'developing' markets. Any notion that these territories are technologically backwards when it comes to smart technology adoption is scotched by powerful evidential trends. Mobile and smart phone penetration rates in some emerging markets are only two or three years behind 'developed' nations (Mallaby 2013). Even in sub-Saharan Africa the percentage of adults with internet access through smart phones, tablets or PCs has reached 70 per cent in some countries (notably Nigeria, Chad, Namibia and South Africa) due to the ease with which wireless technology can be rolled out. Combine these levels of penetration with price comparison site availability and extremely promiscuous buyer behaviour and retailers are faced with the same heady commoditising 'cocktail' that they face in their 'developed' markets. One form of competitive advantage that internationalising firms possess is the fact that they have had experience in grappling with 'multi-channel' challenges in their home territories and thus, theoretically, have been able to steal a march on their local competitors. This however has been of transient benefit as local multi-unit enterprises have caught up and proved just as (if not more) adept at leveraging the opportunities that smart technology has afforded more agile organisations over the past few years.

1.4.2 MICRO CHALLENGES

Combined with these external macro challenges to international firms there are a number of micro issues that emanate from the operation of the standard multi-unit model. The ability of multi-unit enterprises to mitigate their effects, harnessing the principal benefits of standardised scale, has a major influence on the performance of these enterprises. The main challenges faced by the international multi-unit model fall into five categories, as follows.

1.4.2.1 Optimising local human capital

Multi-unit enterprises are 'B2C' (business to consumer) offers that are highly dependent upon labour in order to deliver memorable customer service. Problems stem from the fact that the model is reliant upon the perfect *functional* execution of multiple transactions and 'connective' *emotional* delivery during numerous customer 'touch points'. However, the standardised multi-unit model – in its efforts to ensure consistency and dependability – restricts human autonomy and discretion, acting as a break against individual expression. Issues are exacerbated by the fact that in some 'developed' economies service-facing roles are perceived as having low status and (in relative terms) poor pay and conditions. Front-line service providers in western retail, leisure and hospitality have therefore drawn heavily from pools of labour that are drawn towards this work through necessity: migrants, students, transient workers and part-time female labour. Where 'Generation Y' workers are involved inter-generational issues can occur between different worker age groups and problems occur with regards to attitude and commitment. Youngsters who have constructed their identity around being 'globally connected', becoming (in their minds) 'international brands' through vehicles such as YouTube, Facebook, blogs and Twitter feel constrained by the mundaneness of menial work – leading to potential issues such as sabotage, resistance and non-conformance.

There might be a presumption that internationalising multi-unit enterprises do not face the same issues when expanding into 'growth' and 'developing' markets because they are offering secure and (in relative terms) well-remunerated employment. This is manifestly not the case; indeed, some of the same counter-pressures continue to apply. In some countries and regions such as India and the Gulf States retail work is perceived has having relatively low status and is unattractive to educated local nationals who have higher aspirations. The pool of labour that is left open to internationalising firms is therefore restricted to relatively uneducated sections of the population or (in the case of the Gulf States) diaspora migrant Asian labour. In other markets such as China, given the exponential growth rates of the service sector, labour turnover in retail is high because of low rates of pay in the sector – although recently moves have been made to increase the minimum wage by central government, a move that might help retail close the gap with other sectors. In addition, in some societies, female employment and advancement is 'discouraged', restricting labour supply, whilst in a number of international contexts (see Chapter 4) there is a complete lack of cultural appreciation for a 'service ethic' requirement within a customer-facing multi-unit service environment – a position that proves problematic for internationalising multi-unit firms that are intent upon replicating home-based service systems and standards.

1.4.2.2 Consistency of standards

Given the multi-unit form's heavy reliance on service operatives in numerous locations delivering 'customer order fulfilment' at rapid rate it is easy to understand why service and standards consistency is susceptible to frequent breakdowns. It is a fact that with their wide geographical spread – particularly within an international context – multi-unit firms constantly grapple with problems of time, distance and space which threaten the dependability and reputation of their offer (Olsen et al. 1992). Spatial and span of control issues are the enemies of the co-ordination of standardised product quality and service. Consumers experiencing variable and indeterminate quality across a range of supposedly standard units are unlikely to trust the offer, leading to high levels of non-repeat business and low net promoter scores. In international contexts firms might achieve 'first mover' advantage against indigenous competition when they first arrive, due to superior systems and blueprints. In comparison to the extant 'independent' competition they will almost certainly be differentiated in terms of hygiene, consistency and quality. However, when local operators 'catch up' they are in a far better position (due to proximity) to relentlessly improve the consistency and execution of their offer. International organisations, like Napoleon in Russia, can find themselves overstretched and surrounded unless they have granted sufficient resources and authority to their local teams to ensure uniformity of standards.

1.4.2.3 Standardisation versus localisation

Although all international multi-unit firms will aim for uniform operational excellence they need to be sensitive to the product, place, positioning and price of the *subsidiary* offer to country and regional market needs. Layered on top of this is the fact that at a micro area level, non-standard unit footprints (due to site availability constraints), regional tastes and customs, customer demographics, levels of ambient competition and differing local labour markets all impinge upon the operations of *single* site units. This can give rise to tensions within the multi-unit model where the parent company (for reasons of efficiency, scale and certainty) favours conformity, whilst local operators (both at subsidiary and area levels) constantly bargain and transact for flexibility with regards to capital investment decisions, range, wages, layout and promotional offer, etc. Often the parent will encourage and sanction local adaptation (although its 'recognition speed' might vary), a good example being McDonald's in India where, unlike operations elsewhere, 50 per cent of its menus are vegetarian-based and two units situated next to temples in Amritsar are set at a 100 per cent mix (Kazmin 2012: 16). Other IMUEs such as Starbucks have transmogrified from virtual standardisation to a mantra of 'seeking local relevance' (through store design, item range and taste) in different markets (Walsh 2012: 51). The dangers of increased localisation are obvious – complexity, sub-optimal decision-making and (potentially) increased cost – threatening the very premise upon which multiples were founded, namely, consistency and efficiency. How do international multi-unit enterprises deal with this conundrum? Some apply a metric of 'fixing', establishing 'non-negotiables', or standardising their operation at 80 per cent whilst allowing 20 per cent flexibility at a local level; others might grant total autonomy to local decision-makers, albeit within a prescribed strategic and operational framework.

1.4.2.4 Head office versus subsidiary tensions

Given the natural inclination for subsidiaries/partners to seek local autonomy in order to service local preferences/needs juxtaposed against the propensity for parent companies to assert control through shared 'soft' and 'hard' systems it is of little surprise that significant tensions can arise between the two parties. Boundary tensions can spring up between head office functions (such as finance, marketing, HR, audit and supply chain) and subsidiary-based operations. Whether the organisation is designed according to vertical, horizontal or matrix-based principles the potential for conflict, mistrust and game play remains high. Put simply, the head office will always see itself as the senior partner in the relationship being the final arbiter on strategic decision-making and (most significantly) revenue budget-setting, global talent and capital allocation. The subsidiary/partner will always feel a degree of resentment regarding the parent's primacy and anxiety regarding its *true* strategic intentions.

To be sure, in truly international multi-unit organisations, subsidiaries cannot be seen as independent entities; they generally compete with a range of other interests and subsidiaries to secure scarce human and financial resources. The process of bargaining for more resources or greater latitude with regards to local needs can be a debilitating and exhausting process which, if financial performance metrics are poor, can only exacerbate the subsidiary's feeling that it is under constant scrutiny (i.e. de facto control) by its owner. If, however, the subsidiary/partner is deemed to be 'doing well' there might, indeed, be a granting of licensed autonomy on the basis of continued superior operational performance – a position which one senior respondent described as 'profit-related indenture or freedom'.

1.4.2.5 Format, channel and contract complexity

The previous section described the *multi-channel* pressures that are faced by international multi-unit enterprises in 'growth' and 'developed' contexts converging with their 'developed' country experiences. This inevitably brings a higher degree of complexity to the international organisation which is forced to respond to local markets not only with regard to land-based human and physical architecture but from an 'omni-channel' perspective. Given that the parent might already be stretched for technical resources in its home territory with regards to dealing with 'click and brick' challenges, this attendant pressure threatens to impose an immense strain upon the technical expertise of the organisation. Added to this issue is the fact that during the roll-out (or adaptation) of their product in foreign territories companies might be constantly updating *format* designs. Within multi-unit estates constant refreshment, innovation and adaptation are necessary in order to respond to competitive pressures and/or meet changing consumer demands and requirements. Given the vital importance of *location* to site performance, multi-unit chains will often designate units 'core' and 'non-core', leading to twin-track capital and people investment programmes. Again this is problematic to both consumers – who will notice inconsistency – and unit staff in the 'non-core' units who feel like victims of an informal class system: neglected and under threat, resenting their lack of access to resources in comparison to 'higher caste' members within the system.

This process of acquiring/developing new brands/formats or opening up additional multi-channel routes to market – as an adjunct to existing offerings – is clearly problematic for a parent organisation which might be facing capital and knowledge starvation to fund all of its existing/proposed new ventures. It is made doubly complex by the fact that most international organisations will not be operating to the same *contractual* and agreement terms in each of their foreign territories. It is not unusual (for reasons discussed in Chapter 2) for organisations to have managed, franchised, concession, licensing and/or JV arrangements in 'simultaneous flight'. Operating within this multiplicity of forms, with each contract (potentially) having its own idiosyncratic legal rules and (potential) liabilities, places huge pressure on the parent. How does it co-ordinate conformity and operational excellence within the realms of each contract/ ownership structure?

1.5 The Host Country Multi-Unit Leader (HMUL)

One of the most important organisational actors in addressing some of the aforementioned challenges should be the HMUL (more commonly known as regional manager, retail operations manager, area manager or district manager), who can be defined as somebody who is directly responsible for the performance spectrum of two or more standard managed or franchised units. Within the host country subsidiary/ partner hierarchy they typically report to a vice president, regional, area or operations director but their main defining characteristic is that they have direct P&L accountability for a defined number of units. The questions addressed by this section are, what do we know about the genesis of the MUL role and what does previous academic research tell us about them?

1.5.1 GENESIS OF THE ROLE

In 'developed' markets as multi-unit organisations grew in the late nineteenth century and more layers of senior management were created, the hierarchy of larger chains mimicked the command structure of mechanistic and bureaucratic forms of manufacturing organisations. At first, in the absence of central technology, these managers assumed a policing role at unit level, being titled 'agents', 'store supervisors' and 'store inspectors' (Mathias 1967). As businesses developed paper-based stock taking, pricing, merchandising and ledger systems these 'inspectors' ensured that units were run professionally and consistently according to company policy. One major innovation that brought the importance of MULs into sharper focus was the growth of franchise retail in 'developed' markets in the late 1960s. For instance, in the US it is believed that a significant mediating factor in the proliferation of fast food offerings was the area manager, although observers have noted how little is known about their early duties, responsibilities and impact (Ritzer 1993). However, given the systemisation of food production and strict franchising rules some research has indicated that they played a pivotal role in ensuring consistency of standards and execution (Umbreit and Smith 1991). Further contemporary analysis of the role (DiPietro et al. 2007) indicates that the role has extended beyond merely checking and enforcement into 'coaching and leading' unit managers and their teams. The advancement of technology, some commentators have argued, has freed up MULs to concentrate on 'softer' value-added HRM functions – although significant empirical evidence gathered by Edger (2012: 96–104) would indicate that the role today is perceived by MULs themselves as very close to the compliance and 'checking' model conceived in the early twentieth century.

1.5.2 PREVIOUS RESEARCH

This book takes as its subject of enquiry host country MULs (HMULs) who work in the subsidiary or partner elements of international multi-unit enterprises – particularly in developing markets. What extant research exists about this *specific* cohort? The answer is very little research has been conducted into this important stratum – although there are a number of literature streams that help us place their role within context. Thus, this section will consider a number of streams of literature that – by association – are pertinent to this research: that of global management, home country/expatriate management, host country national management (HCNs) and generic MUL literature.

The concept of 'global management' or 'geoleadership' (Lane et al. 2009) has at its heart the view that transnational organisations should pursue *polycentric* approaches to subsidiary leadership in order to adopt a 'best of each' approach across international markets. Here the 'global manager' is conceived of as culturally adept, with the capacity to adjust his/her style according to circumstance and environment (see Chapter 4). Successful transnational organisations are those that have developed an international cadre of 'global managers' whose behaviours and capabilities are transferable across national boundaries. The issue with this literature is its excessive reliance upon cultural 'flexibility' to embed best practice as an explanation for success, marginalising and downplaying other key attributes that 'global managers' need to possess such as technical/sectoral expertise and the ability to confront the world 'as it is' rather than 'as it should be', especially in high-growth or nascent business environments. This is particularly the case in international business schools that make great play upon their ability to educate 'global leaders' of the future:

> ... many MBAs (in International Business Schools) retain an emphasis on (western) theory, with much time spent on case studies of best management practice, but the reality of working in emerging markets such as Brazil, Russia, India and China can be a world away from the textbooks. Intransigent bureaucrats, corruption and persistent logistical headaches are a characteristic of the Bric markets, and managers working in them need a grasp of the realities on the ground. (Morarjee 2012: 37–9)

Also, the literature and such aforementioned institutions make the presupposition that many corporate managers have either the capacity or willingness to be culturally 'programmed', given that learned behaviours and prejudices are extremely difficult to 'unlearn'.

Outside this stream of literature (it being a lucrative teaching product for international business schools) the other major body of work around this area alludes to more *ethnocentric* approaches to international management through home country managers or expatriates being implanted in subsidiaries to provide assurance on cultural, strategic and operational conformance. Why? Vance and Paik (2005: 590–606) conceive of senior subsidiary roles comprising four vital elements:

- *MNC Strategy* – the implantation of parent company (MNC) strategy;
- *MNC Culture* – the transference of parent (MNC) company culture;
- *Advanced Operations* – advanced technical system operations;
- *Local Strategy* – subsidiary business-level strategy.

Given that the first two elements imply a close knowledge or familiarisation of parent objectives and ideology, it is unsurprising that most MNCs adopt an ethnocentric approach to recruitment and selection at senior levels within their subsidiaries. In fact, the literature relating to home country/expatriate management is voluminous with academic enquiry examining problematics such as expatriate adjustment, acclimatisation and acculturation (Mahajan 2009), performance/success factors (Arthur and Bennett 1995), knowledge flows (Gupta and Govindarajan 1991, 2000, 2002, Bresman et al. 1999), conformance and control (Edstrom and Galbraith 1977, Kobrin 1988), experience 'curves' (Bartlett and Goshal 1989), gender, development and mentoring (Carraher et al. 2008). The fact remains that for most internationalising multi-unit enterprises the dominant approach to international management remains the implantation of 'home knowledge' at the head of subsidiaries – certainly during start-up, growth and/or crisis stages – and, indeed, in the middle of organisations (i.e. one in 1,000 Tesco International employees are home market expatriates; Leahy 2012: 279) in order to give them – perceived or otherwise – assurance of replication, consistency and control.

The argument whether or not 'home' or 'host'-grown management has more favourable performance outcomes is considered in the far smaller, more *geocentrically*-based, host country national (HCN) management literature (Tharenou and Harvey 2006). The argument pursued in this limited genre is that whilst home country managers might provide an effective transmission mechanism 'downstream' for the parent, they are ineffective as regards to translating strategy and change into action given the idiosyncrasies and nuances of unfamiliar local markets:

... while the expatriate manager clearly affords a higher level of control over strategy formulation in the subsidiary s/he is equally clearly at a disadvantage vis a vis a HCN, all else equal, when it comes to control over strategy implementation. Effectively directing local managers and employees from a different national culture, and confronting the unique social, political and institutional characteristics of the subsidiary's operating environment constitute the 'textbook' problems of cross-cultural management – problems with which the HCN manager is more familiar, and therefore better equipped to deal. (Volkmar 2003: 96)

The other benefits that accrue from appointing HCN managers to senior positions in the subsidiary include: empowering the subsidiary within its local markets, avoiding high expatriate costs (eliminating resentment over expatriate salary and benefit inequities), reducing political risk when dealing with local authorities/agencies (due to language and institutional knowledge) and the positive outcomes of perceived progression opportunities within host country firms (Toh and DeNisi 2003, Schaffer and Hyuk 2005). An emerging phenomenon over the past decade has been the emergence of ex-host country national managers (EHCNs) – nationals returning to 'growth' economies from 'developed' markets – a dimension that has been labelled a form of 'positive brain circulation' or 'human systems flow' aiding international company expansion (Tung and Lazarova 2006, Tung 2008).

With specific reference to MULs, there is virtually no literature relating to their activities, behaviours and characteristics within an international multi-unit context. What does exist however, are, first, texts that refer to the role and function of 'middle management' beneath subsidiary leadership level and, second, those which refer to the generic success factors which apply to MULs within national multi-unit contexts.

The first stream of commentary, that of 'subsidiary middle management', considers the various activities and essential knowledge pertaining to the role which are broadly classified as:

- *Local Operations* – supervision and general technical operations management;
- *Expatriate Assistance* – expatriate coaching and adjustment;
- *Intermediary* – liaison role between parent company expatriates and lower-level HCNs; and operatives (Vance and Paik 2005: 590–606).

In general – given its hierarchical position – this role is conceived as one of implementation rather than policy-making. In terms of knowledge transference – in their liaison role as 'middle men' between the top and bottom of the subsidiary – they are seen by some commentators as filling a vital role in knowledge transmission; although it must be said that most texts see senior subsidiary actors as being the vital interlocking cog between the host and parent (Bartlett and Goshal 1989, Bresman et al. 1999, Hocking et al. 2004). What *is* widely agreed is that international organisations penetrating 'growth' and 'developing' markets have found great difficulty recruiting and retaining sufficient managerial talent at this level of the organisation – especially during start-up and roll-out phases of operations (ATKearney 2012). Given that this is a universal observation (certainly across the international retail sector), one must assume that this also applies to the HMUL cohort, implying serious consequences for internationalising multi-unit enterprises.

With regards to generic MUL research within national contexts a full elaboration of the literature is contained in my first book on the subject (Edger 2012: 22–8). The main points contained within this literature – which is almost entirely based on studies conducted within the US fast food industry – are that academics believe that there are a number of critical success factors or job dimensions pertaining to the role and moreover, there are certain managerial practices which, if applied, can result in more effective performance.

With regard to the former – the vital components of the role – Umbreit's groundbreaking analysis established that there were five critical dimensions: *operations, financial management, HRM, marketing and promotions management* and *facilities and safety* (Umbreit 1989). Further studies sought to test the relative importance and hierarchy of these aspects, concluding that operations and HRM were deemed to be the most important job attributes followed by financial management, marketing and safety (Umbreit 1989, Mone and Umbreit 1989, Umbreit and Smith 1991, Ryan 1992, Muller and Campbell 1995, Reynolds 2000). Repeating Umbreit's study, little divergence to these findings was found either within a care home context (Brezezicki 2008) or in the UK pub industry (Jones and Inkinci 2001).

These and further texts also considered the transitional difficulties that unit managers encountered moving into multi-unit management (MUM) roles, the major issues relating less to technical issues (due to their previous unit manager experience) than to HRM and leadership ones caused by managing 'remotely at a distance' (Umbeit 1989, DiPietro et al. 2007, Rivera et al. 2008). Stress, tension and quit rates within this cohort were found to positively correlate to lack of HRM skills and the burdensome demands of the job (Umbreit 1989, Ryan 1992). In order to be successful MUMs had to learn to delegate key functions and activities across their areas in order to 'de-stress' the role, learning to 'manage the managers' rather than seek to 'manage every unit' and create and leverage broader support networks within the organisation (Umbreit and Smith 1991; BHI 2005a, b).

Continuing these important studies I undertook a major research project from 2007 to 2012 which sought to devise an integrated model of effective MUL (Edger 2012). It departed from previous research in that it extended across multi-unit sectors (i.e. retail, leisure and hospitality), triangulated the views of senior operators, MULs and unit managers and attempted to devise a guiding framework that captured the key activities, behaviours and characteristics of effective MULs. This multi-method study concluded that the main activities of effective MULs revolved around *systems* implementation, *standards* and *sales-led service* execution (3Ss). These activities were facilitated by *commitment, control* and *change*-led behavioural practices (3Cs) driven by personal characteristics of *expertise, energy* and *emotional intelligence* (3Es).

The major insight provided by this study was that a guiding theory applied to this domain, namely, portfolio optimisation through social exchange (POSE). That is to say, due to their high levels of interdependence with their followers juxtaposed with *'distance'* issues, coupled with the fact that each of their units differed to some degree (i.e. location, site layout, serviceable market, labour access, etc.), effective MULs optimised their portfolios (areas and districts) through emotional and practical *'currency exchanges'* which could be subdivided into four main categories with sub-components (see Figure 1.1).

- **mutual goal attainment**
  - ○ local direction setting and prioritisation
  - ○ ability to influence
- **free market exchange**
  - ○ positional patronage
  - ○ protection from punishment
  - ○ promissory speed
  - ○ permission to innovate
  - ○ scarce resource access
- **compensated costs**
  - ○ public recognition
  - ○ granting of autonomy
  - ○ emotional capital
  - ○ 'treats'
  - ○ portable skills
  - ○ behavioral coaching
- **uncovering hidden value**
  - ○ knowledge transfer
  - ○ valuable insights

Figure 1.1   Effective MUL 'Currencies of Exchange' (Edger 2012: 250–61)

Also, I found that in addition to transacting vertically, effective MULs also did so horizontally with colleagues (through 'tangible and intangible asset swaps') and support staff (through empathy, recognition and execution). They also actively encouraged 'inter-unit reciprocity' between units or within 'clusters' and/or geographical 'families' where hard and soft exchanges were made to benefit the portfolio as a whole. The study concluded that:

> Given the distance of the MUL from their sites, their high level of interdependency with their followers and the ambiguities and complexities of operating in an (often) chaotic and disorderly multi-unit context, it is the effective MUL's ability to exchange social, emotional and practical currencies both horizontally and vertically – encouraging value-added reciprocation from his/ her followers, peers and other providers – that marks them out as outstanding local leaders. (Edger 2012: 268)

The issue with this study – as with others before and after it, such as Leader-Member Exchange by Bligh and Riggio 2013, Schyns 2013 – is its almost exclusive concentration on MUL practice within 'developed' markets such as the UK and US. Whilst it does touch on the internationalisation of multi-unit enterprises (Edger 2012: 72–80) and, indeed, contains case studies that refer to foreign-owned entities (i.e. Jewson/St Gobain, Pasta Hut/USCo, Jeweler Co/USCo) and firms with international cover (i.e. Haagen-Dazs), it fails to unpack the specific problems which multi-unit firms from 'developed' markets face when seeking to exploit 'growth' and 'emerging' markets. How do they recruit, retain and *develop* HMULs? What activities, behavioural practices and characteristics do effective HMULs display? The pertinence of this question is made all the more important due to, as stated above, the international management literature's (self-serving?) obsession with 'geoleaders' and expatriates rather than HCNs and – most pertinently with regard to this text – subsidiary middle managers such as HMULs.

1.6 A Model of International Multi-Unit Leadership

This text is intended to address a gap in the literature highlighted above; namely, to date there has been little empirical, conceptual or theoretical elucidation of the HMUL position. In addition there has been virtually no focused enquiry as to how they might be *developed*. This is an important omission given that most commentators agree that local management capability is a critical enabler in determining internationalising firms' success. The ability to translate strategy and policy into action whilst adapting it sensitively (and imaginatively) to local nuances should (theoretically) rest heavily upon this cohort. This section will, first, outline the research base for conducting an investigation into their activities and development and, second, consider the overarching conceptual framework that informs the structure of this book.

1.6.1 RESEARCH AND METHODOLOGY

Using the effective MUL model from Edger 2012 as a start-point and comparator for the expert respondents, the principal questions that the research posed to the 'panel' for this book were:

1. What growth paths are IMUEs pursuing?
2. What do HMULs do? What do they focus upon?
3. How do they operate effectively, overcoming extant contextual issues and barriers? How and with what practices?
4. What development mechanisms do IMUEs deploy to improve the capability of this vital cadre of employees?

At this point, it is necessary to consider the method of data collection and analysis for this study, followed by a consideration of its strengths and limitations.

1.6.1.1 Data collection

The data collection method for the primary research of this book followed an inductive multi-method approach over *two distinct phases* over the period 2007–2013. In *phase one* (predominantly 2007–2011), effort and focus was mainly concentrated upon MUL research in 'developed' contexts (with some HMUL data capture); *phase two* (2011–2013) concentrated exclusively on the activities, characteristics and developmental requirements of HMULs operating in 'growth' or 'developing' environments.

The actors selected for analysis during *phase one* of the analysis were located at senior and middle-management levels in both 'developed' *owner/parent* and 'growth' and 'developing' *subsidiary/partner* contexts. In *phase two*, the author assembled a 'panel' of experts drawn from practitioners, academics and consultants who had extensive knowledge of either managing and/or developing multi-site managers in growth markets. In all there were 20 respondents (see the acknowledgements section at the front of the book), some of whom generously gave their permission for case study material to be published based upon their insights and expertise. The IMUE multi-site 'talent development' knowledge of these experts was extensive, covering Confucian Asia (including China), Southern Asia (including India), Eastern Europe (including Russia), Middle East (including the Gulf States) and Latin America (see the précis to each case study). Having received a draft or first edition of Edger (2012) these respondents were, first, interviewed to establish responses to the broad questions outlined above and then, second – when specific points of interest arose – were 'funnelled' to give detailed accounts of HMUL activities and *development* requirements within certain organisational, cultural and local contexts.

In addition to these sources the author was able to draw on two other major *action learning-derived* sources of data (experiential and previous research) which helped shape and inform this study:

1. *Participant Observer Status* – During the mid-1990s the author acted in a HCN manager capacity as Commercial Director for a UK leisure corporation, facilitating the franchised entry of two US leisure brands into the UK market (Dave and Busters and Wendy's). From 1997 to 2002 the author operated as a parent company executive in an MNC organisation (turnover £2 billion, EBITDA of £220 million and 10,000 employees) with a wholly owned business in the Czech Republic (3,000 employees) and a joint venture in China (2,500 employees). In his position as Commercial and HR Director he had a 'dotted line' functional responsibility for these territories, resolving expatriate/HCN talent deployment and HRM alignment. In addition, following two major takeovers by foreign corporations (North European and US) – for the sums of £2.3 billion and $1.7 billion respectively – the author fulfilled a role as part of the host country executive leadership team. More latterly (2008–2010), the author was HR and Productivity Director (i.e. member of the parent company executive) of the largest casual dining chain in the UK which also owned a multi-unit hospitality business in Germany. In this role he was involved in both expatriate and HCN manager selection and contract negotiations.
2. *Previous Cross-Border M&A Research and Teaching* – In 2008 the author was awarded a PhD from Warwick Business School, UK, in connection to the research he had conducted in the area of international HRM and cross-border M&A. During the course of the data collection for this award he collected primary research from both owner and subsidiary respondents in order to build an inductively-based conceptual model of 'International HRM and Cross-Border M&A'. During the period 2007–2012 he has taught 'Behavioural Perspectives on Cross-Border M&A' to over 400 students on the International HRM module element of the Executive and Distance Learning MBA at Warwick. The process of interaction with the students (many of whom have included both parent and subsidiary multi-site executives and managers) has been extremely useful in framing multiple approaches and perspectives within this book.

In addition to these primary sources, during the course of this research the author also secured and made use of secondary sources such as:

- Job descriptions and competency models;
- Training and development material;
- Balanced scorecards;
- Operational manuals, etc.

Other sources such as trade magazines, financial press cuttings, annual reports, blogs and web-based data also provided additional data – particularly with regard to international strategising and the economic dynamics of 'growth' and 'developing' markets.

1.6.1.2 Data analysis

Having completed data collection the researcher must engage in a process of data analysis, being comfortable with both ambiguity and fluidity (Miles and Huberman 1994). In the case of this research, and its pattern of setting a broad research question (i.e. what do HMULs do and how are they *developed*?) rather than hypotheses, the selection of complementary research tools and identification of suitable research sites followed Eisenhardt's (1989) recommended route of data analysis and conceptual construction. The first step of the data analysis process was, as previously outlined, a 'cross-site analysis … which give[s] investigators a rich familiarity' with the data (Eisenhardt 1989: 540). Second, the interview evidence captured from informants/contributors, when combined with prior action-based learning (i.e. participant observation, PhD research and student interaction during international MBA teaching), was analysed to expose important critical aspects of the subject of analysis (i.e. the activities, practices and *developmental* needs of HMULs) from which iterative narratives began to flow. The third step involved structuring emerging patterns and themes from these narratives into an integrated account.

The benefits of such a multi-method, cross-sector/profession, internationally-focused approach were twofold. First, it allowed the functions and characteristics of HMULs to be investigated across a range of multi-unit service organisations in a number of 'growth' and 'developing' contexts. Second, and most significantly – in comparison to previous research methods – it afforded a degree of triangulation by different cohorts of IMUE experts (i.e. practitioners, consultants and academics) on the functions, practices and *development* of HMULs. Conversely, its weaknesses or drawbacks include its scope for repeatability (given its multi-method dimensions, time and context) and, to date, the lack of rigorous scientific testing of its emergent conceptual framework (in spite of its positive 'sense testing' with notable international multi-unit actors). The author also acknowledges that his position as a 'situated observer' (as an ex-parent owner executive, HCN manager, MUL author and teacher) is open to accusations of contamination and bias with regards to research construction, data collection and interpretation.

1.6.2 CONCEPTUAL FRAMEWORK AND BOOK STRUCTURE

The conceptual model (see Figure 1.2) which emerged from this in-depth research and prior action learning is an extension of the previous effective MUL model (Edger 2012), being based around four main clusters: country forces, parental international performance factors, partner/subsidiary local performance factors and 'host' multi-unit leader functions.

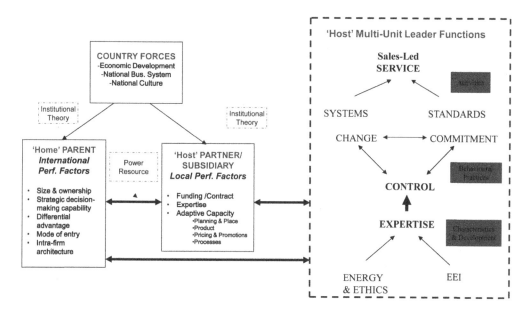

Figure 1.2   International Multi-Unit Leadership Model (© Chris Edger)

1.6.2.1 Clusters, constructs and critical dependencies

As stated, the model (which informs the structure of the book) is framed around four interlinked clusters which are mediated by two theoretical forces (see 1.6.2.2 below).

Country forces include the critical drivers of economic development, national business system effects and national culture. These forces have an impact on performance factors at both 'home' and 'host' level. With regard to the *'home' parent* a number of performance factors feature: size and ownership, strategy-making capability, differential advantage, mode of entry and intra-firm architecture. These considerations have an impact on *'host' partner/subsidiary* performance although 'local' factors such as levels of financial funding, expertise and adaptive capacity with regard to planning/place, product, pricing/promotions and processes have a high contingent effect. The cluster at the end of the chain reflects where policy is operationalised at field-based HMUL level. This *HMUL function* cluster has three main elements: activities (including sales-led service, systems and standards), behavioural practices (control, commitment and change) and personal characteristics (expertise, environmental emotional intelligence – EEI – and energy and ethics). Although this cluster is closely linked to the 'host' subsidiary level, it has a direct link – for developmental and knowledge transfer purposes – to the 'home' parent.

1.6.2.2 Theoretical underpinning

Two explanatory theoretical perspectives emerged from narratives captured by this research, governing the linkages and dependencies within the conceptual model:

- *Institutional Theory* – This sociologically-based 'structural' approach is based around the insight that differing national business systems have idiosyncratic rules, laws and procedures which have an effect on the organisational structures which inhabit each system's domain (Whitley 1999, Hall and Soskice 2001). Whilst there might be degrees of convergence due to the effects of globalisation or the agency of international (or supranational) authorities, nation-state legislatures and local custom-based divergences remain pertinent to the understanding of *required* and *permitted* organisational and (indeed) individual behaviours in certain territories (Smith and Meiksins 1995). In the case of Figure 1.2 it is posited, on the basis of the research, that country of origin and host country institutional effects are a mediator between parent/owner and local (subsidiary/partner) firms. Also, institutional forces (particularly with regard to national culture) are linked to HMUL activities, behaviours and characteristics.

- *Power Resource Theory (PRT)* – This sociologically-based 'power' perspective emphasises the relations between two *interdependent* parties being contingent on the 'law of reciprocity' (Cropanzano and Mitchell 2005). Intra-firm owner-subsidiary/partner relations cannot be conceived purely in hierarchical terms (i.e. the owner governs), but rather as a political space where resources such as information, money, services and goods (Foa and Foa 1980) are traded in order to establish power and authority (in the owner's case) or local autonomy (in the subsidiary's case) (Ferner and Edwards 1995). This is certainly true of the owner-subsidiary respondent narratives contained within this study, with high levels of profit/ROI (i.e. money in RET terms) conferring a high degree of autonomy for the subsidiary BUT high levels of owner control being applied when returns are deemed unacceptable. Thus, in Figure 1.2 PRT is represented as a strong governing force between the owner firm and local subsidiary.

1.6.2.3 Book structure and arguments

The structure of this book follows the conceptual framework outlined in Figure 1.2. Chapter 2 (Internationalisation Performance Factors) analyses what the academic literature has said to date on the mediating variables that have a contingent effect on internationalisation success or failure, concluding that the dominant conundrum posed by these commentaries is how IMUEs should rationally *calibrate* market opportunities alongside a deep emotional *cognisance* of context. Chapter 3 (Activities and Issues) combines both academic insights and practitioner Case Studies to consider the factors that lead to subsidiary/partner success, concluding that to be successful IMUEs must simultaneously ensure both organisational *congruence* and local *customisation*. The consideration of field-based HMUL practices is then dealt with over the next three chapters – practical empirical commentary/Case Study evidence being prefaced by academic insights. Thus, Chapter 4 (Ensuring Control) begins with an elucidation of control typologies and consideration of cross-cultural determinants, followed by HMUL control practices and preferences, concluding with the triangulated observation that in order to gain *co-ordination* (through bureaucratic and value-led means) IMUEs must facilitate high levels of *consent*. Chapter 5 (Generating Commitment) examines the international service, leadership style and HRM literature, progressing on to consideration of the practices that HMULs deploy in order to engage their teams, concluding that in order to bolster levels of local leadership *capability*,

IMUEs must ensure local *compatibility* of their HRM systems. Chapter 6 (Implementing Change) précises the top-down, bottom-up and middle-up-down change/knowledge diffusion literature and then considers HMUL practices in this area, concluding that IMUEs must increase individual *capacity* (i.e. abilities and motivation) with regard to change/ knowledge dissemination processes, which in turn will encourage *collaboration* and cross-fertilisation. Chapter 7 (Characteristics and Development) considers the personal characteristics and interventions that are required for effective HMUL *development*, Edger's (2012) model being supplemented by constructs such as courage, humility, respect and ethics. Chapter 8 (Conclusion) expands on the key themes of the book that represent a number of *conundrums* and *dualisms* that IMUEs must consider/address in order to be successful both at a strategic level and with regards to HMUL development.

2 *Internationalisation Performance Factors*

Chapter 1 referred to some of the macro and micro challenges facing internationalising multi-unit organisations at the present time, including the growing significance of local competition. As Figure 1.2 demonstrates, there are further interlinked forces and contingent variables that need to be considered in a contextual consideration of the subject in question. These will be elaborated upon in this chapter which will delve deeper into the processes and success factors of internationalisation: broader dependencies which determine the success or failure of HMUL operations. A combination of academic insights and case studies will illuminate the constructs which populate owner and subsidiary context drivers highlighted in Figure 1.2.

Most academic texts concern themselves with analysing internationalising organisation performance factors at two levels, usually defined as 'firm and country-level' (Chan et al. 2011) or 'cultural and business level' (Evans et al. 2000). The overarching theoretical position that is postulated in this literature is that the success of internationalising firms is contingent upon the degree to which the parent reduces the *psychic distance* between itself and its foreign markets in order to pursue effective strategies, policies and practices:

> *... psychic distance can be defined as the distance between the home market and a foreign market resulting from the perception and understanding of cultural and business differences. (Evans et al. 2000: 376)*

In this theoretical paradigm it is not physical or cultural closeness that assures success (the point being made that many Canadian retail businesses have failed to successfully transfer to the US market); rather, it is the *accurate perception* of differences. Hence intervening variables such as *strategic decision-making* and *managerial attitudes* and *characteristics* are extremely important in helping internationalising firms to make the right *market entry choices* in order to pursue their *differential advantages*.

This chapter will firstly deal with *country-level forces* which impact the distance between 'developed' owners and 'growth' and 'developing' subsidiaries through *institutionally-based effects* such as the *economic environment*, country of origin/host country *national business systems* and *national culture*. Second, 'business' or 'firm-level' success factors at *owner* level will be discussed including *size and ownership, strategic decision-making, differential advantage*, mode of *market entry choice, intra-firm architecture* and ongoing *resource commitment*. Finally the chapter will consider the dynamic relationship between the two parties, arguing that whilst performance might be affected by the degree of *psychic distance* between the two parties, with *institutional forces* playing a large part in determining business systems and culture, intra-firm relations are *also* regulated by *agency forces* (particularly with regard to 'contract-based' relationships) and *power resource forces* (in the case of wholly or partially 'owned assets') which either facilitate a relationship characterised by reciprocity/commitment or resistance/resentment.

2.1 Developed 'Home' Country of Origin-Level Factors

Implicit within the concept of psychic difference is the notion that significant differences exist between regional and/or national business systems and cultures (Beckerman 1956, Vahlne and Wiedersheim-Paul 1973). Institutionally-based perspectives develop this position further by viewing organisations as social entities that seek approval for their structures and activities in legally and socially-constructed, coercive environments (Powell and DiMaggio 1991, Scott 1995). In order to survive, organisations must conform in order to gain legitimacy and acceptance (Meyer and Rowan 1977, Zucker 1977). This means that internationalising firms must achieve a difficult balancing act – melding their policies and structures effectively to gain legitimacy both home and abroad. At times their attempts to achieve conformance in their home markets will shape their perceptions and actions with regards to foreign markets, eventually impacting upon host institutions. Although there is some debate as to whether 'societies in dominance' (i.e. US, Western Europe and Japan) have globalised certain practices (Smith and Meiksins 1995), the overwhelming view remains that regional, national and local characteristics, shaped by powerful indigenous national business and cultural effects remain embedded, requiring careful consideration by internationalising organisations (Whitley 1999).

If it is the divergences that count, from a 'developed' country perspective, what are the dominant economic, national business and cultural characteristics that might prove problematic for internationalising companies? Defining a coherent number of national business system and culturally-related characteristics is difficult given that 'developed' markets are marked by stark differences; however, commentators (i.e. Jones 2012) have elucidated a number of universal factors that shape managerial perceptions and organisational behaviour; namely:

- Economic development – Advanced economic development has enabled 'developed' organisations to grow 'economy of scale'-sized business models supported by sophisticated industrial and commercial infrastructures.
- National business system – Political stability and the rule of law have framed dependable operating environments for 'developed' economy businesses: rules and procedures that, if followed, lead to (relatively) certain outcomes.
- National culture – Most advanced economies are characterised (according to Hofstede's 1980 typology – see 2.2.3 below) by a high degree of individualism and low power distance, avoidance and diffusion. That is to say that there is a high propensity for individuals to seek autonomy and self-expression, a medium/low regard for status, a willingness to accept ambiguity and a clear separation between work and relationships.

Such 'developed' country of origin characteristics often frame managerial expectations of those seeking to internationalise their operations (O'Neill 2011). In order to close 'perceptual distances', greater understanding is required of growth' and 'developing' host country differences in order to ensure international success. But what are the generic factors that might aid internationalisation performance? The sections below will now provide an account of these variables.

2.2 Growth and Developing Host Country-Level Factors

At a 'macro' host country level within emerging markets what are the mediating factors upon performance that internationalising companies from developed territories take account of in order to provide some assurance of success? This section will argue that there are three main factors including economic and retail market attractiveness, national business systems risks and idiosyncratic cultural features. These will be considered in turn.

2.2.1 ECONOMIC AND RETAIL MARKET ATTRACTIVENESS

Numerous academic studies have pointed to the size and growth potential of developing markets as a major factor in internationalising success (Alexander 1990, Quinn 1999). In particular moderately developed economies offer the best opportunities for growth performance if organisations enter at the beginning (or just after) the ascendant economic curve (Coe and Wrigley 2007). What factors should companies take account of when examining foreign markets? Academic commentary, allied to empirical analysis of organisational behaviour suggests four areas should be examined with regard to economic market attractiveness including growth and fiscal stability, demographic and social indicators, infrastructure and supply chain development and nascent local competition.

2.2.1.1 Economic growth and fiscal stability

Obvious indicators for decision-makers with internationalising firms include GDP growth, service sector expansion and per capita income trends (which have a mediating effect on discretionary household spends). Other indices of importance relate to the degree of national fiscal control: tax raising abilities, serviceability of the national debt, combined with anti-inflationary capabilities (Leahy 2012). The latter point is significant. Internationalising organisations do not want to be exposed to the vicissitudes of rampant inflation that threaten to degrade their costly land-based investments and carefully crafted business models.

2.2.1.2 Demographic and social indicators

Linked with the economic growth factors above is the demographic architecture of the market and associated social indicators. Whilst overall population size is a major attractor, of greater interest might be the size of different demographic groupings. Countries with a proportionate weighting towards a younger rather than ageing population are more attractive, promising increased future consumption patterns (particularly when allied to some of the positive economic factors outlined above). Also, social indicators such as urban growth, unemployment, education, skills and social mobility are important 'attractiveness indices' (Mallaby 2013). Urban conurbation growth providing high population densities represents geographic centres of (potential) high/concentrated demand. This indicator is made even more powerful when linked to adequate housing provision, low rates of unemployment and adequate educational systems facilitating higher skill levels that accelerate social mobility.

2.2.1.3 Infrastructure and supply chain development

Another factor – particularly with regard to retail market attractiveness – is the degree to which target markets have sufficiently robust infrastructures and supply chain capabilities to enable businesses to 'scale up'. Taking Russia, for example, specific issues relate to customs officialdom, affecting supply chain responsiveness:

> *Russia is a lot more bureaucratic than India or Brazil and you lose a lot more time in red tape than in other markets when founding a venture and dealing with logistics … The distances involved are huge so that presents another complication … Shipments of goods can get stuck at customs so the company has to maintain a much larger stock in its central warehouse than branches in India or Brazil. (Morarjee 2012: 39)*

From an infrastructure perspective, positive features in growth markets will include (existing or planned) transport systems (road, rail and air), power supply and utilities and communications networks (telephony, internet and media). In addition the strength of local services is pertinent, especially with regards to land-based branch formats. How competent are local service firms such as builders, architects, lawyers, real estate professionals, etc.? In terms of supply chain provision – where companies might wish to locally source products to reduce freight charges or bypass customs restrictions (see above) – what are the strengths or weaknesses of other sectors such as agriculture and manufacturing?

2.2.1.4 Local competition

On the face of it many developing markets look attractive because retail saturation levels appear low. However, the Introduction hinted at how internationalising organisations can often under-estimate the actual *or* potential strength of local competition. This competition can essentially take two forms: other subsidiaries of international organisations or home-grown competitors. In the case of the former, organisations that have spotted a market opportunity are unlikely to be alone. In the grocery sector, for instance, behemoths such as Walmart, Carrefour and Tesco are most likely to be jostling one another to, first, gain entry through an appropriate vehicle (see 2.3.4 below) and, second, gain primacy over one another in any given regional or national market space. With regards to the latter, local retail firms will, most likely, adopt a 'follow the competitor' strategy, imitating the best aspects of the new entrant (say operational systems and merchandising) whilst adapting their offer to local tastes and preferences. Also, given their in-depth knowledge of the local marketplace, they are in a better position (if funding is available) to – crucially with regard to land-based multi-unit enterprises – determine and exploit the best sites and locations for rapid system growth.

2.2.2 NATIONAL BUSINESS SYSTEM RISKS

The national business system literature makes the argument that MNCs domiciled within specific national or regional business systems operate according to norms, standards and procedures that will differ from those of the companies that they may acquire or operate outside these spheres (Whitley 1999). The extent to which they are able to export practices or conform to local environments, following the acquisition of companies in foreign territories, remains a pertinent debate within this stream of literature (Hall and Soskice 2001). Whilst internationalising companies *might* have a preference for operating under the same codes of conduct and rule of law as exist within their own home markets (see 2.1 above), they need to be cognisant of endemic institutionally-embedded risks – which might threaten the efficiency and viability of their business model – that are associated with doing business in emerging markets, namely, political corruption, legal opaqueness and regional fragmentation (Jones 2012).

2.2.2.1 Political corruption and uncertainty

Unlike western liberal democracies where there is a (relatively) clear separation between politics and business, many emerging economies are characterised by having a political class that has extremely strong ties with commercial interests (FT Analysis 2012a: 10). In these contexts – where '*hard* positional' as opposed to '*soft* democratic' *power* prevails – important contracts and planning decisions might be traded by politicians with multi-unit companies in exchange for self-serving financial gain (Robertson 2012: 40). Indeed, in some cultures nothing is seen as being wrong with this, 'kick-backs' and 'back handers' being seen as an entitlement by the corrupt ruling political elite:

> *Almost everyone in China agrees that corruption is endemic ... the (Communist) party itself is above the law ... 'Whereas corruption in Japan and South Korea was "structural" and institutionalised, in China it was anarchic and predatory', Andrew Wedeman, an expert on Chinese corruption, writes in his new book, Double Paradox ... 'corrupt officials were not ... scraping off a share of the gains companies earned from the government's pro-growth policies: in most cases they were simply preying on companies, stealing a share of their profits in return for not harming them or, in many cases, stealing from the state itself'. (Hille 2012: 4)*

The problem that arises for international organisations that decide not to be complicit in such activities is that they can fall victim to 'revenge tactics', where other companies (most likely locally based) are given preferential treatment over them, or they find themselves being punished for minor misdemeanours. In addition, political uncertainty with regards to regime change where, for instance, liberal free-market policies are instantly substituted by new protectionist rules, remains an ever-present threat in territories with intemperate/unstable political elites/systems.

2.2.2.2 Legal opaqueness

In tandem with this risk of a corrupt and uncertain political environment there is likely to be the existence of a high degree of – what might be speciously called – legal opaqueness (Clover 2012: 1). That is to say that *even* where there might be laws, rules and procedures pertaining to the pursuance of trade within particular territories, they might not be particularly well observed or enforced (Chilkoti and Jopson 2013). As Rahan Tata, an eminent Indian industrialist, commented:

> ... *different agencies in the [Indian] government have almost contradictory interpretations of the law, or interpretations of what should be done ... this game of appeasing or surrendering to a venal system, the soft option – the easy way out – is a compromise. (YahooFinanceUK 2012)*

A close formal or informal relationship between the judiciary and politicians in some countries has, on occasion, led to laws being 'mysteriously' interpreted and applied against the interests of international organisations. This lack of justice, especially with regards to fraudulent activity relating to title, copyright and intellectual property, has grave consequences for organisations with proprietary products or brands. In addition, censorship and dubious human rights protection – especially where countries are not signatories to worldwide conventions – mean that deploying home country nationals might be fraught with danger.

2.2.2.3 Regional fragmentation

It is not only at national government level that international companies need to understand national business system effects, but also – in huge territories that pass through multiple time zones and languages – with regard to the relevant powers relating to regional officialdom. For instance, in India there are 26 regional governments presiding over expansive terrains encompassing over 22 official languages. With significant tax raising and planning powers these local governments, in a nation famed for its endless bureaucracy, can present significant barriers to international firms. Also, given that in some countries, such as China, local governments have been charged with building new towns and cities – often at huge cost (partially due to uncommercial contracts) – the threat of unsustainable property bubbles causing regional insolvency makes certain micro-markets extremely high-risk candidates for expansion.

2.2.3 IDIOSYNCRATIC CULTURAL FEATURES

National culture is defined as the values, beliefs and assumptions learned in early childhood that differentiate one group of people from another and has been argued by some scholars to be an important and relatively stable component of countries (Beck and Moore 1985, Hofstede 1993, Newman and Nollen 1996). National cultural features embody the 'software of the mind', deeply embedded in everyday life, and are fairly resistant to change (Hofstede 1980, 1991, 1993). It is argued that while internationalising firms have so far paid attention to visible national business systems, such as laws and regulations (see above), when deciding how to operate in foreign locations, they have been less analytical concerning national culture-driven social customs and patterns of behaviour that are acceptable to the general population (Florkowski and Schuler 1994).

In the context of national variations, the classic account of national cultural differences within organisations was provided by Hofstede (1980), through his extensive international study of IBM. In this research he categorised differences between the distinctive national traits within geographical units of IBM as being related to *uncertainty avoidance*, *power distance*, *masculinity* and *individualism* (and their polar opposites). Since its publication this typology (which has since been extended to five measures to include *short/long-term view*) has been used as a proxy – by innumerable academics and consultants – to describe and measure differences between cultures. With regards to this study, aspects of both Hall's (1976) and Hofstede's (1980, 1991) models are pertinent to analysing cultural factors affecting internationalising businesses transitioning from developed to emerging markets – particularly with regard to how they conduct their business on a day-to-day basis in these territories; namely, *power distance*, *collectivist*, *uncertainty avoidance* and *diffusion effects* (for a more comprehensive overview summary of the various constructs see sections 4.2.2.2 and 5.2.2).

2.2.3.1 Power distance effects

Power distance refers to the degree to which members of a group or society are conditioned to either consciously or unconsciously submit to the dictates of higher authorities. 'High power distance' cultures demonstrate a high level of submission to those 'in power' (usually men), whilst 'low power distance' cultures have a balanced/sceptical regard for those in authority. Many emerging markets are characterised by the former state, their cultures being notable for extreme deference to seniors, hierarchy and status. This condition persists even when privileged agents of power perform poorly or corruptly through what might be politely termed dishonest opportunism. A lack of legal recourse to protection from retribution in the past (particularly in totalitarian regimes) has created a form of 'Stockholm syndrome' where the 'oppressed' have submitted to the will of their 'captors'. The growth of social media and (soft) democracy, it is argued, might dilute these power distance effects over time as those abusing their positions are brought to account for their actions. However, it is remarkable how embedded deference for authority has remained in many emerging states, meaning that internationalising companies must understand that for many emerging nation citizens 'country comes before company' – particularly if it is from foreign climes.

2.2.3.2 Collectivist effects

Combined with these effects is the extent to which many emerging markets continue to embrace – in marked contrast to the individualistic west – their collectivist-type cultures. In the societies of many emerging markets there remains a precedence of 'family and group' before 'company' (Asma 2012, Clark 2012). Unlike in developed nations, families in emerging nations form strong support structures, living in an extended form. There is strong group identification in these societies, with a village-type mentality persisting amongst their members. The effects of this translate into behaviours at workplace level that might prove difficult for managers from developed markets to understand and/or ameliorate. First, high degrees of nepotism occur where individuals attempt to serve the interests of their direct social networks rather than the organisation. Second, workers are inclined to avoid blame through covering up for one another. Third, as showing initiative might show up other poorly performing members of the group, employees are likely, in a perverse attempt to remain loyal to their colleagues, to remain silent. In addition, as there is little tradition of encouragement and praise at the workplace level in many of these societies, attempts by organisations to exhort workers to higher levels of discretionary effort through autonomy and engagement-led practices are likely to fail.

2.2.3.3 Uncertainty avoidance effects

Allied to the fact – for the reasons outlined above – that levels of worker initiative in some emerging markets are low, there is also a high propensity for workers to seek unambiguous, explicit instruction on the minutiae of what they are expected to do. Employees in 'uncertainty avoidance' cultures find ambiguity and uncertainty disorientating, requiring detailed rules and instructions on how tasks should be performed. Expectations from management have to be clearly stated in order to ensure subordinates feel comfortable. This means that when requirements are not communicated effectively, operational systems are at a severe risk of breaking down. This problem is further compounded by the fact that in order not to be shown up or 'lose face', workers (see above) seem programmed not to request clarification but pretend that they know what is expected of them. Such behaviour is mystifying and annoying to managers from developed markets where workers are apt to request clarity when they fail to understand 'standing orders'.

2.2.3.4 Diffusion effects

In parallel to the cultural dimensions above, many emerging markets are domiciled in societies which possess *high context* 'diffuse characteristics'. That is to say, as relationships are regarded as being more important than business outcomes, western patterns of 'sequential management' practice are doomed to failure. Time management skills are poor as managers and workers place greater value upon relationships rather than rules. Planning systems are regarded as anathema given that most outcomes are believed to be determined by random sequences of events. This leaves western managers, some of whom are steeped in Blanchard and Covey-style learning, at a loss when exhorting employees working in these 'diffuse' environments to 'start with the end in mind'. In fact, it could be argued that all of the cultural traits above that apply wholly – or in part – to emerging markets, militate against the application of widely touted 'universalistic' best-practice US HRM and Coveyesque principles.

2.3 Parent Firm-Level Factors

The sections above referred to some of the challenges that are posed, at both national country of origin and host country level, for internationalising firms – not least the fact that there might be some distance between the economic, national business and cultural factors that govern the ambient business environments in both contexts. But what are the specific factors which mediate internationalisation performance at owner firm level? The retail internationalisation process literature tends to characterise international retailers as mirroring two forms: either multi-national or global (Salmon and Tordjman 1989). Multi-national retailers are dextrous at adapting their model to fit local exigencies whilst global retailers are apt to retain their standard formats (see 2.3.3.4 below). The reality is that organisations rarely take a binary approach, adjusting their strategy according to internal and external considerations. Some of these firm-specific dimensions affecting performance will be discussed below, including *size and ownership*, *differential advantage*, *strategic decision making capability*, *mode of entry*, *intra-firm architecture* and *resource allocation*.

2.3.1 SIZE AND OWNERSHIP

The size and ownership of an international firm is believed by commentators to be a key factor in assessing performance (Agarwal 1994). Empirical evidence suggests that international retailers tend to be larger, at least within their domestic environments. Why are both these factors contingent upon success?

2.3.1.1 Enterprise scale

As stated, several academics have found a relationship between retail multiple domestic scale and its international spread (Vida et al. 2000). The reasons for this are largely common sense: larger companies are more likely to have the resources and capabilities to fund costly overseas expansion (Evans et al. 2000). In addition, they are more likely able to absorb, and deal with, some of the risks associated with international growth – particularly in emerging markets. Larger firms can offset some of the downside by being able to afford to commission more detailed research, fund best-in-class legal support and engage experienced third-party providers who are experts in their target territories.

2.3.1.2 Type of ownership

Type of ownership is also seen as a mediating factor on performance. Publically owned enterprises in developed economies are likely (due to open share registers and regular financial reporting) to take a fairly short-termist approach. Investor scrutiny and criticism will build particularly if 'foreign adventures' are adjudged to have turned sour – making them extremely risk-averse to 'future excursions'. Hence management in these enterprises are under intense pressure to make their foreign investments work instantly, demonstrating a quick positive ROI. Privately owned companies, however, can take a more pragmatic long-term approach. In the early years of investment owners can absorb losses outside of the public spotlight (because it's their money), refining and improving their formats and products with a view to long-term sustainability (a good example being Aldi in the UK in the early 1990s).

2.3.2 STRATEGIC DECISION-MAKING CAPABILITY

The strategic decision-making capability of the firm has a major impact on whether a firm is internationally successful, having a strong intervening effect on the challenges posed by psychic distance. As the section below will elucidate perceptual gaps will be reduced if decision-makers have high levels of experiential knowledge and apply a proper process to the business of foreign expansion.

2.3.2.1 Experiential knowledge

The voluminous academic literature on knowledge coalesces around the central insight that firms with a rich systemic body of knowledge can develop unique capabilities which will generate valuable outcomes (Nelson and Winter 1982, Barney 1991). In an international context the literature points to experiential knowledge as being essential (i.e. knowledge garnered through direct experience). Essentially there are three types of experiential knowledge that are useful for decision-makers, namely, *international*, *host country* and *sectoral*.

- International experience – A useful aptitude that decision-makers can possess is what some commentators term international market portfolio management (IMPM). Indeed, it is postulated that international firms that possess IMPM perform better than those that don't (Etgar and Rachman-Moore 2008, Chan et al. 2011). What is it? Essentially decision-makers with IMPM skills have deep experiential knowledge of the processes and potential pitfalls of international expansion. They have learnt from previous successes and failures and are able to codify best-practice systems, operations and entry approaches in order to optimise success. An oft-cited example of IMPM is IKEA who, having learnt from mistakes made during their China entry, applied their learning on entering the Russian market (Jonsson and Elg 2006).
- Host country experience – A useful attribute is also personal knowledge of the political, cultural and business characteristics of the host market which might pre-empt any major mistakes being made with regard to product or place. Such a position facilitates a more accurate perception of psychic distance between the organisation's proposed offer and systems and its 'contextual fit'. Such in-depth experience is also useful in terms of 'spatial pre-emption' (see 2.3.4.1 below), aiding decision-makers to leverage first-mover advantage (especially in key urban sites) due to their superior country knowledge (Kerin and Varadarajin 1992).
- Sectoral experience – In addition to the above, the possession of specific retail portfolio management (RPM) capabilities is highly beneficial to strategic decision-making outcomes (Chan et al. 2011). Experience in areas such as multi-format/ channel expansion – once market entry has been achieved – can assist rapid system growth. Locking down 'gold brick' sites (in malls, retail parks, high footfall streets, etc.) in key urban conurbations and then driving aggressive roll-out is one aspect of RPM. Another is the appropriation of sufficient warehousing, logistics and supply chain capabilities to service demand for the expanding network of stores.

2.3.2.2 Attitudes and decision-making process

Experiential knowledge suggests that decision-makers will be able to act rationally, according to information which is founded upon, and interpreted according to, their deep insights. However, such a normative account of decision-making fails to account for major factors such as decision-maker personalities and – in the absence of some of the factors above – their own subjective attitudes, tastes and preferences which have been moulded by prior home experience. Perception of knowledge, meaning and reality in international markets can differ amongst decision-makers not least when some personalities are characterised by a lack of self-awareness, ego, arrogance or over-confidence. For instance, success in one market can lead decision-makers to become overconfident that they have found a 'universal approach' that can apply internationally. Indeed, research has indicated that whilst some companies start off successfully in their international expansion plans, they are derailed by 'over-exuberance' in later forays (Haleblian and Finkelstein 1999). In the absence of direct experiential knowledge, some commentators have argued that education can be a mediating factor in fashioning international outcomes, there being some connection between the education of decision-makers and advanced cognitive and thinking, which aids management of the expansion process. The one factor that most commentators agree upon, however, is that companies who fail internationally have not applied a rigorous analytical approach to the decision-making process:

> ... the root of the problem appears to lie in the retailers' lack of preparation and understanding of individual markets. (White 1995: 52)

Hence the lack of appropriate 'real time' information leads to a lack of appropriate analysis and insights, leading to misguided managerial action on the ground – a notable example being the UK DIY chain B&Q in China:

> Kingfisher (owner of B&Q) was one of the very first international businesses to set up shop in China, opening its first store in 1999. But it completely misunderstood the market. Yes, there was a property boom and millions more middle-class Chinese, but they didn't want a traditional B&Q. [CEO Ian Cheshire commented] 'They have a completely different mindset. There is no DIY in China. If you've got the money you need ... it's beneath you to do your own manual work' ... So what on earth is B&Q still doing in China? Cheshire is adamant that since he took the helm and shut down a third of the stores, annual losses of £62m at their peak in 2009 have been reduced to £9m last year. (Wallop 2012: B9)

2.3.3 DIFFERENTIAL ADVANTAGE

Firms can posses scale and decision-makers with experiential knowledge, but their internationalising efforts will amount to nought unless their business model possesses some form of product, branding or operational differential advantage *which can be adapted to context*. Internationalising organisations are most successful when they deploy a unique, differentiated offer – offering customers something that they need/want *and* is not already in existence (or readily accessible) in their own marketplace – *but*, at the same time, is cognizant of local tastes and preferences. Thus, differential advantage for international multi-unit enterprises comes in their overarching *business model, product and brand concept, operational capability* and *adaptive capacity.*

2.3.3.1 Business model

The firm's business model incorporates the end-to-end value chain of the commercial enterprise incorporating some of the elements referred to below. In least-cost business models where a 'lean' philosophy might prevail it is important that multiple interlocking processes are designed around the principles of economy. Premium business models are generally constructed around end-to-end levels of quality, amenity and service. The *individual components* of these models might be replicable; however, it is the transference into international contexts of the *'integrated system'* (from supply chain through to customer order fulfilment) that can afford distinct competitive advantage.

2.3.3.2 Product and brand concept

Certain elements of the firm's business model will be perceived by decision-makers to act as a basis for differentiation in under-developed markets, none more so than its products and/or brands. In terms of multi-unit enterprises, product can be conceived of as format type rather than the manufacturing conceptualisation of products as factory-produced goods. Internationalising firms can export or adapt extant formats for export, something that has been achieved successfully by a number of *mass merchandising* companies (such as grocery, household good and healthcare) over the past 30 years. For instance, Carrefour was extremely successful in the early stages of the foreign expansion of its grocery 'hypermarket' concept in the 1990s. There is strong evidence that *premium/specialist* retail formats travel particularly well as they are (in comparison to mass merchandise) easily transportable and, when in situ, avoid direct competition (Dawson 1994, Muniz-Martinez 1998). Branding is crucial in premium formats such as fashion and accessories which usually incorporate proprietary product lines. In this environment an alluring *'status-led'* brand image validated by distinctive, well-crafted merchandise acts as a formidable barrier to entry for competitors (Wigley and Moore 2007, Thomas 2012).

2.3.3.3 Operational capability

An important aspect of differential advantage – but one that is often overlooked or minimised by academics and commentators – is the degree to which firms have superior operational capabilities which transform inputs through a number of value-added process stages into valuable outputs (Slack et al. 2009). 'Transforming inputs' – staff, technology, buildings and machines – underpin the vital processes that service 'transformed outputs' such as customers, materials and information (Johnston and Clark 2008). These 'transforming inputs' such as the operational team, IT systems (incorporating ERP planning systems, EPOS customer order capture, replenishment systems, etc.), warehousing, fleet and logistics, etc. are vital components of multi-unit firm success. If these capabilities can be leveraged over multiple formats/brands in any given territory, then firms are able to extend their 'efficient frontiers of production' through effective asset optimisation (something that Inditex has achieved in a number of territories it operates in multiple forms).

2.3.3.4 Adaptive capacity

The final component of differential advantage is the ability of firms to intelligently modulate, adapt and then *constantly meld* some of the factors outlined above to fit the dynamic contexts of the markets in which they operate. To a large extent, the capacity to perform this activity will be highly contingent on the levels of integration, intra-firm architecture and the amount of tangible and intangible resources it deploys (see below). However, within the conceptualisation of differential advantage, academic studies have consistently demonstrated that the failure of many international operations is partially connected to the lack of adaptation of their retail offer. Those firms that adapt *at least* some elements of their offer will appear generally to perform better than those that adopt a uniform, standardised approach (Evans et al. 2000). In addition, where management perceive greater cultural differences, they are more likely to 'fit' their offer to the extant conditions, a recent example being provided by the UK 'better' sandwich chain Pret a Manger:

> Unlike British rivals in food and retail which have failed to break the US and Asian markets, Pret has managed to find a formula that translates to markets outside the UK ... 'You have to tweak the model when you go abroad' said Mr Schlee (CEO, Pret a Manger) ... 'In Asia, there are more hot food options and meal deals'. (Ebrahimi 2013: B3)

However, there is little agreement amongst academics on what the optimal position on adapting an offer should be (Chhabra 1996). Elements that academics believe should be *standardised* – based on empirical evidence – include distribution and product (Cavusgil and Zou 1994) and a worldwide definition of store décor, pricing and service (Salmon and Tordjman 1989). On the other hand, components of the offer that should be *adapted* encompass promotion and merchandising assortment (Salmon and Tordjman 1989) and pricing and promotion (Cavusgil and Zou 1994). In reality decision-makers will base their decisions on which elements of the offer to adapt and (most crucially) constantly refresh based on the evolving retail characteristics and cultural idiosyncrasies of the addressable market.

2.3.4 MODE OF ENTRY

In spite of some of the factors outlined above (such as experiential knowledge) 'internationalisation theory' dictates that internationalising firms typically adopt a *low-risk* strategy to enter markets due to lack of perfect information in uncertain foreign environments (Rugman 1981, Rugman and Hodgetts 2003). Other studies have shown that, with regards to entry, first movers generally gain a competitive advantage through '*spatial pre-emption*', that there are certain *size and product dependencies* relating to entry selection and that, in the same way that firms transition through a product *life cycle curve*, international retail has its own 'entry to exit' cycle.

2.3.4.1 Spatial pre-emption

As previously stated, scholars have noted the degree to which 'first market entry shapes future performance' (Chan 2011: 1006). Indeed, many commentaries demonstrate a positive relationship between the timing of entry and sales, market share and growth (Gielens and Dekimpe 2001). Spatial pre-emption enables internationalising organisations to secure markets and the best sites in advance of their competitive set, reducing the likelihood that there will be significant investment by followers. Having established a 'beach-head', successful international entrants, having also established proof of concept, often move decisively in securing primary locations.

2.3.4.2 'High' and 'low'-risk modes

Modes of market entry can be subdivided according to risk (Dawson 1994). Typically high financial risk options – which require a high degree of planning and research by the owner – include:

- Acquisitions – Buying a local firm lies at the extreme end of the risk profile for internationalising firms. The advantages are that they gain complete control of an asset that they can either modify or change to mirror the differential advantages pertaining to their own standardised format, acquiring knowledge, presence and a springboard to rapid roll-out in one bold step (i.e. Tesco in Poland and Thailand: Felsted 2012). However, as most academic research has shown, most M&A ends up having a value-destructive, rather than enhancing, effect. The reasons for this generally relate to financial (overpaying), strategic (wrong target), integration (poorly planned and implemented) and socio-cultural issues ('hard' versus a 'soft' culture) (see Edger 2012: 75–80).
- Organic growth – Firms can enlist local consultants (such as consumer insight, marketing and property) to help their management build a business in foreign territories on a site-by-site basis. Theoretically, the merit of such a strategy is that the right sites can be purchased for the brand format and the firm avoids any integration issues that arise from acquiring. Issues arise, however, if firms select the wrong sites due to lack of market knowledge and/or fail to adjust the consumer proposition appropriately if the initial stores fail to deliver to initial expectations.
- Joint ventures – Companies might choose this option believing it to be a soft route to entry, framing a local joint venture agreement where it utilises the knowledge and expertise of a local firm to help it adapt and roll-out its format, whilst ensuring that risk is equally spread between both parties as the local partner is strongly incentivised (due to its financial tie-in) to make sure that the venture succeeds. In time the internationalising firm might grow in confidence to the extent that it assumes majority control of the jointly owned asset. Common drawbacks to such arrangements relate to issues such as cultural incompatibility or lack of trust between the two parties leading to fractious legal disputes and/or a complete breakdown in relationship.

Low financial risk modes of entry include:

- Web-based – Advances in web-based technology have enabled multi-unit firms to adopt a new low-risk market penetration strategy of setting up online order catalogues backed up by warehousing. This approach is designed to raise consumer awareness, minimising capital outlay on store infrastructure, whilst the next stages of expansion are examined. To date this is a strategy that has (for infrastructure reasons) been mainly pursued in 'developed' to 'developed' market transmissions (i.e. Debenhams in Germany and Marks and Spencer in France).
- Concessions and licensing – This approach involves the retailer granting legal entitlement to foreign companies to use its brands in their own format, sometimes in the form of implants (say in department stores). The only risks to the retailer in these types of agreement are non-payment for goods, a lack of control over the general environment in which its goods might be sold (potentially diluting its brand equity) and the fact that long-term agreements might be difficult to exit, inhibiting its ability to pursue its own organic strategy.
- Franchising – A slightly higher-risk strategy involves the licensing by the owner to a franchisee (single or multiple) of the intellectual property (typically the operational blueprint and design) of its standardised format in exchange for a fixed fee. Additional fees might also be charged for use of proprietary technology, marketing and promotions support and supply chain access. Risk here lies for the owner/franchisor in the form of franchisees undermining the essence of the brand through imperfect execution. Also, insufficient support to franchisees (along the lines of that promised in the licensing document) could lead to costly claims and reputational damage for the owner.

2.3.4.3 Size and product dependency

Although it is difficult to generalise upon which mode of entry is best – beyond making the obvious point that most firms will adopt a low-risk strategy – academics have found there to be two main dependencies with entry, relating to firm size and retail offer. Smaller firms tend to concentrate on rapid geographic expansion through franchising, licensing and concessions, whilst larger firms are likely to pursue market consolidating, acquisitions and joint venture strategies (Dawson 2007, Coe and Wrigley 2007). With regard to retail concept, premium specialist retail is reliant upon organic growth or closely supervised franchising, whilst mass merchandising utilises joint ventures or acquisitions as its preferred market entry mechanisms (Dawson 1993, Chan et al. 2011).

2.3.4.4 Internationalisation life cycle

One aspect of the internationalisation literature is its virtual exclusive concentration upon 'pre-entry strategy' and 'mode of entry' mechanisms to the neglect of 'post-entry', 'assimilation' and 'exit' stages (Dawson and Mukoyama 2006). Internationalisation performance is contingent not only upon entry choices (as outlined by Alexander 1997,

Alexander and Myers 2000, Evans et al. 2000) but upon the whole life cycle – as outlined by Figure 2.1 below illustrating Dawson and Mukoyama's empirical findings:

Process Form Stage	Functional	Spatial	Temporal	Structural
Pre-Entry	Market Analysis	Local Research	Previous Experience	Strategy Review
Entry	Format Design	Market Choice	Entrance Timing	Entry Mode
Post-Entry	Brand Development	System Development	Roll-out Speed	Finan. Mgt.
Assimilation	Social/Cultural Integration		Full Ownership Timing	Subsid. Creation
Exit	Estate Rationalisation		Sale	

Figure 2.1   End-to-end internationalisation process (adapted from Dawson and Mukoyama 2006: 35)

The utility of the framework presented above is its clear elucidation of *post-entry* stages, with Dawson and Mukoyama making the point that during the *functional process* element of this phase, not only do decision-makers need to address the issue of retail brand development but also – during the process of doing so – ensure that appropriate knowledge flows are transferred to Head Office to inform decision-making. This is facilitated by intra-firm architecture, the next major factor in internationalising firm performance which is addressed below.

2.3.5 INTRA-FIRM ARCHITECTURE

As stated, the process literature relating to retail internationalisation tends to focus upon pre-entry and entry stages, rather than post-entry activities. This is a major omission given that what happens after an organisation enters a foreign market is as important as what happens beforehand. Major mistakes can be made in terms of format adaptation, site selection and system development. The question is how can firms expanding into developing terrains minimise these missteps? One way internationalising firms can minimise mistakes is to diligently agree, prescribe and monitor the *activities* of its local foreign extension, something that will be discussed in Chapter 3. Internally, however, it is necessary to have the appropriate architecture (i.e. structure and processes) to optimise intra-firm relations. This section will elucidate conceptualisations of forms of intra-firm architecture by referring to both *generic* and *retail integration* typologies, followed by *knowledge capture/transmission mechanisms* and levels of *resource allocation*.

2.3.5.1 Generic integration typologies

The classic approach to analysing international owner-subsidiary integration was developed by Perlmutter (1969), who characterised three dominant integration approaches according to culture and the centralisation/decentralisation of decision-making processes:

- Ethnocentric – cultural extensions of the parent were implanted in the subsidiaries;
- Polycentric– the subsidiaries adopted characteristics of the local culture;
- Geocentric – both entities converged towards a common culture.

The concept of 'regiocentric' was added later (companies taking a regional view of their operations based on cultural overlaps, i.e. Confucian Asia, Latin America, etc.). Overall, Perlmutter also conceived his framework as a dynamic construct, with international companies transitioning from ethnocentric approaches during the beginning of the relationship with their subsidiaries, to decentralising polycentric and then geocentric (i.e. global convergence) approaches occurring during maturation.

Further developing this integration typology, Bartlett and Ghoshal (1989) proposed an explicitly evolutionary model of the international firm, distinguishing four types:

- Multinational – has a series of dispersed and loosely co-ordinated subsidiaries and tends to be highly decentralised;
- Global – has developed a more co-ordinated and centralised approach to international operations;
- International – places particular weight on the exploitation of parent-company skills through worldwide adaptation; it tends to have a federal structure;
- Transnational – reflects the inability of any other of the structures to handle the growing complexity of markets. This type is characterised by differentiated contributions from each national team, with knowledge being shared, having more of a matrix, and less of a hierarchical organisation, than has been traditional (Kim and Mauborgne 2000).

An additional contribution from the M&A field (Bower 2001, Schweiger 2002) stresses the importance of aligning the integration approach with the intended M&A strategies of the acquirer. Both scholars use a similar typology of integration which they attach to their five generic strategies; namely:

- Consolidation – bringing functions and activities together;
- Standardisation – best-practice implementation across functions;
- Co-ordination – a lighter approach where products may be sold through existing channels but with little change to function or process;
- Intervention – where poor performance in the target requires remedial action by the buyer.

Useful as the frameworks above are they mainly conceive of parents as owning their subsidiaries outright. A useful contribution to integration and intra-firm architecture is made by Whitley who differentiates between three types of owner control based on contract relationships:

Characteristics	Types of Owner Control		
	Direct	Alliance	Mkt. Contracting
Involvement in management	High	Some	Very Low
Concentration of ownership	High	Considerable	Low
Owners' knowledge of business	High	Considerable	Low
Risk-sharing and commitment	High	Considerable	Low
Scope of owner interest	High	Considerable	Low
Exclusivity of ownership	Considerable	Limited	High

Figure 2.2   Characteristics of owner-control types (adapted from Whitley 1999: 35)

The point that Whitley makes is that levels of control are a fundamental determinant of owner and subsidiary/partner behaviour. High levels of control are exercised when the owner has direct control (through ownership) with looser controls being exercised in 'market contracting' relationships. Such a typology has obvious implications for brand franchisors whose brand equity and reputation is (under this model) threatened with (relatively) low levels of influence.

2.3.5.2 Retail integration typologies

Specifically with regards to the international retail process literature (i.e. Martenson 1987, Treadgold 1991), integration is conceptualised through the structural architecture of the firm, taking three forms:

- Centralised – In this structure the aim is standardisation, with decision-making being taken at centre. Inevitable problems occur because decision-makers at Head Office are too far away from local operations to make informed decisions, leading to incorrect assumptions being made with regard to product and merchandising requirements (Martenson 1987).
- Geographically divisionalised – Such structures (often denominated as 'regions') are usually the consequence of attempts to ensure appropriate adaptation of the offer (Treadgold 1991). Often product, merchandising, pricing and promotions decisions are devolved in order to cater for regional/national preferences, needs and differences.
- Decentralised – In this structure subsidiary/partner management is predominantly local. Host country MDs with local retailing and market knowledge are granted autonomy (within an agreed strategic framework) to optimise the retail concept in what is likely to be an evolving, dynamic competitive context. This structure is usually adopted during the late growth/maturity stages of the subsidiary's life cycle when it is under severe competitive pressure (Evans et al. 2008). The advantages of such structures (especially as large compound growth rates tail off) are that they reduce the distance between executive decision-making and local context.

2.3.5.3 Knowledge transmission mechanisms

Reference was made above to how international companies must attend to parent-subsidiary knowledge transfer flows (Dawson and Mukoyama 2006). But how do international firms construct viable *formal* and *informal* processes that ensure that valuable information and insights will provide added value to the decision-making process over a range of issues (i.e. product, merchandising, price, etc.)? The answer is that whilst there is a large literature which relates to *explicit/codified* and *tacit/relational* knowledge *per se* (i.e. its creation, diffusion and adoption within organisations) very little is known about how international multi-unit organisations effectively leverage knowledge over large distances. Generally, the literature describes *types* of parent-subsidiary knowledge transmission mechanisms, common examples being:

- Formal mechanisms
  - Talent deployment (either at head office or subsidiary level – i.e. expatriates, inpatriates, etc.);
  - Job rotation/placements/short assignments;
  - Functional/matrix-structured reporting lines;
  - Working/project groups;
  - Conferences, meetings and courses;
  - Telephony and web-based communication platforms.
- Informal mechanisms
  - Head office/local country field visits;
  - 'Social capital' networking opportunities (i.e. development programmes).

The main issue within international contexts is that due to issues such as language, distance, cultural and contractual constraints, the process of knowledge transference is highly difficult and complex. Which methods work best in any given context? One organisation that deploys 'real-time' knowledge applications is Intidex, the owner, amongst other brands, of fast-fashion chain Zara (5,500 stores worldwide). In this organisation qualitative feedback is sought on the latest launches from regional managers, unit managers and staff from the centre of operations in Spain the day after placement (Keely 2012). 'Trend information' on what colours and designs the customers (dis)liked is sought immediately and, when linked to quantitative data, informs decision-making in succeeding ranges within local markets:

> *A system is in place for retail staff to transmit information [-(on ranges]-) straight to the design team at Arteixo. (Hume 2011: 23)*

> *Store Managers hold daily staff meetings to discuss hyper-local trends, such as which colour of pastel trousers are selling well in Dubai, or what hemlines are it in Bogota. Information which is then fed back to headquarters. (Johnson and Felsted 2011: 13)*

Such sophisticated knowledge feedback loops within international firms, however – according to both previous academic studies and empirical research for this book – seem to be the exception rather than the rule.

2.3.5.4 Resource allocation

The relationship between parent and subsidiary/partner must not be considered (as it usually is) in isolation from the fact that in many major international organisations it forms only one element of a firm's networks and interests. To this extent subsidiary/ partner firms must vie with other entities for resources from a parent who is constantly analysing and appraising where the best use of its resources lies. How can these resources be characterised? In classic terms they can be defined as 'hard'/tangible (i.e. capital) or 'soft'/intangible (i.e. knowledge). However, given that both parties exist in a state of mutual interdependence where a high degree of reciprocity is required for optimal outcomes, definitions provided by resource exchange theorists prove useful in this context, particularly in light of all the exchange constructs referred to above. Adapting Foa and Foa's (1980) framework, essentially six resources are traded between the two parties:

- Money – In 'owned' relationships the parent deploys capital in return for profit whilst in 'licensed' situations contracted partners deploy finance in expectation of a return whilst giving up a proportion of their revenue in fees.
- Information – As stated above, parent owners will disseminate knowledge relating to the offer (i.e. blueprint), whilst subsidiary/partners are expected (dependent on the level of integration) to transfer local information and insights to Head Office.
- Cultural capital – Often the parent will diffuse the most pertinent aspects of its company culture as a means of binding foreign workers into its 'vision, values and brand essence'.
- Goods – In certain sectors (such as fashion and accessories) goods will flow from the parent's supply chain.
- Services – Best-practice IT platforms (i.e. merchandising, stocking and EPOS), format design and logistics capabilities might be transferred from Head Office with back-up support and help desk facilities.
- Status – Conferring on the subsidiary and/or its leadership elevated status (with regards to titles, PR and position) is a form of 'emotional resource' allocation from the parent in return for buy-in and discretionary effort.

If the right levels of resources are applied and traded *both ways* so that *benefits* outweigh *costs* for both parties, then positive *performance* outcomes stand a higher chance of occurring. However, as Chapter 3 will illustrate, intra-firm relations in an international context are rarely that simple.

2.4 Chapter Summary

This chapter has attempted to summarise the literature which elucidates some of the factors relating to whether or not internationalising firms perform successfully when they expand into foreign territories. It started by considering 'home' and 'host' country forces – the characteristics of the expanding firm's 'country of origin' having an impact on the way in which decision-makers 'see the world': perhaps taking an individualistic universal 'society in dominance' perspective (Smith and Meiksins 1995). From a 'host' country standpoint, country forces such as rates of economic development, its national business system and culture have contingent effects on the degree to which they permit or facilitate successful product/market overlays to be made by internationalising organisations. Other contingent factors were then considered for 'owner' success including size and ownership, strategic decision-making capability, differential advantage, mode of entry and intra-firm architecture; the overwhelming impression being conveyed that the process of ensuring high performance internationally is multi-dimensional, making it highly complex and ambiguous for decision-makers.

However, in order to simplify understanding and aid our digestion of these commentaries, two broad themes emerge that would seem to encapsulate what internationalising companies should do when analysing developing market opportunities. First, they should take a rational approach to economically *calibrate* the relative market attractiveness of their business activity, dispassionately assessing the prospects for their 'product-market' combination (see Kottler 2000). In addition to this 'scientific' approach, decision-makers should demonstrate a high degree of emotional *cognisance* to idiosyncratic national business system/cultural nuances that will play a major role in determining whether or not they understand the market sufficiently well to meld their product/brand, policies and practices appropriately to ensure success (i.e. closing down levels of psychic distance). Thus, decisions should be derived from both rational *calibration* and deep emotional *cognisance* of potential opportunities. Such an approach will often be symbolised by the way in which organisations enter markets, provide funding, align their structures and utilise local expertise to develop their products and services – matters which will be discussed in the next chapter.

3 *Activities and Issues*

The previous chapter examined performance factors relating to internationalisation from a parent company perspective. It highlighted the fact that there has been a great deal of research and empirical analysis around understanding *why* and *how* IMUEs expand internationally and the variables which threaten to impinge upon their success. Much of the literature pertaining to internationalisation takes an 'owner/parent' view – but what about the subsidiary/partner perspective? Given that the focus of this book is trained upon local 'field-based' leadership it is pertinent, at this juncture, to consider IMUEs from a subsidiary/partner point of view. What activities do they expedite and what issues do they face? This chapter will address this question by, first, examining interlinked factors relating to local performance from a subsidiary/partner standpoint such as *funding* and *alignment*, *expertise* and *adaptive capacity*. It will then examine issues in the relationship between parent and subsidiary from both a theoretical (*agency* and *power resource*) and practical (*operational* and *strategic*) point of view. Activities and issues will then be examined with regard to field-based local leaders in IMUEs – what do they do and what practical problems do they face on a day-to-day basis? Following chapters in the book will then consider how effective local leaders are developed in order to ensure that the 'rubber hits the road' in IMUEs.

3.1 Local Performance Factors

From a subsidiary/partner perspective performance will be contingent upon three main factors: the degree to which they are financially equipped and aligned with parental KPIs, the level of local expertise at their disposal to translate the parent's concept into reality on the ground and their adaptive capacity; that is, their room for manoeuvre in melding product, place, price, positioning, etc. to local exigencies. These will be considered in turn, followed by a discussion of the issues and tensions between themselves and the centre.

3.1.1 FUNDING AND ALIGNMENT

The entry point for understanding subsidiary/partner performance is the degree to which they are sufficiently funded for the first few stages of launch and growth in new *start-ups* and redesign and expansion in *acquisitions*. Land-based multi-unit investment is both capital and revenue intensive both from a site and infrastructure perspective. As discussed in 2.3.4.3 in the previous chapter, IMUEs will generally favour the low-risk approaches to market entry through alliances (i.e. joint ventures) and market contracting (i.e. franchising, concessions, licensing, etc.). What their partners have to demonstrate – beyond obvious factors such as compatibility, knowledge and ambition – is sufficient financial resources. Thus, what is the cash position of the partner, what are their lines of credit, how are their existing commercial interests faring, do they have sufficient financial muscle to underwrite the first three years' business plan? Often IMUE expansion can founder in certain territories due to the fact that their franchisees/licensees in certain regions are insufficiently capitalised to exploit growth opportunities, rather than the concept itself being defective (see Case Study 1 below). In the case of acquisitions or alliances (where partners have extant estates) subsidiaries will be highly dependent on the parent providing sufficient finance during redesign and roll-out stages – how committed is the parent for the long haul, what are their short and long-term ROI expectations, when do they expect the subsidiary to be accretive and earnings enhancing? Often the pressure for acquired entities to perform quickly in conformance with ambitious targets that have been shaped through the (high) EBITDA multiple paid, can place unrealistic expectations upon local managers who are put under immense pressure by the centre (almost on a daily basis through conference calls and requests for information) to account for performance.

Obviously the funding of the foreign operation will be connected to the type of entry mechanism chosen by the parent with the subsidiary/partner, assuming higher or lower forms of risk/pressure according to specific arrangements. The types of *contracts* deployed will also place a framework around the working arrangement – particularly in alliances/market contracting situations – where the financial obligations of both parties are detailed in full. In direct ownership positions the internationalising disposition (i.e. ethno/poly/geo/region-centric) and architecture of the IMUE (see 2.3.5) will affect financial structures and monitoring. However, what generally remains constant across IMUEs is KPI alignment, allowing the parent to drive performance and make benchmarked comparisons across the portfolio (Case Study 1). Thus, international hotel groups will apply a generic set of KPIs across their estates – whatever the local ownership structure – incorporating measures such as REVPAR (revenue per average room), customer service, employee engagement, etc. Indeed, subsidiary/partners will be competing against one another on either an international or regional basis, with upper quartile performers being more immune from central interventions and/or favoured for extra investment than those in the lower echelons. What does emerge from any analysis of IMUEs, though, is the complexity that is derived from the 'multi-layered' approaches that are adopted as companies approach regions and territories on a 'case-by-case' basis, as highlighted by the following case study.

Case Study 1 – Subsidiary/Partner Alignment in Peugeot Citroen

Bryn Thomas is a Senior Executive at Peugeot Citroen and has extensive subsidiary/parent-level experience in both multi-site Commercial Sales and Finance. Peugeot Citroen is one of the world's pre-eminent vehicle manufacturers and multi-unit retailers with strong footholds in both developed and growth markets through direct (owned), alliance and contracted mechanisms.

The way in which Peugeot Citroen (PSA) is configured internationally varies according to each particular country market. It has wholly owned subsidiaries, joint ventures, importer distributer (akin to 'master franchisees') and third-party assembly/distribution types of arrangements. The factors that influence the structure of each entity relate to the scale of the opportunity (i.e. in sizable markets, owned subsidiaries are the preferred approach), the degree of risk (i.e. in smaller/emerging markets or those with a high degree of political uncertainty/cultural specificity the joint venture or importer/distributer model is favoured) and circumstance (i.e. for pragmatic reasons full ownership is deployed when an importer/distributer folds). Whilst other commercial vehicle manufacturers also apply the same 'mixed model' in relation to their 'dealer networks' it is notable that companies such as Volkswagen have a 'total franchise' model with no 'owned' outlets. The question is how do we knit together what, to outside observers, seem quite a complex set of arrangements and networks?

The answer is that, first, each country has a PSA management team whatever the owner/contractual configuration. This team will either (if it is an owned subsidiary) run the territory (incorporating in some instances both manufacturing and an owned/franchise multi-unit dealer network) or (if it is set up as a joint venture or importer/distributer model) monitor/work with the partner on the ground. Second, the contract is important in maintaining consistency and quality throughout the whole multi-unit network. For instance an importer/distributer might have its own network of units, plus a 'sub-franchised' set of multiple or single franchisees. What we run through all the contracts is a set of minimum pre-requisites (i.e. PSA promotional support, franchisee capital and liquidity requirements, base volume targets, prescribed standards, audit rules, proprietary IT platform usage/subscription, etc.). Third, and most importantly, we have a set of KPIs that pretty much run throughout our entire multi-unit dealer/showroom operation which consist of four fundamental metrics: volume, market share, profit and quality. These will be measured on a weekly and monthly basis ... the data gives the organisation 'line of sight' on how units are performing, be they owned, 'master franchisee', 'franchisee', etc.

What does differ from market to market is, first, the degree to which we 'animate' the dealer network and, second, the level of brand segmentation. With regard to 'animation' (i.e. how we motivate both dealers and consumers), different markets will have different preferences. In the case of franchisees, multi-unit field operations (particularly zone area managers) will have some flexibility as to what incentives can be deployed for the dealers themselves (i.e. extrinsic cash or intrinsic treats) or the end-consumer (i.e. cash off, free 'add-ons' or finance-based offers). The point is that 'one size does not fit all'; local field operations can choose from a menu of items to 'animate' either the dealer or the consumer. A finance offer might work in one territory whilst a loyalty/service-based offer might work in another – it is a matter of local judgement as to what will work and why! Second, some markets like China have a segmentation strategy, unlike other markets – here PSA, which operates via joint venture arrangements. The Peugeot brand has a single joint venture in place and so has a single dealer network. Citroen has two joint ventures in place, one building the value-based 'C' class range and the other building the more premium-based 'DS' range ... Consequently, Citroen has split its commercial dealer network into two to reflect the joint venture and brand arrangements ...

I suppose the general conclusion that can be drawn from the way in which we do business is that we operate a 'multi-layered/tiered' multi-unit network which is bound together through coherent contracts and KPIs, but with a high degree of flexibility as to how local operators 'animate' their networks and end-consumers within given markets!

3.1.2 COUNTRY EXPERTISE

In section 2.3.2 above, reference was made to the necessity that central decision-makers either possess or *co-opt* expertise in the territories they are targeting for access, in order to limit the potential for missteps. Once the decision has been made to go ahead they will assemble a team with a range of talents and insights that – according to the mode of entry – will either liaise with the local partner or directly run the acquired entity. A combination of 'talent-types' are available for deployment consideration (see section 1.5.2: expatriates, TCNs, EHCNs, HCNs) – although, in the initial phases at least, it is likely that IMUEs will favour the placement of expertise that has an understanding of the firm's values, modus vivendi and product concept. Increasingly, given the growth of western-educated managerial cadres in developing markets, IMUEs are able to select subsidiary/partner leadership from 'locally attuned' internal and/or external pools of labour, to fill vital senior roles such as Country Manager, FD, HRD, Supply Chain, Estates, etc. This is particularly the case where IMUEs already possess regional footprints in areas such as Southern Asia or Latin America (see Case Study 2). Whilst the recruitment of 'local management' for senior regional and country-based positions in IMUEs is very much in vogue due to the perceived advantages of having a 'cultural' bridge – where individuals who understand the local culture, language and market interact with policy-makers at the centre – issues remain; not least, talent scarcity in some areas and tensions between individualistic, short-termist perspectives of Anglo-American managers and a collectivist, longer-term approach of managers in 'high-context' developing territories.

Case Study 2 – Growth in 'Local' Subsidiary/ Partner Appointments: Korn Ferry International

James Hyde is Senior Client Partner of the global executive search and development firm Korn Ferry International. He has had over 20 years of high-level recruitment, selection and development experience working with a broad range of international blue chip clients (including a number of IMUEs), handling assignments to search for top-tier leadership: chairmen, CEOs, functional heads and other senior executives.

Over the past five years IMUEs have relied less upon deploying expatriates into international operational theatres (indeed, experienced 'expats' are fighting over a decreasing pool of jobs!), rather appointing leaders of 'local' origin to positions of influence in subsidiaries/regions ... For instance, I was on a conference call this morning with two Southern Asian-based HRDs (both – incidentally – 'locals') of a major international hospitality firm who discussed senior 'local' appointments with me ... the issue is, however, there is a short supply of 'local' talent, conversant with 'western business practice' and discourse (either through immersion or education) and very often a 'bidding war' ensues for the best talent, which has a propensity – due to the large number of opportunities – to move frequently ... But why is there such a high demand for 'local' leadership talent, what value do they add and what are some of the tensions that are caused through their appointment? ...

The need for 'local' leadership to populate senior positions in the subsidiaries/ partnerships of IMUEs has arisen for three main reasons. First, 'local' leaders (at SVP and VP level) are perceived as being far more adept at adapting the IMUE's strategy, product, policies and practices to 'fit' local exigencies ... they can also interpret what is needed and 'go back up the line' with a fair degree of credibility to get the right resources and backing to 'do the right thing' in local markets ... Second, in tandem with the first point, they bring a level of what I term *'fusion'*; for instance in US-owned IMUEs blending meritocratic, *'individualistic'*, performance-based cultural approaches with local cultures (especially in Asia) that favour more *'collectivist'* loyalty, relationship, 'longevity' and trust-based approaches ... 'local leaders' are appointed on the basis that they have the courage and 'nous' to adopt a hybridised 'best of each' approach ... Third, from a market-based perspective, things are fast moving in many growth markets with dynamics such as an expanding young, aspirational middle class who are quite different – from a consumptive point of view – compared to their parents ... their levels of expectation regarding service quality (reinforced by social media, travel and high disposable incomes) place far greater demands on multi-site operators ... they expect/demand extremely high levels of service and are quite sophisticated and discerning about what constitutes great service ... this means that multi-site operators must – in some instances – devise service delivery systems and consumer-friendly products that exceed standards in developed contexts ... If you take Starwood's W brand in Asia, it really has set a template for four-star and five-star hospitality ... These expectations in a fast-changing, dynamic context demand 'local' leaders who are sensitised, empathetic and attuned to consumer micro-trends and can drive change quickly through an understanding of what strategic leadership approaches work best in which context ... the problem lies in finding the people who can do it or be trained to do it! ...

Inevitably clashes do occur between 'home' central policy-makers and these 'local' leaders ... for instance, 'process driven/outcome-led' Anglo-American managers might struggle to understand the need for a more 'highly diffuse' approach towards 'getting things done' in certain markets ... in short-termist cultures where there might be a focus on 'delivering the quarterly plan', there might be frustration relating to the patient, long-termist approach adopted by some 'local' leaders ... Also, in management practice terms it might be perceived by 'developed' managers that 'local' multi-site leaders do not necessarily follow the *'rational'* managerial best-practice manual, relying instead on more *'intuitive'*, 'unscientific' approaches in cultures that are derived from a more small-family-business, entrepreneurial mindset.

3.1.3 ADAPTIVE CAPABILITY

As stated in the previous chapter (see section 2.3.3.4), the degree to which companies will be successful in transporting their product/concept will rest (to a large degree) on the extent to which they can adapt it to local conditions. Firms can reduce their so-called *'psychic distance'* by getting emotionally and physically closer to territories through deploying the right people and creating an appropriate structural and communications 'architecture' (see sections 2.3.3.3 and 2.3.5). But what activities do senior personnel in local subsidiaries/partners actually expedite in terms of added value for the owner? In general, their contribution lies not only in executing the parent's will (framed through KPIs and contract conditions) but also in helping central technocrats (property, HR, marketing, etc.) locally adapt the product/concept and all its supporting processes. Questions that subsidiary/partner leadership will be seeking to address in order to adapt elements of the business model/proposition, to achieve optimal performance, will gravitate around a number of areas – not least product, place, pricing and promotions, people policies and processes:

- *Product concept* – What consumer need does it fill in the existing/future market? What is the 'market space with a market place' for the product in its current form? What changes (i.e. range, specification, quality, etc.) are required for local tastes?
- *Place* – Where will the launch of this product be most impactful (footfall and visibility)? Where is its optimal demographic fit? What is the 'cluster potential' around the site? How commercially viable/secure are the terms of the site lease? How can we build a quick pipeline?
- *Pricing and promotions* – What is the optimal pricing structure (i.e. price elasticity equation)? What are the best promotional mechanisms and channels?

- *People, policies and practices* – How do standard company contracts comply with local laws and regulations (i.e. hours of work, holidays, maternity, etc.)? What is the requirement for organised representation? How transferable are company training programmes (given learning styles, cultural sensibilities, idiomatic language, etc.)? What is the local wage structure?
- *Processes* – Can the local supply chain support the current offer? Is logistics fit for purpose? Can IT systems be transferred in their current form?

3.2 Problems and Issues

The notion that with the right funding/alignment, locally-based senior expertise and adaptive capability, high performance will occur at subsidiary/partner level seems compelling. However, many previous academic studies – particularly those taking agency and power resource theoretical perspectives – suggest that relations between owner/parents and subsidiary/partners are highly ambiguous and complex. For, in addition to cultural and institutional explanations of divergence or convergence, MNCs – and particularly IMUEs – should be seen as being riddled with highly contested spaces at best, and chaotic and disordered ones at worst (Ferner and Edwards 1995). Scholars operating out of a power and politics paradigm note that international organisations, due to a multiplicity of competing interests, personalities and hierarchies, can be riven by conflict and disharmony. After considering intra-firm *theoretical perspectives* on subsidiary-owner relations, this section will also consider common *strategic* and *operational* dislocations that occur.

3.2.1 INTRA-FIRM THEORETICAL PERSPECTIVES

Within the academic literature there are two theoretical perspectives that help explain the 'micro-reality' of intra-firm relations in IMUEs. The first, *Agency Theory*, applies to 'contracted' relationships: the low-risk modes of entry referred to in section 2.3.4.2 above. Here relations between the principal (i.e. owner) and agent (i.e. contracted party) are governed by the perceived equity and fairness of the contract (Quinn and Doherty 2000). If the agreement is imbalanced, disproportionately favouring any given party, debilitating levels of conflict, resistance and sabotage can arise. The second perspective, *Power Resource Theory*, is more applicable to 'owned' situations, and refers to the degree to which the subsidiary is able to bargain for extra resources from the parent based on the power they derive from matters such as local knowledge, networks and influence (Birkinshaw and Fry 1998). Both theoretical perspectives will be considered in turn.

3.2.1.1 Agency

One of the issues that internationalising companies have when they pursue 'low-risk' market entry strategies through licensing their format and blueprinted operations to single or multiple operators is that they are drawn into a contractual situation with 'agents' who have a range of different expectations and capabilities. Indeed, the balance of power in the relationships will vary according to agreed contractual terms and the relative strategies, strengths and weaknesses of the signatories (Hough 1986, Moore et al. 2004). In addition, differences in knowledge or skills by the 'principal' or 'agent' can lead to issues such as 'information asymmetry' (i.e. unequal knowledge possession), which shifts the balance of power between them (Quinn 1999). This implies that

> *... to be successful in the long term ... effective management of the relationship, the monitoring of the information flow and clear demarcation of respective partners' interests become crucial to the international business. (Wigley and Moore 2007: 284)*

Often, following the initial 'honeymoon' of the agreement, disputes will arise between the brand owner and contracted party if the former believes the latter to be failing in their delivery upon initial implied/contracted promises (i.e. profit, brand execution, roll-out, etc.) and they are in receipt of imperfect information about the state of the licensed business or, in the case of the licensee, it is felt that the 'principal' is providing insufficient support (see resources in section 2.3.5.4 above).

3.2.1.2 Power resource

An exceptionally powerful contribution to our understanding of owner-subsidiary relations is Ferner and Edwards's paper 'Power and the Diffusion of Organisational Change within Multinational Enterprises' (1995). In this paper they propose a framework (loosely based on Lukes's 1975 'three faces of power' theory – which itself can be traced back to Weberian categorisations of bureaucracy and power) categorising the varying sources of power within an organisation, and showing how the distribution of these sources shapes conflict and, subsequently, negotiations between the organisational groups. One source of power is derived from formal authority roles (*authority relations*), but power can also be obtained by using the culture of the organisation (*culture relations*) to legitimise certain courses of action and, most importantly perhaps, the control of resources of value to others in the organisation (*resource-based power* and *exchange relations*). Ferner and Edwards argue that in MNCs, the control of resources becomes a particularly important source of power, since many assets that the organisation possesses are strongly embedded in subsidiaries' distinctive national contexts, within the direct competence or control of local managers. Consequently the ability of individuals and groups within MNCs to influence outcomes can be dependent on the ability and willingness of local actors to mobilise resources in the owners' interests. These types of power relations can be seen as cross-national channels of influence in which complex intra-firm interactions take place between actors. Such a framework is useful in scotching the notion that subsidiaries and their executives, whatever the form of strategic integration, are merely passive recipients of owner/parent strategies, initiatives and practices.

In addition to this lack of recognition concerning the role of power, an overemphasis on structure and institutional forces has also led to the downplaying of *organisational politics and conflict* in the view of some scholars such as Edwards and Kuruvilla:

> *... many models and empirical studies fail to address the political nature of the global–local issue; it is political in that various groups of organisational actors will seek to either extend or limit the extent of global policies in order to defend or advance their own interests. (2005: 11)*

Edwards and Kuruvilla cite Kristensen and Zeitlin who had argued that

> ... *a multinational should be seen as a battlefield amongst subsidiaries representing and mobilising their own regional capabilities and national institutional means against the rest. (2001: 192)*

This is a view that accords with Morgan et al. (2003), who characterise the multinational as a 'transnational social space' which is 'inherently disordered', with global policies constituting only one mechanism through which 'order is instilled'. Therefore, according to all these perspectives, the balance between global and local pressures (or convergence versus divergence) is not the result of a one-off, rational calculation by top managers, but rather is something that is contested, over which there is an ongoing struggle, and consequently shifts over time.

This view of the complexity of owner/subsidiary interactions has been empirically endorsed by scholars like Forsgren (1990) who, in his analysis of the subsidiaries of Swedish multinationals, found that the 'hierarchical' power of corporate HQ is counter-balanced by the resources deriving from subsidiaries' participation in 'industrial networks' with suppliers, customers, governments and local unions. It was therefore his contention that

> *(MNCs are) loosely coupled political systems rather than tightly bonded, homogenous, hierarchically controlled systems. (1990: 264)*

This is useful in moving beyond a view of the MNC as a strict hierarchy. Forsgren's central point, like that of the scholars cited above, is that co-ordination is not practised effortlessly and that power is a necessary component in the process.

There are other works in which the concept of power and conflict is highlighted (Martinez and Ricks 1991, Taylor et al. 1996). Taylor et al. (1996), for example, note that MNC headquarters

> ... *will attempt to exert high levels of control over their global innovators, but these affiliates will simultaneously have the power to resist these central efforts. (1996: 975)*

However, in this body of work there is little elaboration of the dynamics of parent-subsidiary power relations, a gap which is addressed in the works of Birkinshaw (i.e. Birkinshaw and Fry 1998, Birkinshaw and Hood 1998, Birkinshaw 2000). His analysis is pertinent to the issue of policy transfer, since it throws light on the resources available to subsidiaries to negotiate the 'terms of transfer'; thus subsidiaries engage in a political process, based on 'proactive, pushy and sometimes Machiavellian tactics' (Birkinshaw and Fry 1998: 52), whereby they acquire credibility, reputation and a 'track record'. Local actors network with key personnel at the corporate centre and construct international alliances and coalitions with other groups within the MNC. If subsidiaries obtain and build power resources and possess the ability to resist transfer, then it is likely that transfer of policy such as acquirer HRM practices will be a negotiated process.

Additionally, notions of evasion, resistance, manipulation or 'space at lower levels' (Broad 1994, Ortiz 1998) within subsidiaries are a counterbalance to institutionalist arguments pertaining to the determinism of 'country of origin' forces from the parent:

> *Institutions condition the behaviour of actors within MNCs as they do in all organisations, setting limits to what is feasible and attractive, but they do not close off the scope for choice: there remains a degree of 'space' for actors within institutional influences. Since the priorities and preferences of different groups of actors are bound to vary, the inevitable outcome is that courses of action will be shaped by the exercise of power within the MNC. (Edwards and Kuruvilla 2005: 15)*

Nonetheless, to balance the equation, as Oliver (1991) argues, it is in principle possible to synthesise the insights of institutionalism with those of a power-based perspective. Oliver explores the scope for owners/parents in MNCs to negotiate over the terms of their conformity to localised institutional pressures. Organisations are able to deploy a range of strategic responses, running from *full adherence*, through *avoidance* (e.g. hiding non-conformity under a façade of ritual compliance), *compromise*, to full-blooded *resistance*. In general, the variables that influence such strategic responses include the dependence of the organisation on the source of the institutional norms (for performance), the perceived legitimacy of the norm, the efficiency gains from conformity and the multiplicity and consistency of institutional constituents.

3.2.2 STRATEGIC

The power-based theoretical perspectives outlined above provide some explanation as to why friction occurs between parents and subsidiaries/partners in IMUEs. In addition to this 'micro-political' frame of reference, however, dislocations can often occur around strategic matters (see Case Study 3 below). Often country managers and their teams can be at odds with their 'lords and masters', as one respondent stated, 'because they really don't get the fact that strategy must be backed up by tactics, and if the global strategy is wrong then what we do on the ground is naturally impaired'. At times there will be disagreement over the vision and mission set out for the IMUE, although – more likely – fall-outs will occur around the way in which resources are allocated behind which products/concepts within which markets. As the centre in most IMUEs largely fulfils a resource allocation role (capital, revenue, knowledge, human capital, etc.) the strategic thrust of local subsidiaries can naturally be impaired if they are subject to scarcity. Often country management will be responsible for running a multi-branded/formatted estate; but which brand is currently well-supported in strategic terms by the centre and which ones have fallen out of favour? At times there might be variances in what the centre deems strategic priorities and what actually works on a local basis. Also, the complexity of the way in which IMUEs are configured across national boundaries in a variety of ownership structures and agreements only adds to 'multi-layered/tiered' complexity, making the expedition of strategy extremely complex.

One means by which multi-brand IMUEs have sought strategic clarity and 'line of sight' has been to disband regional/country management structures in favour of global branded structures. For instance Accor, the French hotel IMUE, announced in December 2012 that it was appointing chief operating officers to run each individual brand 'to put itself ahead of the curve when it comes to anticipating trends', with its President Yann Caillere commenting:

This organisation structure will enable us to develop first-rate specialists in each market segment and rely on teams that are entirely focused on their brands and have a perfect knowledge of both their customers and their competitors. (Brumby 2012: 1)

Hence, strategy and resources are built around single branded entities (especially in hotels and casual dining) where global MDs with 'brand-specific' marketing and operational teams – drawing down on shared service support in particular territories (i.e. HR, property, IT, supply chain) – are totally aligned to the purpose and symmetry of the concept. Although this, in itself, does not eradicate all the issues that pervade parent-subsidiary/ partner relations, greater clarity and 'shared vision' promises greater understanding and customer responsiveness.

Case Study 3 – Resolving Strategic Tensions in Sodexo

Andy Vaughan was a Senior Strategy Director with Sodexo, the 'on-site service solution' experts (offering single and multi-unit catering, facilities management, security and outsourcing services). Market-listed in France, Sodexo has grown from managing services in a single unit in Marseilles to become an E18 billion organisation operating in over 80 markets.

Sodexo is an extremely successful services company which has grown rapidly over the past ten years – particularly in 'growth' markets. It operates in a very competitive sector (alongside other companies such as G4S, Compass, Mitie, Serco, etc.) and has increasingly had to take more of a global '*sector-based*' rather than 'country-based' approach over the past couple of years ... What does this mean? ... Fundamentally the organisation has – due to the demands of global clients such as P&G – had to take more of a '*global solutions*' approach rather than a national one ... this has meant that rather than dividing the business up by region and/or country, the company has gone down the route of dividing the business internationally by six or seven specific sectors (such as business and industry, education, 'seniors', event management, healthcare and defence, etc.) ... *Global sector directors* are now hard-lined into direct reports in each territory, with the view being taken that technical expertise needs to be shared 'within sector' and that, in some cases, such as senior contract relationships – across national boundaries – sector specificity and key account management need to be combined ... accounts can also be managed on a global basis allowing better line of sight (in terms of ROI, P&L, etc.) and allowing more focus on *growth sectors* within given markets ... at national level sector specialists are able to draw down skills and resources regarding each particular service (such as catering, facilities management, energy/green, etc.) ... However, there was *one other major reason* for this drive towards sector specificity – the need to temper what had been perceived as the *inhibiting power of local country management* ...

In any IMUE there will always be tension between the centre and its subsidiaries due to distance, although in the case of Sodexo, two issues seemed to generate tension: *culture* and *strategy* ... In the case of *culture* the fact that Sodexo was a French-owned company and the fact that it operated within a 'relationship-based' service context, meant that as there was an aversion to face-to-face conflict, and that most things were usually agreed outside of meetings! ... compared to Anglo-American IMUE companies I have worked for there was also a more 'ambiguous' approach to task-setting (more deliberating and discussion) and performance management; which is not say – incidentally – that things were done any less well! ... With regards to *strategy*, conflict between the parent and its subsidiaries largely occurred around managing contracts/operations across national boundaries (with the Sodexo CEO having to step in at times to 'order' things to be done cross-nationally) and the sharing of best practice ... Country management could also argue (quite justifiably in my view) that because our business is about *'context-based service provision'* (i.e. the regulation of human behaviour within specific cultural contexts, according to particular employment rules and regulations) the centre would never get the 'localness' of our business ... my sense is, actually, that this is a local business (due to local labour laws) and in-country operators will still need to retain a lot of autonomy (in spite of global sector management) ... Also, in countries where local management was doing particularly well in terms of performance against targets and year-on-year growth they were obviously in a strong position to tell the centre 'where to go'...

This 'difficult' behaviour (hopefully resolved by the new global sector structure) mainly manifested itself in *mature* territories – in *growth* areas such as the BRICs and emerging markets, there seemed to be a lot more 'synergy' between the centre and the local businesses ... Perhaps this was because – at least in the initial phases – there was more of a parent-child type of dependency where behaviour was to some extent regulated by outside 'experts' (expats and secondments from the centre) ... also these younger subsidiaries were in the fortunate position of having less hierarchy (especially in the initial phases) and of being more focused upon quite staggering levels of growth, concentrating upon building networks and relationships rather than 'fighting' the centre ... Take markets like Mexico and Brazil – urbanisation and the growth of industry (both manufacturing and service-based) meant that more facilities were being built with large single-site workforces who needed to eat! ... a perfect opportunity for canteen and catering provision ... The capacity of these markets to grow at an exponential rate is obviously attractive to companies like Sodexo although I would like to caveat this view with the proviso that companies put their 'brightest and best' out into the markets to develop locals to eventually manage the entities rather than using them as 'parking lots' for 'problem managers' in mature markets! ... to this extent IMUEs need extremely good talent management systems to ensure that 'very average' people don't get dumped in very promising growth environments!

3.2.3 OPERATIONAL

In addition to strategic issues giving rise to issues between the centre and international business units, distinctive problems can arise around operational matters. Disagreements can occur around the way things are planned and organised within different territories due to differing national business systems, cultural or competitive pressures (see sections 1.4.2, 2.2.2 and 2.2.3 above). Often the centre can be 'behind the curve' in terms of what is required at a local level to ensure operational effectiveness. Centrally conceived initiatives – particularly those relating to employees and customers – can be opposed at a local level because they are perceived as mistimed or irrelevant. More pertinently, given the power of some regional/country operators – conferred either through their performance or closeness to the Global CEO (see Case Study 4 below) – they might, as one respondent stated, 'choose to pursue different operational means to achieve the same KPI ends'. Thus centrally-driven L&D, IT and supply chain programmes might wither on the vine, as regional/country 'barons', far away from the centre and protected by their own 'power resources' (see 3.2.1 above) pursue their own paths to secure operational success.

Case Study 4 – Centre Versus Regional Tensions in PremCo

This case study is a truncated summary of a round-table discussion that was held by the author and the Chief People Officer and Head of Global Talent in one of the world's fastest-growing premium IMUEs (PremCo). In this discussion they refer to the operational tensions between the regions and the centre – particularly with regards to embedding a uniform approach to training and L&D across the group.

In PremCo we have experienced exponential growth – doubling in size every three years over the past nine! This is as a result of our 'own store', franchised/licensed and wholesale international expansion ... Also our stores are getting bigger and we have now segmented our range ... I have just got back from visiting x with the Board where we have just opened our largest store in Southern Asia at xksqft ... our formats and products are now segmented into three sub-brands backed up with extensive social media and internet ordering channels ... hence we are now a *multi-channel/product/brand* with different operational format sizes ... this inevitably brings immense operational challenges ...

The retail management structure in PremCo is split into four regions (US, Europe, Asia and Developing Markets). Each MD has a fair degree of autonomy and has an idiosyncratic style of leadership and focus that reflects their functional background (say finance, multi-channel or operational) or nationality (Mexican, UK, etc.). Ramping up this complexity, the 'regionals' (MULs) as we call them have different job titles, job descriptions and objectives in every region! ... As such we do not have any formal development programme for our MULs, many of whom originated from store management level ... even at store level – *would you believe!* – we are only just developing a proper store manager training programme! ...

What have been the forces that have militated against the development of a company-wide L&D culture? As I have learnt to my cost, this organisation does not take to centrally-driven company-wide programmes ... there is a huge amount of *'try before people buy'*... There is *always* a need to pilot L&D initiatives on a limited scale before they generate buy-in and momentum ... I would compare this directly with another major British iconic company I worked with where we could go company-wide as soon as key decisions were made by the policy-makers. In PremCo *because of the power and authority of the (four) International Regional Company MDs* there has to be real buy-in ... in a large part they challenge the utility of group-wide development programmes because of local 'fit' *but* also because of the influence they wield over key decision-makers at the centre due to their (seemingly) unstoppable profit momentum (which seems to confer *complete autonomy!*) ... what they say is 'we are delivering so why would we listen to you!' ... In order to get our messages over and secure buy-in we use international conferences to get group-wide initiatives embedded but these are sometimes delayed or deferred ... Another factor working against us is the complete power of the CEO within the organisation – very few decisions are made without his sign off ... as he supports the existing balance of power and does not want to upset the regional 'operators' our job is made doubly difficult. Another issue we have is the fact that many of the head office functions are fractured ... for instance the Service and Productivity Department is very close to the field and drives retail programmes ... it is difficult for us in HR centrally to 'get in' and make group-wide L&D interventions ...

Other reasons for an under-developed retail management L&D system stem from lack of company-wide integrated reporting systems of capturing and disseminating HR data ... The rapid growth in employee numbers ... a move from a wholesale/ licensing model to a managed retail one ... a concern for FOH aesthetics and product/store design rather than BOH managerial form, structure and process ... the fact that the employment brand has not kept pace with the retail brand ... all of these issues pose immense issues for the strategic HR team as we move forwards!

3.3 Field-Based HMUL Activities

Whilst leadership at the subsidiary level – whether structured on a brand sector or country basis – busies itself with interacting with the centre (global or regional) in order to secure plan sign-off and resources for development and expansion, IMUEs are reliant on one specific cadre of employees to bring the strategy alive on the ground; namely, its field-based operators. Previous commentary provides an overview of the typical tiers of field-based operatives (Edger 2012: 67–72); suffice to say that the most important actor in translating plans into action is the host multi-unit leader – HMUL (see section 1.5). Usually called area/territory/district/city manager or coach, these individuals (usually promoted from general or unit manager positions) are tasked with three main activities: to implement operational *systems*, enforce brand *standards* and execute flawless sales-led *service* at point of purchase. A detailed account of their duties and the specific issues that they face is surfaced comprehensively elsewhere (Edger 2012: 85–106); however, a brief reprise – with the inclusion of additional activities that the 'expert panel' for this book believed that HMULs despatched in IMUEs (see *bold* insertions below) – is appropriate prior to successive chapters which consider the behaviours and development interventions they require in order to expedite their roles in developing market contexts:

3.3.1 SYSTEMS IMPLEMENTATION

a) *Labour processes*
 - Labour ratio tracking – Ensure units keep to forecast and/or budget/cash target.
 - Rostering and deployment: Ensure that units are fully manned to undertake duties required during peak and non-peak trading sessions. Check seasonal rostering plans; ensure sufficient labour capacity to service volume. Check 'right person, right place, right time'. Check for 'ghosting' (i.e. staff that are on the payroll but are not working at the establishment).
 - Employment law compliance – Ensure that units are operating legally and in accordance to cultural/religious norms (i.e. following working-time rules, migrant diaspora workers have permits/passports, proper age, gender and diversity regulatory/religious adherence, etc.).
 - Unions – Deal with local representatives of organised labour where necessary. Ensure good relations are sustained for operational efficiency purposes.
b) *Standard operating procedures*
 - BOH tasks – Ensure standard back of house task lists and section 'details' are adhered to (i.e. data uploads, delivery checks, storage, security, etc.). Monitor food production procedural adherence within catering and dining contexts.
 - FOH tasks – Monitor front of house tasks such as: pre-opening procedural adherence, 'daily duty manager' sweeps, section accounting, till procedures, etc.
c) *Availability, stock and waste processes*
 - Availability – Ensure appropriate stockholding is in place to service demand. Monitor replenishment and check supply chain to ensure constant availability.
 - Reconciliation – Ensure cash takings reconcile with sales and stock.
 - Theft and shrinkage: Check security and surveillance processes to minimise pilfering, 'knock-offs' and shrinkage.
 - Waste – Monitor and minimise non-consumable *and* perishable waste.
d) *Sales and pricing monitoring*
 - Daily/weekly sales – Check daily and weekly sales against budget and last year.
 - Timeslot analysis – Monitor sales flows by timeslot; check throughputs and efficiency.
 - Pricing accuracy – Check coding exception reports; ensure pricing accuracy.

- Ad hoc discounting – Check 'end of line'/'out of date' pricing and sales times (too early?).

e) *Due diligence and essential maintenance processes*
- Safety – Check fire safety compliance (testing, extinguishers, etc.). Monitor on-site customer incident book.
- Hygiene – Check adherence to statutory and company procedures. Ensure food hygiene standards are compliant (i.e. 100 per cent food hygiene training for food handlers). Check pest and rodent control systems. All equipment maintained and serviced?
- Legal compliance – 100 per cent under-age alcohol sales training (in territories where legally permitted).
- Hazards – Ensure all essential maintenance requests are actioned on time and to specification.

f) *Ad hoc processes/change initiatives*
- Pre-opening – Oversee new opening processes; staffing, stocking, training, handover, etc.
- Local suppliers – Maintain and monitor 'local suppliers' list (product and maintenance contractors).
- New product launches – Train and communicate new product launches.
- Change initiatives – Act as conduit for all new change initiatives (i.e. promotions, operational systems, etc.).
- *New site locations – Scan for new site opportunities.*

3.3.2 STANDARDS ADHERENCE

a) *Merchandising and display*
- Planogram checks – Ensure merchandise is displayed according to specification (i.e. facings and perishable range display).
- Promotions – Check promotions (signage, posters, shelf pricing, gondola ends, etc.).

b) *Internal environmental management*
- Cleanliness – Check cleaning rota and cleanliness (especially toilets and trading areas). In addition check BOH stock rooms, staff changing and rest rooms, etc. – the cleanliness of these areas will be linked to FOH standards.
- Sound, lighting and 'smell' – Ensure all 'sensory' sound, lighting and (where appropriate) 'smell' systems are functioning appropriately. Check speaker systems and background music loops, ensure the store is properly lit for security, safety and product illumination purposes and check 'perfume' and ersatz 'odour' systems.
- Air conditioning and heating – Check functionality and effectiveness.
- Fixtures and fittings – Ensure fixtures and fitting are maintained and presented to the required standard.
- Store security – Check the robustness of the store security systems (both mechanical and human).

c) *External environment*
- External agencies – Fulfil a troubleshooting, problem resolution and 'relationship' role with local officials, authorities, landlords, environmental health, safety executives and external auditing agencies engaged by the organisation.

– Competitive scanning – Monitor local competitive activity. Respond (where permitted) and/or feedback to senior management/head office (if feedback loops in place).
– Social responsibility – Check links with local community (i.e. charities, fund raising, job schemes, perishable food distribution, etc.).
– Local PR – Ensure units have a high degree of local visibility through the local press.

3.3.3 SALES-LED SERVICE EXECUTION

a) *Unit-based HR*
– Roles and responsibilities – Check that roles and responsibilities are clearly denominated, assigned and understood. In particular, ensure shift leaders have clearly specified pre- and in-session duties and tasks.
– Recruitment and selection – Appoint managers and assistants with appropriate behaviours and capabilities. Check store recruitment systems and hiring mechanisms to ensure 'meritocratic' attitudinal and skills testing.
– Coaching and training – Ensure that appropriate coaching and training mechanisms (in terms of operational requirements AND culture/language) are in place and are being rigorously followed.
– Compensation – Check compensation levels against local market; ensure that sufficient talent is being attracted and retained.
– Performance appraisal – Ensure that regular team/staff appraisals are taking place to the required standards of development and performance metrics.
– Store leadership – Check and audit staff satisfaction/engagement, absence, grievance data, etc.
b) *Service concept adherence*
– Service flow – Ensure that customer 'touches' are applied in the appropriate manner (sympathetic to local cultural norms) at each stage of the service cycle.
c) *Customer survey follow-up*
– Mystery customer – Monitor and action outputs from 'mystery customer' visits.
– Online surveys: Monitor and action outputs from online survey data.
– Web-based feedback – Regularly check and (where permitted) answer feedback on web-based forums and channels.
d) *Service promise and complaints resolution*
– Service promise – Check that the service promise (i.e. no quibble return) is fulfilled, particularly in relation to 'click and collect' services.
– Complaints – Ensure that complaints are answered and rectified both in-store and at head office in accordance with company procedure.

3.4 Chapter Summary

Following on from the previous chapter, which took a predominantly 'owner' perspective on international performance factors, the account above started with concentrating upon 'host' subsidiary/partner success variables. It was argued that the starting-point for success was appropriate funding and expansion capital to address the market opportunity, whatever the contractual arrangement. Also, as Case Study 1 (PSA Peugeot Citroen) highlighted, diffuse organisational/contractual arrangements could be 'synergised', giving both parent and subsidiary/partners heightened mutuality, if generic KPIs existed to 'bind' the IMUE together in a common purpose. By the same token Case Study 3 (Sodexo) showed how a movement to a single, as opposed to a multi-channel/brand country management structure, can be deployed to improve 'lines of sight' and create more effective 'communities of practice'. However, as Case Study 2 (Korn Ferry International on five-star hotels) demonstrated, the degree to which IMUEs deployed local expertise was becoming increasingly important – not least because of the way emerging markets are maturing, with tastes and preferences changing in tandem with increasing levels of affluence. Hence the adaptive capability of subsidiary/partners is crucial in terms of responding to dynamic changes in local customer behaviour. The chapter then progressed onto problems and issues faced within international companies generally, through principal-agent 'information asymmetry' (exacerbated over long distances) and owner 'power' over the subsidiary/partner being heavily mediated by factors such as cultural/national business insight and resource access/exploitation. Such theoretical perspectives provided some explanation for the strategic and operational issues that beset IMUEs, which were most forcibly highlighted in Case Study 4 (PremCo).

But what are we to make of these narratives and academic insights? What starts to emerge from these accounts and, indeed, resonates with those given by respondents in succeeding chapters, is the tension that exists between the need for IMUEs to achieve some form of *congruence* whilst simultaneously allowing degrees of *customisation* for effective market 'fit'. In economic terms, IMUEs must calculate the returns provided by the degree of alignment they *should* impose juxtaposed against the degree of autonomy they *must* permit. The end part of this chapter – on local field-based HMUL activities – is highly pertinent to this debate. Local leadership within IMUEs has a significant role to play in ensuring *consistency and adaptability*. Hence, the way in which IMUEs train and develop HMULs to dispatch the duties and activities outlined in section 3.3 above is discussed in the succeeding three chapters.

In these chapters consideration will be given to how IMUEs exert control, generate commitment and implement change through their field-based HMULs in developing market contexts, which present a set of issues that are – in some instances – far more challenging than in developed market situations. Previous research into developed market MUEs found that MULs 'managing at a distance', sandwiched between the centre and their units, were troubled by excessively compliance-led regimes (a factor partially attributable to the developed market downturn many MUEs confronted after 2007), which degraded levels of employee motivation and commitment (Edger 2012: 96–106). In such contexts the problems that MUEs and their MULs faced were, primarily, how to generate commitment in order to gain some semblance of control. However, the issues that IMUEs faced in growth markets were different: most notably how – in cultures that exhibited highly diffuse characteristics – they could first gain control, prior to generating commitment and change.

4 *Ensuring Control*

The previous chapter considered the activities and issues connected with international multi-unit leadership – particularly with regard to subsidiary/affiliate and operations-level leadership. But what practices do subsidiary/affiliates apply at a local field level within a multi-unit context to ensure control? How do they ensure efficiency and effectiveness at unit level where the proverbial rubber hits the road? In my previous book I argued that in *individualistic* developed market contexts such as the US and UK effective MULs needed to generate commitment before they could ensure control (Edger 2012). However, within international contexts, due to increased distance and major cultural divergences, organisations – for dependability, resilience and quality purposes – must ensure that they, and their members, exert *control prior to generating commitment*. This is in spite of the fact that managers from a variety of cultures rank control activities as the least attractive part of their role unless they are appropriately trained and rewarded (Konrad et al. 2001). To this extent this chapter needs to understand the nature, deployment and effects of control in cross-border international multi-unit situations. How do different organisations from differing cultures ensure operational and financial control through *formal* (i.e. hierarchy, policies/practices, procedures, rules, laws, monitoring, compliance, punishment, reward, etc.) or *informal* (i.e. relational, social, network, personalised contacts, etc.) means? Which control approaches are appropriate in which contexts? Why?

In order to address these questions this chapter will first address the literature on control considering, in turn: generic frameworks of control (models and typologies), cross-national control mechanisms (bureaucratic/contract and culture/values) and control preferences at both organisational and individual levels. Second, this chapter will then go on to simultaneously consider *how* organisations guide and develop HMULs and *what* HMULs do themselves to ensure control at portfolio and unit level. In doing so it will be argued, in contrast to the literature, that organisations and HMULs do not adopt a binary position – deploying bureaucratic or culture/values-led control mechanisms – they do both. Four control mechanisms will be advanced in this regard: *blueprint execution, output prioritisation, values transmission* and *confessional security*.

4.1 Frameworks of Control

My previous book examined managerial control theory and the broader managerial literature looking at their roles, the processes which they adopt for success (such as distributed delegation), the essential paradoxes and conundrums they face and the 'critical management' perspectives relating to what they do (Edger 2012). What this analysis lacked was a proper elucidation of managerial control frameworks and a consideration of what management and control 'means' in a cross-national context. With regards to the former, some reference was made to the origins of the study of managerial control, beginning with the 'legal rational approach' advanced by Weber in the late nineteenth century, the 'administration view' propounded by Fayol (1916) and the scientific management perspective that sought to expand the 'efficient frontiers of production' (Taylor 1916). These were essentially dispassionate, impersonal approaches, whose fundamental flaws were based around their conception that humans would act rationally, according to scientific law rather than human emotion. Following these studies various schools of thought addressed the behavioural aspects of production, including psychologically-anchored human relations and, more latterly, the HRM fields of analysis. With regard to economic, psychological and sociological perspectives, issues relating to control were examined with regard to decision-makers being constrained by 'bounded rationality' (Simon 1945), operating within a power nexus (Etzioni 1980), the way in which emotions, values, personalities and context mediate levels of control (Fineman and Sturdy 1999) and recipient perceptions of the ethics and morality of control (Barker 2005). In addition, a large literature has examined effects and structures of control (Tannenbaum 1968), the types and transmission of control (Ouchi 1977, 1978 and 1979), control drivers (Eisenhardt 1985), narratives of control (Barley and Kunda 1992), conceiving of HRM and delayering practices as control (Ezzamel and Willmott 1998, Sewell 1998, Legge 2005). As a start-point, however – in order to provide clarity of understanding for the reader and provide context for the discussion of control in a cross-national context – it is necessary to provide an overview of extant control models and typologies that are largely used throughout the literature on control and help contextualise the succeeding narrative.

4.1.1 CONTROL MODELS

There are two rational models that are cited and used extensively in the control literature – cybernetic systems (Green and Welsh 1988) and behaviour/output (Ouchi 1979, 1980):

- Cybernetic systems – This approach involves 'a process which uses the *negative feedback loop* represented by measuring achievement, comparing achievements to goals, feeding back information about unwanted variances into the process to be controlled, and correcting the process' (Hoftstede 1978: 451). Essentially this model mimics technical process control frameworks and is grounded in general systems theory (Green and Welsh 1988). The model itself involves three hierarchical levels which perform specific tasks which are interlinked through feedback loops: *'higher management'* (set standards), *'controllers'* (fulfil measurement, comparison, feedback and intervention functions) and *'operators'* (regulating inputs, the process itself and outputs). This model is both normative and descriptive – many businesses being set up to regulate control in such a manner. Issues with this approach include the presupposition that standards actually exist and that accurate measurement is possible, and its lack of behavioural insights that might account for cheating and/ or resistance.

- Behaviour/output model – This conceives of management control systems (MCS) being distinguished between output and behaviour control (Ouchi 1979, Eisenhardt 1985). *Output controls* are the application of outcome measures to assess managerial performance. They are particularly appropriate when (as in multi-site contexts with a wide distance between 'principals' and 'agents') it is difficult for senior managers to monitor subordinate activity and/or decision choices. By contrast *behaviour controls* are the monitoring evaluation of managerial actions against pre-set conformance standards with effective control in this area being contingent on effective 'clan' selection and training *input controls*. Behaviour controls become pertinent when outputs are difficult to measure or they are unreliable regarding 'real' performance. It acknowledges transformation processes as being imperfect and the availability of measures varying from 'high' to 'low' (Ouchi 1979: 843). Again, the problem with this model is related to its presumption of rational managerial action.

4.1.2 CONTROL TYPOLOGIES

In addition to these 'rational process' models, how is control conceptualised in terms of 'form' and 'purpose'? This section will provide a reprise of some of the control typologies that exist within the literature that, again, advance our understanding of the domain. Seven 'forms' of control will be considered: direct, systems, bureaucratic, multi-layered, concertive, chimerical and socio-ideological:

- Direct – Direct or simple forms of control are characteristic of workplaces that rely upon singular forms power or authority (i.e. nineteenth-century factory owner/ managers, small and medium enterprise – SME – owners). In this context one person, due to the business scale and type of ownership, *informally* interacts (sometimes autocratically) directly with employees. As the firm grows and control cannot be vested purely in one person, levels of hierarchy are built and systems established to ensure conformance.
- Technical/systems – As in the cybernetic model outlined above, process control is achieved through prescribed standards being delivered through operatives whose outputs are measured and monitored by 'controllers'. In this form – especially in production contexts – there is Tayloristic *scientific control* of process systems, stages and throughputs by both management and machines.
- Bureaucratic – This form of control relies upon the use of *formal* rules and laws to regulate managerial control. In this paradigm managers are bound by specified rules and cannot (in theory) act in an arbitrary manner as sanctions for misdemeanours and rewards for success are 'officially prescribed' (there is further discussion of this approach in 4.2.1 below).
- Multi-layered – This approach, favoured within the 'field' operations environments of multi-unit enterprises (as opposed to generic MNCs), conceives of mutually-interdependent systems, standards and service controls being cascaded throughout the operational line to ensure 'line of sight' alignment and co-ordinated effort (Garvin and Levesque 2008, Edger 2012). Hence performance metrics relating to outputs such

as sales, margin, safety compliance, labour ratios and customer service are applied at every level of 'field' hierarchy albeit these measures are tailored to each level of strategic business unit (SBU).

- Concertive – In this post-bureaucratic conception, the frontier of control in organisations is moved to employees through mechanisms such as self-managed teams. Groups of employees are conceived of as being socially self-regulating 'clans' where values and rules are generated consensually amongst co-workers. The benefits of this form of control for organisations are that it reduces costs through managerial delayering and (theoretically) increases worker discretionary effort (Barker 2005).
- Chimerical – This is a hybrid form of control where vertical control is achieved by means of surveillance through machinery and technology (Sewell 1998). Horizontal control is achieved in socialised, interdependent work contexts through teamwork and co-worker assessment.
- Socio-ideological – These MCS forms are purposefully crafted to shape employee mindsets, norms and ideas. Vision, mission and value statements which designate the 'way in which we do business' are calculated managerial attempts to ensure ideological adherence to senior management will by constructing 'meaning' within the organisation through a set of narratives. Ideology co-opts mindsets, underpinning certain laws and rules, prescribing what are acceptable/unacceptable behaviours (Alvesson and Karreman 2004). Such approaches are not mutually independent from bureaucratic, technical and multi-layered MCS, rather they work in tandem. Its benefit to senior management is that it guides individual decision-making and choices into *purposeful action* in complex, ambiguous and uncertain situations where mandated rules might be lacking.

As stated above, some of these MCS are not mutually exclusive in organisations, several forms (due to different forms of industrial activity) being applied simultaneously. For instance, within casual dining, a socio-ideological approach will embrace the whole organisation whilst specific functions like logistics or food production might rely on a technical/systems approach and central administrative functions adopt a bureaucratic form of MCS, with the field relying on multi-layered forms of control.

4.2 Cross-National Control Mechanisms

What MCS do/should organisations transport to their international subsidiaries/affiliates? This is a non-trivial question given, for instance, that certain monitoring and evaluation approaches that are acceptable in the organisation's country of origin might not be culturally acceptable overseas – particularly in emerging markets:

> ... (the) question of whether companies can transport their domestic management control systems overseas, or whether they need to redesign the MCS according to the cultural imperatives of the overseas nations, is of considerable practical significance. (Harrison and McKinnon 1999: 483)

International organisations might, as previously outlined, adopt a specific integration strategy that has particular relevance to MCS deployment ranging from 'loose' to 'tight' based on their business model, stage of international evolution and/or philosophical makeup (Perlmutter 1969, Bartlett and Ghosal 1989). In general, however, the literature categorises two types of dominant control approaches across borders – bureaucratic or cultural (Jaeger 1983). The former conceives of control as being formally applied through rules and procedures in a dispassionate, functional manner in order to ensure operational and financial conformance. The latter sees control as being applied through more informal values-led techniques, where individuals are bound into the 'clan' through shared understandings that shape desired behaviours and activities. Both approaches will be considered in turn.

4.2.1 BUREAUCRATIC/CONTRACT CONTROLS

From a temporal perspective international organisations, in their early stages of subsidiary/ affiliate development, are likely to rely on formal bureaucratic means of control to ensure technical consistency, dependability and quality. According to Jaeger (based on US/ Brazilian MNC research),

> ... bureaucratic control consists of the utilisation of a limited and explicit set of codified rules and regulations which delineate desired behaviour. For an individual to become a functional member of a bureaucratic organisation, he must accept the legitimacy of the organisation's authority, and he must learn the rules and regulations so that he can indeed follow them ... A bureaucratic control system has several implications for the selection, training and monitoring of organisational members. Persons must be found who have the technical skills required (or are trainable) who will accept the organisation's authority and who can learn the organisation's form in accordance with them. (Jaeger 1983: 92)

This paradigm incorporates both the regulation of behaviours and outputs, in line with Ouchi's (1979) model. With regard to *behavioural control* there are impersonal, rational rules regarding selection, rewards and training of locals. Scrutiny and evaluation of activities from the centre takes place through HQ staff, expatriates or socialised locals using procedures, policies, manuals and/or electronic surveillance. Technical competence is valued highly due to these 'direct, formalised and explicit' MCS. Output control is ensured through reporting and monitoring systems where information and data are gathered and analysed in order to apply rewards or sanctions.

The advantages of bureaucratic control systems reside in their low cost (in relative comparison to relational forms) and in that they set the foundations, once rules have been established, for looser forms of co-ordination. Issues relate to the fact that loyalties and 'buy-in' can be weak in extreme bureaucratic forms – particularly in collectivist cultures where relationships are valued more highly than formalised procedures. Such approaches in collectivist cultures also have hidden costs where 'breakdowns' might occur due to non-disclosures caused by a fear of retribution. Also, a reliance on explicit codified direction can lead to information asymmetry (Arrow 1962) where the international owner (the 'principal') applying top-down rules is denied local tacit knowledge and information from its subsidiary/affiliate (its 'agent'), resulting in costly incorrect market solutions being applied.

This situation is most pertinent in international franchising contexts where owners typically exercise control through formal *contractual* mechanisms. The question posed in this literature is whether codified rules and regulations (i.e. the franchise contract) or informal controls (common beliefs and shared values) are the most efficient means of exercising effective control (Quinn and Doherty 2000). Broadly the literature concludes that in the early stages contract is the most efficient manner to regulate relationships through financial surveillance, expatriates and third-party audits. However, if a profitable relationship is to develop, then:

> *In the context of the principal-agent relationship, agency theory highlights the importance of the information transfer, the information asymmetry problem and associated monitoring costs. This information asymmetry problem arises in the principal-agent relationship because agents, being in day-to-day control of a company, have detailed knowledge of its operations. The principals have neither access to this knowledge, nor, in many cases, the ability to interpret the information. (Quinn and Doherty 2000: 360)*

Problems are intensified within franchising contexts when there are conflicting goals between parties, a weak brand or insufficient support activities. Accordingly, a number of studies show that franchising performs better when values and norms relating to the desired attitudes and behaviours of participants are shared (Doherty and Alexander 2004). High levels of personal interaction aid insight and decision-making, allowing a degree of autonomy for the franchisee to evolve over time – important because many of these actors see themselves as 'independent entrepreneurs'.

4.2.2 CULTURE/VALUES AS CONTROL

The alternative form of control posited by the literature is culture and its associated values. In essence scholars (mainly structural sociologists) view culture as a form of organisational and societal regulation and control, a nexus that shapes, guides and informs the behaviours of actors through shared 'meanings' (Sohn 1994, Harzing and Sorge 2003). By their very nature cultures vary, influencing *types* of control within societies and organisations, in some instances incorporating many of the elements referred to above. One pertinent definition of culture is provided by House et al.:

> *... culture is defined as shared motives, values, beliefs, identities and interpretations or meanings of significant events that result from common experiences of members of collectives that are transmitted across generations. It is important to note that these are psychological attributes and that this definition can be applied at both the societal and organisational level of analysis. (House et al. 2004: 15)*

It is self-evident that variances in COO and host country cultures will have a mediating effect upon organisational cultural 'fit' both home and abroad, but what has the most important influence in cross-border contexts – organisational or national cultures?

> *The interaction of national and organisational cultures has been explicitly addressed by several scholars with the finding that national cultural attributes run deeper: ie imposing a parent's organisational culture which is incongruent with the value system of a subsidiary's national culture will be difficult and slow, if possible at all. (Volkmar 2003: 97)*

Hence, organisations need to be careful when transporting their cultures abroad not least because their effectiveness is founded upon the premise that they are bounded, purposive and intentionally structured. By contrast national cultures have more diffuse characteristics, making it difficult to understand idiosyncratic nuances that have profound commercial implications for internationalising organisations. Additionally, national cultures exert a significant force because they embrace their members' whole lives, whilst organisations provide temporal control at a workplace level (Hendry 1999). Thus, both dimensions of 'culture as control', at national and organisational levels, require analysis, both being considered in turn below.

4.2.2.1 National level

Over the past century scholars have sought (on the basis of empirical research) to construct universal categories that describe the structure, agency and form of national cultures. Whilst it is impossible to go into each framework in detail (Schneider and Barsoux 2003, Lane et al. 2009 and Hofstede et al. 2010 all provide excellent contemporary overviews), a brief consideration of the types of cultural categories advanced by certain scholars is useful at this juncture:

- Kluckhohn and Strodbeck (1961) – Members of societies display five orientations: *disposition* (good, evil or hybrid), *relationship with nature* (dominant, harmonious or destructive), *interpersonal relations* (lineal/hierarchical, collateral/collectivist or individualist), *action orientation* (doing, being or containing), *temporal focus* (future, past or present), *conception of space* (public, private or mixed). Scarborough (1998) applied this framework to 'western culture' (which he characterised by an aggressive, active approach to technology, nature and progress with a reliance on scientific method and reason) and 'Chinese culture' (orientated towards passive fatalistic submission with a reliance on precedent and Confucian intuition and wisdom).
- Hall (1976) – Hall considered why cultures communicate in a different way, categorising them as either 'low' or 'high' context. *High-context* cultures (i.e. Japan, China, Korea, Vietnam, Latin Europe and Middle East) display the following attributes: long-lasting relationships, shared 'codes' of communication, primacy of those in authority, reliance on spoken rather than written agreements and 'insiders' being preferred to 'outsiders'. *Low-context* cultures (USA, UK, Scandinavia and Germany) are characterised by: shorter relationships, explicit messages, diffused/delegated authority, written agreements, insider/outsider parity and cultural patterns that are more open to change.
- Hofstede (1980, 1991) – Five dimensions are categorised: *power distance* (hierarchical distance between individuals), *achievement orientation* (self-efficacy-related need for performance), *uncertainty avoidance* (individual/group inclination to accept ambiguity), *individualism* versus *collectivism* (closeness of relations between members), *masculinity* versus *femininity* (division of roles and values within society) and *long-term* versus *short-term* (temporal orientation towards life; also labelled *indulgence* versus *restraint* in Hoftstede et al. 2010).

- Trompenaars (1993) – Building on insights from previous commentators, categories included: *universalism* versus *particularism, collectivism* versus *individualism, specific* versus *diffuse, status, time* and *nature.*
- Schwartz (1994, 1999) – Schwartz identified ten value types: *power, achievement, hedonism, stimulation, self direction, universalism, benevolence, traditional, conformity* and *security.*
- House et al. (2004) – See 5.2.2 in Chapter 5.

Of all these frameworks, Hoftstede's (1980, 1991 and 2010) are the most widely cited and applied. But how do national societies measure up against his model? Figure 4.1 below gives culture dimension ratings for seven countries:

	PD	I	AO	UA	LO
US	L	H	H	L	L
Germany	L	H	H	M	M
Japan	M	M	H	H	H
Indonesia	H	L	M	L	L
West Africa	H	L	M	M	L
Russia	H	M	L	H	L
China	H	L	M	M	H

Symbols: PD: power distance, I: individualism, AO: achievement orientation, UA: uncertainty avoidance, LO: long-term orientation, L: low, M: medium, H: high

Figure 4.1   Selected national cultural dimension scores (adapted from Hoftstede 1993: 91)

It is not just the cultural dimensions specific to each country that are important to note (some scores having slightly changed according to Hofstede et al. 2010); it is the *variance* between countries which is important, bringing into focus how organisations, influenced by their COO national values, can transfer products, assets and practices into societies with such vast differences (note the major divergences between the US and the Indonesia/ West Africa/Russia/China cluster for instance).

Issues with national cultural approaches relate to three main factors. First, they usually involve binary definitions that fail to reflect the fact that many societies' and regions' cultures are rarely captured by such universal caricatures; societal clusters are notoriously unreliable given regional and tribal variances in norms and customs. Second, whilst anthropologists might argue that the cultural core of any group is relatively fixed and coherent through time and space, economic and socio-demographic drivers can move culture, especially at an inter-generational level (see 5.2.3 below). Third, there is the notion that even within 'dominant cultures' individuals can assume multiple identities (i.e. 'acting' in different contexts, masking their true personal preferences) especially if it serves their own personal self-interest.

4.2.2.2 Organisational level

At a corporate level culture can be described as an ideological mechanism to control the mindsets, behaviours and outputs of workers and managers. With regards to parent and subsidiary/affiliate relations, *cultural absorption* usually occurs over time as values are transmitted and either rejected (on account of extant national culture or prior organisational programming) or accepted. But how is corporate culture defined and under what circumstances – particularly during M&A and joint ventures – do culture clashes occur?

The concept of culture as providing an explanation for variance in firms' performance gained credence in the 1980s through the work of notable scholars such as Harrison (1972) and Schein (1985), also being popularised through the work of commentators such as Peters and Waterman (1982). Given its antecedents in anthropological theories of organisation, scholars operating in this area have, as their starting-point, structural notions that the basic values, beliefs and assumptions held by members of a corporation translate into a dominant culture of *shared outlooks and meanings* within organisations. There are typically seven primary dimensions that scholars use to capture, measure and compare the essence of organisational cultures (O'Reilly et al. 1991, Chatman and Jehn 1994, Ashkanasy et al. 2000):

- Innovation and risk-taking – the degree to which employees are encouraged to act autonomously in order to be innovative and take risks;
- Attention to detail – the degree to which employees are expected to exhibit precision, analysis and attention to detail;
- Outcome orientation – the degree to which management focuses on results and outcomes rather than on the techniques and processes used to achieve those outcomes;
- People orientation – the degree to which management decisions take into consideration the effect of outcomes on people within the organisation;
- Team orientation – the degree to which work activities are organised around teams rather than individuals;
- Aggressiveness – the degree to which people are aggressive and competitive rather than easy-going;
- Stability – the degree to which organisational activities emphasise maintaining the *status quo* in contrast to growth.

Scholars contend that companies with an innovative profile, good attention to detail, a focus on results and process, strong people and team orientation, and a strong emphasis on achieving and maintaining a growth profile, are more likely to be successful than firms who do not exhibit these cultural characteristics (Kotter and Heskett 1992, Ashkanasy et al. 2000).

With regards to combining organisational cultures scholars argue that cultural absorption/integration – especially after events such as M&A or joint venture agreements – is dependent on the *nature and types* of cultures being combined (Cartwright and Cooper 1993, 1996). Using the seminal model proposed by Harrison (1972), which refers to four culture types (*power*, *role*, *task/achievement* and *person/support*), they hypothesise that assimilation is easier in some circumstances than others. Their model in Figure 4.2 below demonstrates how they conceive types of culture as cast in terms of either *constraint* or *autonomy* for individuals:

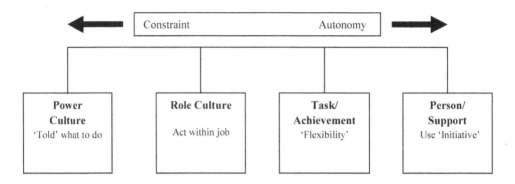

Figure 4.2   Relationship between culture types and individual consequences in terms of constraint/autonomy (adapted from Cartwright and Cooper 1996: 50)

Cartwright and Cooper's central thesis is that cultural compatibility or fit between the combining organisations is essential to effective cross-border combination performance:

> ... *the existing pre-combination cultures of the partnering organisations play a major and fundamental role in determining merger and acquisition outcomes. (1996: 61)*

For instance, organisations with a *power culture* seeking to blend entities (or individuals located in them) with *task/achievement* or *person/support* cultures, risk alienating individuals by placing limits upon their levels of autonomy, increasing the likelihood of resistance, and thus jeopardising the performance of the new combination. A combination of the 'best of each culture' (i.e. *hybrid*) is advocated by these scholars as one means of ameliorating this issue. Their thesis is endorsed by other commentators who add that cultural change is more likely to succeed if changes are imposed incrementally rather than quickly after mergers (Kavanagh and Ashkanasy 2006).

It is important to state that although differences in organisational culture might be one serious explanation for the failure of combining cross-border entities, associated practical issues are also of consequence. Scholars have pointed to the dominant contingent variable relating to compatibility, unity and (therefore) effectiveness being the amount of *autonomy* granted to subsidiaries/affiliates (Weber and Schweiger 1992). Limits to discretion and independent action were also identified as a major factor by Lubatkin et al. (1999), who highlighted the major *strategic/organisational* areas for conflict between the combining cross-national organisational entities (see Figure 4.3).

Both Weber and Schweiger (1992) and Lubatkin et al. (1999) observed that COO executives were annoyed and stressed if they failed to curb autonomous tendencies among HC executives relating to the factors highlighted above. Conversely, HC executives railed against interventionist positions adopted by the parent's top managers with regard to imposing standards, rules and expectations. Are there regional differences between approaches? One important study found that the aforementioned clashes due to organisational/strategic reasons were as pertinent for mergers between continental European companies as researchers had found to be the case in the majority of (mainly) US studies (Very et al. 1997).

- Determination of goals of profitability
- Determination of goals of productivity
- Determination of goals of competitive position
- Determination of goals managerial resources
- Determination of goals of physical resources
- Determination of goals of employee relations
- Determination of goals for public
- Expanding into new marketing territories with existing products
- Introducing new products
- Investing or changing of equipment and/or manufacturing process
- Changing level of expenditures for advertising and promotion
- Changing selling and marketing techniques
- Production schedule and plans
- Purchasing important raw materials
- Determining and changing budget plans
- Financing major investments
- Hiring, promoting and firing high-level managers
- Determining rewards and compensation for high-level managers
- Determining training programs for high-level managers
- Changing product design
- Changing product prices
- Determining research and development budget
- Determining research content

Figure 4.3   Top management perceptions of autonomy removal (adapted from Lubatkin et al. 1999: 70–71)

In summary, there are three advantages of achieving some degree of cultural, strategic and operational compatibility between the parent and its subsidiary/affiliate:

- Patterns of decision-making – The creation of a *shared culture* in which a *similar world view* predominates creates internal *social pressure* and programming that assures patterns of decisions-making choices and behaviours in both benign and extreme commercial circumstances (Boyacigiller 1990).
- Organisational commitment – Under the right cultural circumstances (quite often a *hybrid* position in combinations suffering from high distance) powerful trust-based commitments and mutual interdependencies can develop, strengthening the organisation's ability to move quickly to changing circumstances.
- Social knowledge – Also in cultures where there is an emphasis on control through values transmission rather than *just* bureaucratic compliance, implicit and indirect social interactions and networks yield more value over time:

Compared to a bureaucratic-formal control *system, training and socialisation in* cultural control *are also more important. An organisation member must not only learn a set of explicit, codified rules and regulations, but he must also learn and become part of a subtle and complex control system which consists of a broad range of* 'pivotal' *values. Furthermore, social pressure exists to accept peripheral values. (Jaeger 1983: 94)*

The disadvantages of attempting to impose some form of cultural homogenuity (especially at high distance) are that the means through which this is achieved – expatriate role models, local socialisation programmes, frequent visits from HQ, conferences, seminars, social events – are extremely costly.

4.3 Cross-National Control Preferences

The sections above have outlined different types of *MCS forms* and *functional bureaucratic* and *emotional cultural/values* cross-national approaches to control but what are specific *preferences* of organisations and individuals to control? As stated, different organisations and societies have different control preferences which are likely to differ according to shared values and meanings. This means that as organisational culture cannot be detached from its context, MCS practices and preferences vary from country to country:

> ... *since cultural norms precondition human disposition, behaviours and practices, expecting uniform policies and practices to work effectively across the globe is unrealistic. (Ueno and Sekaran 1992: 660)*

The cultural frameworks in section 4.2.2.2 above made some reference to the dispositions that certain cultures have to particular modes of control, but what is the actual empirical evidence relating to where preferences – both at an organisational and individual level – lie?

4.3.1 ORGANISATIONAL PREFERENCES

A plethora of studies – often using Hofstede's framework to make cross-national comparisons between cases with the US as a control sample – have been made to either validate or dispute 'ideal type' models. The narrative in the literature is apt to make dualisms with, for instance, Anglo companies derived from individualistic cultures, where ambiguities are low, being characterised as using bureaucratic controls and Japanese/Korean companies derived from collectivist cultures, where ambiguity is high, having a preference for relational cultural controls (Mead and Andrews 2009: 348). In fact, scholars have taken varied approaches to the problematic, analysing organisational approaches from three different comparative starting-points.

    The first set of comparative studies analyses what control approaches companies with differing COO take in the same cross-national context. Taking three studies in particular, what are the findings? First, in a study comparing US and European MNCs over foreign subsidiaries in the same territory it was observed that US organisations had a propensity to rely on high bureaucratic output controls, whilst European companies exerted influence through high cultural/values controls (Egelhoff 1984). Second, in a comparison of US and Japanese MNCs with Korean subsidiaries, again, US MNCs were seen to exert high output controls, with the Japanese applying high cultural controls (Chang and Taylor 1999). Third, in a comparison of US and Japanese MNCs, US organisations applied both high input and output controls, whilst Japanese firms placed a greater reliance on cultural control (Pooripakdee 2003). Clearly these studies supported Hofstede's thesis with regards to US organisations having a high level of individualism and achievement orientation, expressed through the close monitoring of financial outputs, with Japanese firms preferring to deal with high levels of uncertainty avoidance through relational means of control.

Another stream of research examines the degree to which MNCs, operating in different foreign territories, adapt controls to fit different societal contexts. What scholars have found is that adaptation is contingent on three factors:

- Distance – Organisations operating in low-distance environments (i.e. 'close to home') are likely to have more social knowledge about the territory and will adopt behavioural control approaches through culture and values. In high-distance contexts where they have less social knowledge, more bureaucratic/input control approaches will be adopted (Hamilton and Kashlack 1999).
- Resource protection – In the case of joint ventures where partners exchange physical and knowledge-based resources, US firms are apt to use strong bureaucratic controls to protect their knowledge, whilst Chinese firms use a variety of control mechanisms to protect their assets (Chalos and O'Connor 2004).
- COO factors – In keeping with Hofstede's findings, COO factors have a greater contingent impact on organisational control practices than other factors (scale, sector, etc.), controls in the international arena being the same as those applied in home-based contexts (Harzing and Sorge 2003). For instance the socio-cultural and political-economic conditions of countries have a profound impact on both control and hierarchy preferences (Tannenbaum et al. 1974).

A well-established cross-national genre has also looked at intra-organisational control preferences. Ouchi and Jaeger's (1978) seminal work found that American (Type A) intra-organisational behaviour emphasised bureaucratic control due to high levels of individualism and labour mobility. Japanese (Type J) intra-organisational behaviour was characterised by culturally-led controls due to high levels of collectivism and a 'jobs for life' philosophy. Type Z American companies (in contrast to McGregor's Theory X) adopted a hybrid approach. Also, in a comparison of US versus German intra-organisational preferences it was found that the former's control preferences were centralised, directive and task orientated (based on the principles of 'universalism' – 'our way is the best'), whilst the latter's archetype rested upon decentralised, participatory and socio-emotional control (Kreder and Zeller 1988). In line with these findings Harzing (1999) concluded, in an important study, that US MNCs had a preference for formal planning, financial, monitoring and central policy-making systems rather than personal control (values) mechanisms.

The issues with much of this research are its reliance on a limited number of conceptual frameworks, qualitative/deductive-led research methodology, its inability to go beyond national levels (or caricatures of analysis), its over-emphasis on US 'matched' comparisons and, at times, its inconsistent and contradictory evidence (see for instance Hall's 1976 'low context' coupling of US and Germany with the findings of Kreder and Zeller 1988 above). One major flaw, however, is its organisational level of analysis that fails to capture the essence of individual control preferences from both manager and recipient perspectives.

4.3.2 INDIVIDUAL PREFERENCES

How do managers and employees from different national contexts perceive control? To what extent are national and organisational cultures the sole affective force relating to general cognitive perceptions – the way in which people think and relate – of control? A stream of literature argues that in addition to some of the affective variables outlined above, preferences and attitudes of individuals from different cultures are also dependent upon:

- Personal factors – Hofstede et al. (2010: 6) make the argument that personality is a consequence of both inherited genetic *human nature* and learned *cultural experience*. But to what extent do fundamental elements of *human nature* (i.e. instinct for survival, nurture, autonomy/dominance, etc.) override *cultural forces* in certain circumstances? Furthermore, some scholars argue that individual control preferences, rather than being solely dictated by learned culture, are driven by factors such as nature, age, gender and socio-economic status, which all offer a far better explanation for loose or tight control preferences (Anthony and Govindarjan 2004).
- Situational position – In addition, the *level* that individuals occupy in both societal and organisational contexts has a mediating effect on perceptions relating to control. Within organisations, levels of worker alienation (ergo their perspectives on control) are likely to be affected by the clarity of their role and perception of supervisor support (Posner and Butterfield 1979).

But how do managers themselves conceive of their roles? In essence managers from different cultures have varying views and interpretations concerning what it *means* to be a manager (Tolich et al. 1999). Importantly, these differences in views affect how they discharge their managerial authority (Sandberg 2000). In keeping with some of the observations made above some studies have attempted to analyse the different ways in which managers from different national backgrounds act with regards to certain tasks/functions:

- Financial controls – Managers have different views with regards to one of their most important functions: budgetary and financial control. One study found that Japanese managers are more likely to use budgets as a communication device, preferring more budgetary 'sleeve' than their US counterparts (Daley et al. 1985).
- Risk and compliance – With respect to discharging their compliance responsibilities, managers are apt to have different attitudes as to what their primary role is with regard to reportage. For instance, in a comparative analysis of Southern Asian and Anglo accountants' views of whistle-blowing, researchers found that Southern Asians were far less comfortable with the concept of 'telling' than their Anglo counterparts (Patel 2003).
- Monitoring and evaluating – An essential part of the manager's role is the process of checking and evaluating MCS. Different views as to what this means prevail, one study showing that Japanese managers conceived MCS as vehicles to disseminate information, whilst US managers saw control systems, which they believed were essential in defining roles and outcomes, from a reward and punishment perspective (Birnberg and Snodgrass 1988).

- Influencing – Managers also differ in terms of their conception and understanding of power and influence *tactics*, with variances being explained by factors such as gender, personality and national cultures (Yukl et al. 2003). According to one study, Type J managers (see above) deploy altruism-based strategies to gain compliance whilst Type A managers apply rewards and sanctions to get results (Hirokawa and Miyahara 1986). Another study found that US managers deploy direct task-related tactics to influence subordinates whilst Chinese managers used informal personal-related strategies (Yukl et al. 2003).

To sum up, studies have shown how, in addition to cultural forces, variables such as age, hierarchy and personality-related factors affect how individuals view control. Managers will also have different control preferences in different cultural contexts. However, an important final point to make is that often managers are labour under an of power and influence (Pfeffer and Fong 2005). This is why studies have consistently shown that managers, whatever their organisational or national contexts, often have a preference to resort to *structural* rather than *individual* ability power sources, opting for legitimate/ rational means of exercising control rather than persuasion or personal ingratiation (Yukl and Tracey 1992).

4.4 HMUL Control-Based Practices

The term organisation itself implies a social structure that is created to provide order, co-ordinated conformance and assured outcomes. Ergo, members of an organisation are expected to contribute to its structural and functional salience by despatching pre-set duties, roles and tasks. In international contexts achieving control within subsidiaries and affiliates is made difficult due to the problems of distance and cultural transference, threatening costly malfunctions to operational effectiveness and efficiency. In part, as Chapter 3 demonstrated, these issues can be resolved at subsidiary/partner level through a number of interventions, but the fact remains that local managers such as HMULs are pivotal in monitoring, discharging and executing controls in MUEs at unit level where the customer directly interacts with both service providers and the product. Given that the literature referred to above acknowledges that control in international organisations is contingent upon organisational preferences (bureaucratic versus values/ideological), host country cultural attributes and individual conceptions of what being a manager actually is, how do effective HMULs ensure control at a local level in such ambiguous and complex circumstances? What are the unifying practices that distinguish high performers in comparison to their peers? In actual fact, unlike the literature that creates dualisms between *bureaucratic* and *values-led control*, effective HMULs pursue a judicious combination of the two. Bureaucratic control is enforced through *blueprint execution* and *output prioritisation* combined with *values transmission* and *confessional security*. These will now be considered in turn.

4.4.1 BLUEPRINT EXECUTION

In order to provide consistency across their formats all MUEs will provide their front-line operations with a blueprinted guide which provides information and instruction regarding how the product should be executed. Often this blueprint will cover a range of standard operating procedures (SOPs) relating to back of house (BOH) functions and policies and practices relating to front of house (FOH) sales-led service execution (Edger 2012: 86–92). In international organisations where offers are adapted according to local conditions these blueprints will have been amended at subsidiary/affiliate level to fit these local exigencies. Commonly, international MUEs will apply a greater degree of conformance to BOH systems with regards to activities such as replenishment, sales data capture and stocktaking so that their stores operate off a common platform for efficiency purposes (enabling uniform monitoring, checking and measurement). For instance, Tesco implemented common supply chain platforms into its international operations as a matter of course:

> *Tesco has a simple doctrine: local, but global. We create local stores that look completely different depending on the continent but run them on our global operating systems. Our common platform is called, suitably enough, 'Tesco in a box'. These are core work processes (the company's hidden wiring and plumbing, completely unseen by its customers) which have been turned into systems and are then used across the group – such as ordering, finance, replenishment, merchandising, customer data handling … good processes in all types of organisations should be capable of being applied universally. When that happens, a company benefits from higher productivity. (Leahy 2012: 177–8)*

In terms of ensuring '*macro-adherence*' against its blueprint, international organisations will often delegate auditing activities to their subsidiaries although Head Office – particularly in the case of franchise operations – will conduct planned or random checks to assess levels of adherence or deviation. In franchised contexts the implications for non-conformance to codified procedures by franchisees (master, multiple or individual) can result in costs such as penalty charges or, in extreme circumstances, termination. Hence the importance of the role of the HMUL in ensuring '*micro-adherence*' to blueprinted standards and systems in international MUEs. But what are the issues confronting HMULs in their local surveillance and application of the blueprint and how do they overcome them?

There are a myriad of issues faced by HMULs in executing the blueprint which can be classified as being *operational, cultural* and *personal*. From an *operational* point of view how accurately has the blueprint been translated from its parental source or to what extent has it been adapted effectively to mirror local conditions? What resources have been supplied to the HMUL to ensure its effective execution – has the necessary capital and investment been supplied in order to enable conformance? For sure, at times, HMULs will find themselves at the point of delivery without the necessary physical and human wherewithal to fulfil the requirements outlined in the operational blueprint. How do they improvise in order to fulfil pre-ordained duties and tasks? Also, from a *cultural* perspective – in *high context* environments where there is a reliance on spoken rather than written agreements (Hall 1976), with concomitant gaps in capability around simple managerial functions such as checking, monitoring and measuring – HMULs might struggle to get their unit personnel to understand and/or implement codified rules and procedures. From a personal perspective, in cultures with high levels of *power distance*, HMULs might be apt to adopt a detached perspective due to their perceived levels of personal power (derived from their hierarchical status), meaning that they are insufficiently in control of what is happening on the ground because they have outsourced responsibility (under the aegis of punishment) to their front-line operatives.

Given these issues how do effective HMULs execute the blueprint? In many cases HMULs in IMUEs, having been promoted from unit manager level, will be familiar with the blueprinted detail and, having been promoted for (amongst other things) their technical competence, will be able fulfil the policing and checking aspects of their role effectively due to prior knowledge and experience. However, it is the HMULs' ability to *manage at a distance* that marks them out as supreme operators. Now they are located off-site with multiple unit responsibility, they have to plan their time carefully to schedule in planned operational audits and due diligence checks alongside spontaneous 'visits with a purpose'. They are also adept at using the resources of their organisation and district to act as additional 'eyes and ears'. For instance at a district level they might use some of their most capable unit managers to run 'interim' or 'dummy' audits to check on compliance, and to provide their units with calibrated trial runs. Utilising other agencies within the organisation such as property and maintenance, HR and internal audit (such as stock takers) also helps 'spread the load', providing invaluable information on adherence. However, in order to be successful HMULs must adopt the *managerial practices* necessary to execute, namely, planning, scheduling, organising, delegating and 'chasing up'. As stated, some HMULs in certain cultural contexts will assume that, given their elevated position 'above the units', they can abandon all accountability to unit level, stepping in only to punish non-conformance when it goes wrong. Successful HMULs do not wait for system failure; they anticipate or fix problems quickly through adopting a *proactive* rather than *reactive* stance.

Given that levels of *action orientation* (i.e. doing, being or containing) amongst middle managers can vary across cultures (Kluckhohn and Strodbeck 1961), how are the HMUL skills with regard to blueprint execution, detailed above, developed? Interventions such as expatriate best-practice diffusion, home country assignments, rotation around exemplar operations and bespoke immersion and training can all lead to the improvement of baseline managerial practices which will form a formidable coupling with technical knowledge. However, getting HMULs to abandon deeply held conceptions of what constitutes effective managerial action (i.e. passively waiting for malfunctions to occur in order to apportion blame to others down the chain of command) requires deep behavioural change. HMULs must understand and accept what the content and *process* of effective blueprint execution looks like across multiple sites. They should be given the tools and techniques of 'managing at a distance' – which given the bounded cultural dispositions of managers in some contexts, is not a concept that is easily understood or accepted.

Case Study 5 – Blueprint Execution in Rosinter Restaurants, Russia

Kevin Todd is the President and CEO of Rosinter Restaurant Holdings, Russia's largest multi-brand casual dining chain (approximately 460 units – one-third franchised – and 11 brands, including Il Patio, Planet Sushi, Costa Coffee, McDonalds and TGI Friday) operating in 10 countries, spread across 44 cities. Over a successful 30-year career, Kevin held several senior executive roles in the restaurant industry and was MD of the franchise arm of Volvo, UK. A Visiting Professor at BCU, Kevin is also a Council Member of the EFSF (European Food Service Forum).

The problems of ensuring consistency across a multi-brand portfolio that is spread across multiple time zones, in different ethnic regions with distinctive local labour/consumer micro-markets is a non-trivial challenge! Getting the local leadership (i.e. regional, territory and store managers) to understand, buy into and execute the 'basics' – the core operating standards – is a hygiene factor for most businesses, but is highly complex in diffuse international contexts due to distance, capability, language and cultural disposition. How do you ensure that the standards and service promise in one of our branded restaurants in St Petersburg is exactly the same as in Kazakhstan? The answer to this is that you need to apply both a *top-down* and *bottom-up* approach … best-practice behaviours need to be *modelled by senior management*, supported by *an operational architecture* which shows what good looks like (i.e. exemplar stores), and by local leaders with clearly defined/appropriate skills, roles and responsibilities, resources and a clear line of sight.

From a top-down perspective you need a *senior team* who *model the correct behaviours* in terms of 'getting it right every time'. In international contexts where (some) 'hierarchies' have 'outsourced' blueprint accountability – 'swooping down' to apply sanctions and penalties only when it goes wrong – you have an inappropriate culture that leaves people demoralized and fearful on the front-line. Senior executives need to model good behaviours because it sets the tone and desired standard down the line … many is the time that I will go into a store and *refuse to 'walk by'* standards that are clearly unacceptable … but having picked up on the deficiency, rather than just losing my cool, *I will seek to understand why and how* the breakdown has occurred; is it because people haven't been trained, got the appropriate resources (i.e. machinery, labour or technology) or worse, they just don't care?! … Whatever the reason you just cannot (especially in 'emotionally-connective' casual dining contexts) just ignore poor practice which might be the symptoms of broader issues … when local leaders become desensitized to sloppiness (especially BOH) and fail to take remedial action to *fix the causes* you've lost it … As CEO I see myself as the standard bearer for great brand/product execution … If I care, then there is a strong chance that my people will care too! …

But modelling behaviour and seeking to understand causality is insufficient in itself … You need to take a *holistic approach to blueprint execution* by, first – from a 'bottom-up perspective – making sure everybody knows what an outstanding store looks like (especially in franchised systems) ... if operators can see what good looks like and how such standards are achieved then you stand a chance of replicating it ... throughout my career, and also here at Rosinter, I have always believed in having 'Centres of Excellence' that are beacons of good practice, spread out across the organization to diffuse best practice ... Second, you need structures, processes, defined roles and responsibilities and clear line of sight metrics that provide assured outcomes ... this might seem tedious and obvious but, in my experience, is something that is done poorly in many organisations ... what great international organisations do is have structures with clear accountabilities and defined cross-functional responsibilities (i.e. field operations with brand marketing for instance) ... I believe that brands are all about relentless focus (in terms of execution and innovation), so operational and functional structures need to be built around brands – even in multi-brand contexts where the costs of applying such structures might seem prohibitive ... you need to get teams together that *intimately* understand and *care about* their customers, service delivery systems, product, etc. ... In Rosinter we have just changed the operational architecture to focus more around *single* rather than *multi-brand sites*, which in turn creates a sense of purpose, identity and (most importantly) *autonomous know-how* (i.e. *how to slightly adapt the format and product sales mix to add value in distinctive micro-markets*) ... This means that right '*hard*' (i.e. refurbishment capital, promotional spend, menu investment, etc.) and '*soft*' (i.e. certificated training, HRM, customer satisfaction systems, etc.) resources can be directed at the right areas, for the right purpose ... in addition, monitoring systems, metrics and reward can also be adapted to be fit for purpose, ensuring people have 'skin in the *right* game!' to perform.

4.4.2 OUTPUT PRIORITISATION

Given the fact that many internationalising MUEs are derived from Anglo-American contexts, many organisations will rely on bureaucratic 'output controls' (Ouchi 1979, Jaeger 1983): a set of outcome-related measures that help 'controllers' and 'senior managers' in the firm analyse and assess performance. In MUEs these metrics will form part of a 'multi-layered net' within the operational line (Garvin and Levesque 2008) so that organisations have a line of sight on the despatching of key priorities. In some organisations these outputs are coupled with inputs in the form of a balanced scorecard where *operational and financial outputs* are bound together with *people and customer-related inputs*. Such frameworks set clear parameters and expectations within the organisation whilst creating a high degree of alignment/congruence, often bolstered through associated reward and performance systems (typically more connected to 'hard' financial outputs rather than 'soft' people inputs).

The issues facing HMULs in prioritising outputs relate, again, to operational, cultural and personal factors. From an *operational* point of view organisational priorities and targets might not be well expressed, constantly change or, as previously stated, over-emphasise financial outputs to the detriment of all other measures. In addition they might be insufficiently cognisant of the local environment, being a direct translation of what is more important in the home rather than the host market. Metrics that make sense in mature home contexts might have little relevance or practicability in emerging foreign markets. How does the HMUL deal with this ambiguity and complexity? In addition, from a *cultural* perspective, HMULs might be operating in contexts with low levels of *achievement orientation* with polychromic *temporal* characteristics which emphasise fatalism rather than science or longer rather than shorter-term time horizons (Hoftstede 1980, 1991, Scarborough 1998). How does the HMUL gain buy-in to short-term metrics and acceptance for the need to respond to urgent organisational priorities in these diffuse contexts? Also, from a *personal* point of view HMULs, given their cultural pre-programming and dispositions, might either be fairly sanguine about the need to respond to certain measures and targets, believing them to be indicative rather than mandatory, or take a literal interpretation of 'what they have been told to do', attempting to (unrealistically) comply with every measure and priority. In certain cultures they might also be ill-equipped – due to ingrained attitudes towards nonconfrontational styles of managerial behaviour – to conduct mandatory performance appraisals where the non-achievement of certain outputs can be openly discussed for improvement purposes.

How do effective HMULs manage outputs to the satisfaction of 'controllers'? The first thing that needs to be said is that given the plethora of measures that apply in most MUEs, HMULs can never (except in exceptional circumstances such as a uniformly underperforming district or unit that they have just taken responsibility for) meet every output criteria set by their superiors or organisation. More likely, successful HMULs conduct a *gap analysis* and target their most serious output variances and/or concentrate on the *causal factors* that have led to underperformance. As HMULs are measured on district-wide metrics, making a significant difference in a small number of serially defective stores can have a disproportionate impact on their overall numbers. To this extent HMULs are portfolio optimisers (Edger 2012), concentrating upon raising metrics through targeted rather than wholesale interventions. This requires high levels of interpretative nous, courage and managerial skill.

However, in some cultures with high *uncertainty avoidance* (Hoftstede 1980, 1991), HMULs might constantly seek affirmation and guidance from above regarding what they should concentrate upon and how they should do it (in order, if things go wrong, to protect themselves from sanctions). Developing and reinforcing managerial behaviours that emphasise a bias towards action based on robust empirical insights is difficult in some cultural contexts. International MUEs can intervene to develop prioritising skills through insisting that their cadres of first and second-line managers go through 'entry level' programmes that teach time management, activity planning, problem-solving and financial interpretation skills. The fact remains, however, that some managers within certain contexts are fearful of acting on their initiative due to a fear (which is justified in many cases) of local retribution – one reason why international MUEs wishing to embed the correct behaviours resort to instituting a generic company-wide set of values which seeks to inform and direct behaviours in an appropriate manner (see 4.4.3 below).

Case Study 6 – Output Prioritisation in Growth Markets

Paul Turner is Professor of Management Practice at Birmingham City Business School and has held senior executive positions in a number of global multi-unit enterprises.

The extent to which organisations specify and define outputs at a local level is dependent on the business sector in which they operate. The extent to which product/service outputs are consistent and 'standardisable' in local contexts depends on nuances, customs, laws and tastes. For instance, professional service firms (with a large number of intangible outputs) will differ compared to car manufacturing! In the case of MUEs there is inevitably the conundrum as to how firms gain international conformity, against a set of benchmarked standards/metrics, whilst retaining some sort of local flexibility. Translating central controls in MUEs down the line seems fine in principle but difficult to do in practice.

Rules and standards transference is complex is because of two main reasons. First, the parent's country of origin and the way it operates (connected with leadership, structure, culture, history, international experience, etc.) will have a direct effect on the way in which management control systems are designed, resulting in either 'tight' or 'loose' approaches. Second, the local culture will (in all likelihood) have a preference for the way in which certain control approaches are dispatched, be they budgeting, auditing, monitoring, compliance, etc. It is not these activities *per se* that organisations have a problem expediting, but rather the approaches and techniques that are adopted in order to ensure conformance. For instance, in some cultures where a high level of literal interpretation applies international MUEs must be careful not to overload those 'on the ground' with rules and procedures, as operatives will feel that they have 'to do everything'. This may result in them doing the wrong things, at the most inappropriate times, for what they believe to be all the right reasons.

How do international organisations get around this? In earlier times, it was common for international MUEs to deploy expatriates who would act as transmission vehicles between the centre and local markets. This has fallen out of favour more recently due to cost and, more importantly, a view that local managers are better able to conjoin central objectives and controls with local predilections. Thus, HCMs (host country managers) have been sent on significant immersion programmes at the parent's centre, exposed to best-practice approaches through business school sponsorship or inducted into organisational 'ways of working' through 'home country' job placements and/or rotation. This has given them behavioural insight into leading-edge practice and/or the way in which 'things are done around here', affording instruction and insight into policies and practices that are deemed to represent the 'glue' of the organisation … Another approach adopted by MUEs has been through reward systems (whether individually or collectivist). This is a developing area although my feeling is that bonus and incentive systems that are linked to certain outcome metrics are more powerful (given 'hygiene' level socio-economic circumstances) in some markets than they are in others.

But given that at the Senior Leaders Conference at Davos in 2011 there was still a major concern expressed that international organisations were vulnerable to global talent shortages, what further insights might apply to ensuring optimal outputs at a local level? For me it is clear that what successful organisations do is appoint managers who have a high level of social awareness and connectivity. What do I mean by this? Frankly, managers that can emotionally connect ... possessing the ability to network ... 'making sense' of the functional central/local linkages. At multi-site field level this means that HMULs must be judicious and discriminating about not only which measures and controls are important but also *how they can be most effectively implemented*. To this extent local managers require good managerial skills training (planning, organizing, delegating, monitoring, etc.). They also require cognitive thinking skills for problem-solving and prioritization ... but also (and most crucially) they require the ability to apply a cultural filter ... sifting through what has come down from 'on high' to make it locally relevant and impactful.

4.4.3 VALUES TRANSMISSION

As outlined in 4.1.2 and 4.2.2.2 above, organisations often develop a type of socio-ideological narrative exemplified through a 'values system' (either tacit or codified – expressed through company web sites, induction programmes, CEO missives, etc.) which provides a set of assumptions that are the basis for ethical action. These are intended to guide purposeful/intentional attitudes and behaviours that provide the moral standards for 'permissible' conduct within the organisational clan. In some instances – most pertinently within international contexts – these act as a corrective against ingrained personal or cultural values which might subvert the way (according to what the organisation wishes) in which people are treated or day-to-day business is transacted. Given that personal values are derived from three principal phases – birth (0–7 years), imprint (8–13) and socialisation (13–21) (Massey 2005) – organisations have much work to do in some cultures in order to overturn or countermand received truths. To this extent organisational values require *bounded* and *purposive* statements of 'the way we do things around here' in order to ensure that, in the absence of explicit instructions, members – rather than falling back on pre-programmed defective behaviours – are acquainted with what is the 'right thing to do' in most circumstances, a celebrated example being the 'self-assembly' furniture retailer IKEA:

> *[An IKEA Senior Executive commented] ... 'we always recruit through values. We spend an enormous effort in strengthening the values:* togetherness, down to earth and hardworking' *... (As such) IKEA's standard jobs questionnaire plays down skills, academic credentials or*

experience to focus on values and beliefs ... Would-be employees can even take a culture quiz on IKEA's website to gauge their suitability ... such a strong culture allows senior executives to have deep trust in country and store managers who are given what IKEA call- 'big freedom within frames' ... (store managers) can decorate showrooms in a way that inspires local customers ... (but store managers) cannot customise products or branch out of the set product range. (FT Analysis 2012b: 11)

The broad reality is, however, that while organisational values are intentional ideological mechanisms that seek assured behavioural outcomes, they will often come up against diffuse, idiosyncratic cultural and personal values in international contexts. Take common value statements such as 'acting as one team', 'listening to others', 'acting with integrity', 'treating others with respect', 'communicating openly', 'no blame culture', 'meritocratic progression'; whilst these values might be taken as a given in developed liberal economic contexts they are not necessarily 'base values' within some emerging economies. In some *'high context'* (Hall 1976) cultures where there is a predisposition to *defer to authority* and where *'insiders'* are far more trusted than *'outsiders'* any notion that managers should subscribe to some of the aforementioned values would be treated with (guarded) derision or subtle avoidance. Even organisations such as Tesco, who have been one of the most successful internationalising MUEs in recent times, have found it difficult to inculcate their core values in societies that take a 'stratified' managerial approach (Leahy 2012: 124).

The question therefore remains as to how, first, HMULs enact corporate values within resistant contexts and, second, how organisations develop and encourage HMULs to ensure adherence to their codes of conduct? The answer is that successful HMULs will be extremely adept at locating ambiguity, recognising how the local cultural norms and values of the people might conflict with those of the company. By making a conscious effort to act as standard-bearers and exemplars for their organisation's values they can set a good behavioural example to their followers. Thus, they will make decisions in conformance with their organisation's values even when they run counter to extant local cultural norms, for instance basing appointments and/or reward on performance rather than relationships. Also, having clearly stated that the values of the organisation are those that underpin behaviours within their districts and units, they can also signal their disapproval of deviant behaviours through visible admonishment or readjustment. But how do they develop these selfless behaviours that might run counter to subordinate and, indeed, their own personal predilections? For sure, organisations operating within international contexts often have well-developed immersion programmes that attempt to inculcate extant values and role models (whether expatriates, exemplar EHCNs or home country senior executive roadshows/'town hall' meetings) from which they can absorb and imitate good behaviour. In essence, though, HMULs must be adaptable enough to modify their behaviour; something that is often associated with age and/or cognitive capacity demonstrated through educational attainment (see 5.2.3 below). Indeed, as some emerging economies become more affluent and democratic, some of the values espoused by international organisations become a better 'fit' for those espoused by transitioning societies.

Case Study 7 – Values Transmission in Middle-Eastern Multi-Site Contexts

Dr Nollaig Heffernan, Chartered Psychologist, teaches resilience, leadership and change-management to multi-site leaders in emerging markets (particularly the Middle Eastern Gulf States). Designer of the ILM 72 psychometric test, she teaches at the EHL (Ecole Hotelier Lausanne), is a visiting lecturer on the MSc in Multi-Unit Leadership at BCBS and is employed as a consultant and coach by many major international corporations. Dr Heffernan has assessed and coached numerous cohorts of emerging market multi-unit leaders with the aid of the MTQ48 personality profiling questionnaire.

One of the typical misconceptions of developed market internationalising companies is that their values will translate easily into the management cadres of their subsidiaries/partners. Imposing parent values (in a faintly universalistic and imperialistic manner), and expecting them to translate and work well, is a mistake. Counter-intuitively perhaps, what successful companies usually do as a start-point is work upon emphasising the *similarities*, convergence and benefits rather than the *difficulties*. Based on my extensive experience of training and coaching numerous multi-site leaders – particularly in the Gulf States – I would point to three insights that can either facilitate or derail values transmission both from an organisational and/or local leadership perspective.

First, from an organisational perspective it is imperative that companies *sell the upsides* of the values they are attempting to inculcate throughout their international operations. One of the main problems I encounter during my training sessions with highly intelligent and motivated multi-site managers in the Middle East is that due to their *'high context'* needs to maintain relationships and family ties outside of work, at times their inability to delegate (due to notions of *hierarchical managerial primacy*) within the workplace causes them stress and anxiety that they are being restricted from sustaining their external networks, debilitating their psychological capacity to act effectively. However, by taking a value such as 'taking responsibility', or 'displaying a can-do attitude' – one which is deployed by most companies – and showing them that this allows them to *delegate purposively* to subordinates that are bound by the same values, shows the benefit of adoption; in this case de-stressing them by facilitating a 'spreading of the load' that, in turn, allows them to devote more physical and 'mental' time and/or connection with their families.

Second, and on a similar theme, companies that expect to impose corporate values lock-stock-and-barrel are likely to be disappointed when they come up against the *collective primacy of 'in-country' value systems* that are actively promoted by governments wishing to promote homogeneity and self-sufficiency. In many territories a sense of 'country first' is propagated and pervades (creating issues for values such as *'meritocratic progression'*). Thus, when choices arise between job/company and country values, the latter will usually always win out, a situation that companies attempt to ignore, overturn or countermand at their peril!

As these emerging nations beome more self-confident, the treatment of 'outsiders' might change as part of a progressive change process – but an understanding of 'insider' mentality is important with regards to the permeability of country values systems.

Thirdly, however, from a *convergence perspective* it should be said that many values such as 'treat people with respect', 'act with integrity', are already embedded as part of the clan cultures and rituals within the Middle East Region. *'In-country'* managerial behaviours to *'insiders'* are remarkably similar to those that have been put forward by western management gurus over the past ten years – most notably 'servant leadership'. Notions of serving other members of the clan in order to gain loyalty and trust are important tenets of local custom. Indeed, with social media, increasing levels of education, increasing egalitarianism (due to a need for skills in the workplace), value systems are not the atypical caricature of perhaps 15 years ago! Also, although managerial action in emerging markets is often characterised as being self-protective, hierarchical and uncertainty-avoiding I would classify it as being little different to within western contexts where due to 'rhetoric' and a certain 'HRM discourse' a *perception* of greater equality and equanimity exists at the workplace! ... For instance, in some ways there is, due to *'low mood management'*, perhaps more (rather than less) honesty in some emerging market contexts in the Middle East!

So I would say that international companies attempting to impose their values within emerging markets should think twice about doing so and adopt a hybrid approach. It should respect the differences (whilst upselling benefits of new approaches) but work hard on leveraging and emphasising the similarities. There is no doubt in my experience this is what discriminating local leaders in multi-site operations do anyway!

4.4.4 'CONFESSIONAL SECURITY'

An important dimension of HMUL activity in relation to ensuring control is the provision of confessional security which enables followers to 'safely' own up to (serious) breaches so that effective remedial action can be taken immediately. Although the voluntary admission and/or acknowledgement of the wrongs/sins of oneself or others are the central tenet of many religions, open disclosure of malfunctions or corrupt practices is anathema in some cultural contexts. Due to a fear of penalties and sanctions members of some societies would rather risk business failure than seek redemption/rectification. Thus, 'covering up', 'lying' and 'cheating' within some contexts are deemed far more preferable to disclosures which might herald severe sanctions. In order to prevent this information asymmetry – where 'controllers' believe that there is seamless adherence and conformance in contrast to the real 'hidden' situation on the ground – successful operators within MUE contexts are apt to grant 'amnesties' and protection for individuals who come forward with information that could protect (in extremis) the reputation of the organisation. For, whilst senior organisational actors might believe that they are in control of issues such as quality, safety, security and consistency, the reality is that MCS can be manipulated and corrupted to deceive.

The way in which organisations usually approach the detection and resolution of serious compliance breaches (outwith normal channels of spot audits, etc.) is the provision of an organisation-wide 'whistleblower' facility, usually presided over by the company secretariat or legal office. Here, individuals that believe they have witnessed or heard of major lapses that run counter to the organisation's ethics or procedures, are afforded anonymity whilst their claims are investigated. Useful as these channels are, empirical evidence continues to suggest that in some cultures members are hesitant or unwilling to use such vehicles to surface malfeasance (Patel 2003). Why? First, potential 'whistleblowers' do not trust the promises made by senior managers that they will be granted surety of protection due to deep-rooted fears relating to oligarchic brutality (i.e. shoot the messenger as well as the perpetrator). Second, particularly in '*high context*' societies (Hall 1976), 'telling' or 'showing up' friends or colleagues – even if it prevents something such as a major health and hygiene infraction – is deemed to be disloyal, close relationships being placed before those of the organisation. Hence matters such as endangering staff/customers through 'cutting corners' (i.e. reducing essential maintenance), breaking employment conventions (i.e. bullying subordinates and applying 'sweat shop' hours) and/or corruption (i.e. stealing, pilfering and/or nepotism), continues unreported until detected.

The question remains therefore, how in such circumstances HMULs in certain developing market contexts ensure business resilience through 'confessional security' and how organisations develop these skills? In part it is down to HMULs developing trusting relationships (see 5.4.5 below) with followers, in order to get them to believe they can share important information in a safe and secure manner without immediate repercussions. This will usually occur in informal circumstances where confidences can be shared in a non-threatening environment. In order to harvest such interactions, however, the effective HMUL needs to build up respect and followership through high levels of visibility, transparency and exchange (i.e. resolving problems and fulfilling promises). The HMULs' task is made easier if such behaviours are mirrored further up the organisation by their regional and managing directors. Organisations that wish to encourage openness and honesty need to ensure that best-practice behaviours which remove fear of retribution are transmitted throughout the organisation.

Case Study 8 – Ensuring Confessional Security in KUE Inc., Southern Asia

John Woodward is an Executive Board Member of US-owned, Singaporean-based KUE (Knowledge, Universe and Education) which has 'early year', school and adult educational multi-site businesses spread throughout Southern Asia (i.e. Singapore, India, Malaysia, etc.). A successful serial entrepreneur and founder/CEO of the Busy Bees chain of nurseries in the UK (214 units), John has extensive international experience, advising multi-site 'early year' and educational chain leadership in the US and Southern Asia.

Having built up (through organic growth and acquisition), run and sold a number of businesses located in the 'early years' multi-site domain, the central insight I would offer is that our success has been built not upon replicating 'sameness' but '*seeing the differences*' ... What do I mean by this? ... That is to say every business serves a unique micro-market that has salient differences with regards to customer segment, skilled labour, competitive set, land and buildings, etc. To this extent our success in building a multi-site portfolio has been built upon not ubiquity but micro-market differentiation ... important because with regard to customers who entrust us with their child's well-being and safety (a highly emotional transaction) addressing what they require cannot necessarily be prescribed by a process or system but has to be met through in-depth understanding of specific needs and aspirations ... we are not dealing in – from a multi-site business perspective – 'Kentucky Fried Children'! ... In international operations such as those in Southern Asia where I have been involved as both an advisor and executive of a major firm attempting to build a 'scale' educational business ('early year' to adult provision), understanding and adapting the offer to local conditions is vital ... I call it being 'deliberately naive' – approaching a market with no preconceptions in order to ensure that the right offer can be melded to local requirements ... Given the product I am involved with – 'early year' childcare and education – although it is important to 'fit' the product to the local market it is also essential, given the 'emotionally'-based human dimension, to ensure our area and unit managers are sensitised and capable of 'tweaking' the offer to certain customer needs and speak up (without fear of being penalised or disciplined) if they make mistakes, believe that we are providing insufficient resources for great childcare or see malpractice in the estate that is going unreported ... But what are the behavioural similarities and differences regarding 'speaking up' in Southern Asia and the UK?

With regards to similarities area and unit managers have to do two things well – run a strong P&L whilst ensuring that the educational/duty of care needs of their charges are attended to ... this is the same in 'growth' as 'developed' territories ... however, running a great P&L is an *output* founded upon the *input* of selecting and leading highly motivated staff (who are intrinsically driven by the challenge of 'early years' provision) who are bound into the business to provide consistency and familiarity for the children ... Often we will have bought units or small chains from 'founders', incorporating them into the group ... and whilst we improve standards and systems we must (if the 'founder' leaves) *equal or exceed parental perceptions* of the 'new' versus 'old' regime if we are to increase capacity utilisation ... Take one business we took over in Singapore 'Pat's Schoolhouse' ... these seven units were of an extremely high quality, loved by parents, where Mandarin and English (a 'must' in certain Asian countries) were taught ... what we did was increase occupancy through better systems and processes but also by ensuring the managers and staff kept their 'bonds' with parents ... How did we do that? ... Through empowering managers on-site (in the same way we do in the UK) ... by giving them the training and the systems that give them the courage and confidence to provide a great service that they could take *pride* in ... any serious problems that arise are resolved by virtue of the fact that local leadership (i.e. area, regional and board level) are close to the businesses – regularly out in the field and/or easily accessible to *generate confidence* ... to help rather than punish ... By employing highly competent people whom we invest heavily in, backed up by leaders who *listen* rather than just monitor and pounce ... we believe things are rarely hidden from view (no more so than the UK) ...

In terms of differences, we obviously have strong health and safety audit procedures that apply to any of our units on a global basis *although* the cultural/regulatory standards that require adherence vary from territory to territory ... In certain Southern Asian businesses for instance aural 'temperature checks' are required of any visitor due to certain epidemic risks ... also in one territory only Muslim women are allowed to be employed to look after children in certain locations and boys and girls must sleep (during 'time outs') in different rooms ... in addition, in one territory due to government strictures (due mainly to special constraints) we are only able to lease sites on three-year agreements (posing issues in levels of infrastructure investment, staff longevity, etc.) ... All these challenges might seem to pose problems at a micro-site level, raising issues around consistency, compliance, adherence, etc. ... yet it is remarkable how local teams cope and adapt ... Again I would stress that in this business it is important to liberate front-line staff so that they are passionate, flexible and responsive to service individual customer needs ... this is a 'high emotion' business; you have to match the service to individual requirements to satisfy customers ... after all, parents are entrusting us with their children! ... But the high levels of loyalty you get in Asia, through their commitment to raising children (kith and kin relationships, extended families, etc.) means that people will 'speak up' if things are wrong because of the emotional connectivity they feel with what they are doing ... Such behaviour is essential in this business because it really is our people that 'fill in the gaps' ... systems and processes can only go so far in uncovering bad practice – which in our business it is absolutely essential (from a reputational and ethical standpoint) to avoid.

4.5 Chapter Summary

This chapter referred firstly to the literature pertaining to control – especially with regards to international contexts – and then, secondly, elucidated respondents' accounts as to how IMUEs and HMULs gain control at a field-based level. The sections relating to the literature surfaced the different ways in which control has been modelled (i.e. cybernetic and behavioural/output) and conceptualised as typologies (i.e. direct, technical, bureaucratic, multi-layered, concertive, chimerical and socio-ideological). It then progressed, widening our understanding into cross-national control mechanisms concentrating on the two typologies most frequently referenced by scholars in this domain, namely, bureaucratic/contract and culture/values (Ouchi 1979, Jaeger 1983). Preferences for either approach were then discussed from national, organisational and individual perspectives. The principal observation that can be drawn from this complex (and sometimes contradictory) literature is that managers from different cultures – due to societal conditioning – have been found to have different preferences for control types. Anglo-American managers are seemingly conditioned to prefer individualistic, output-driven bureaucratic controls, with Asian managers (to select one broad cohort) having societally-grounded preferences for 'collectivist relational', values-based controls. In addition, scholars have emphasised that distinctive national cultural values are almost impossible to transcend with organisational values.

This juxtaposition poses a major problem for internationalising IMUEs, particularly with regard to how they ensure control 'on the ground'. The sections dealing with *how* IMUEs gain control through the practices of their HMULs refer to both bureaucratic and values-driven approaches. But given the aforementioned divergences that exist in the literature, what do these empirical accounts tell us? What emerges from this discussion of IMUE approaches and HMUL practices, in the second part of the chapter, is that in order to ensure some semblance of *co-ordination* down the line – through both bureaucratic and values-based means – organisations must achieve *consent*. That is to say that the way in which they train and *develop* their HMULs to exert control – in a manner which leads to changes in embedded behaviours – must involve the *willing* co-option of recipients. With regards to bureaucratic controls (blueprint execution and output prioritisation) the two Case Studies in this area (5 and 6) demonstrated that HMUL development benefitted from strong modelling, good basic managerial training and ensuring MCS (management control systems) were simple to understand and easy to implement. With regards to getting 'buy-in' to organisational values, Case Studies 7 and 8 highlighted techniques such as proving how adopting company values could help 'clan' members actually fulfil their cultural/societal obligations and how demonstrably protecting people from punishment could remove abiding 'fears of retribution', unlocking empowered and honest/confessional behaviours. But having gained some degree of *co-ordination* through *consent* at field level, how do IMUEs get their field-based local leaders to engage and motivate their followers to deliver excellent sales-driven service? This is now dealt with in the next chapter.

5 *Generating Commitment*

The previous chapter dealt with managerial conceptualisations of control within an international organisational context. It was argued that given the fact that in some emerging markets people's allegiances fall firstly to their family (and in some cases their state) rather than their company, internationalising firms must ensure that they achieve *managerial primacy* in order to ensure conformity in both 'owned' and 'contracted' environments before they address issues such as generating behavioural commitment. With regards to expediting control through its crucial middle-management cadre of HMULs it was posited that companies concentrated on ensuring *blueprint execution*, 'line of sight' alignment through *output prioritisation* and, crucially, an uncompromising approach to *values transmission and confessional security*. These 'sociological control' approaches, however, are not in themselves sufficient to ensure effective performance of HMULs and their followers; a range of psychologically/intrinsically-based interventions are also required to generate commitment.

Within the academic literature commitment is typically portrayed as a behavioural construct that determines an individual's psychological commitment to their firm (see Edger 2012:109). The implication is that individuals with a high level of organisational commitment will be more productive, displaying more discretionary effort and concern for executing their job tasks more efficiently and effectively. But how do companies generate commitment in emerging market contexts where the means by which they do so might be fundamentally different (according to national cultures and preferences) than in developed regions? For instance, in the previous book *cross-portfolio involvement* was cited as an important component of generating commitment but this construct was located in cultures where there is at least some tradition of participation and self-expression.

In order to explore the nature of commitment within emerging market contexts this chapter will explore, first, commentary relating to international services management, second, international leadership style preferences (particularly at middle-management level) and, third, international HRM. What becomes apparent when addressing the evidence and arguments elucidated by these three literature sources is that although service-delivery systems, operational leadership and HRM are highly contingent upon context, there are some 'universal' aspects that apply to all areas. For instance, although there are significant variations in leadership style preferences according to societal values, 'leader team orientation and the communication of vision, values and confidence in followers are deemed highly effective leadership behaviours across nationalities' (House et al. 2004: 7). Also, the deployment of certain 'best-practice' HRM (equitable wages, job security, benefits, training and development, etc.) approaches is becoming commonplace across the board amongst internationalising firms.

Following a discussion of these three streams of literature, consideration will be given to the behaviourally-based practices that international organisations put in place to generate commitment from their HMULs. These include five approaches: *local vision, talent attraction, tailored development, portfolio teamworking* and *trust and communication*.

5.1 International Services Operations Management

Whilst the generic services operations literature is significant, its subset – international services operations management (ISOM) – is still developing as academics attempt to understand how different service systems are applicable within different cultures. The generic literature (mainly US based) takes a fairly universalistic approach with commentators such as Albrecht and Zemke (1995) and Reichheld and Markey (2011) advancing frameworks and propositions that they argue are applicable in most contexts. Albrecht and Zemke's 'service management concept' (SMC) argues that effective service-based organisations take a long-term 'total service approach' underpinned by unrelenting management focus concentrating upon ensuring *resource availability, capacity for local decision-making, high levels of service skills, aligned reward* and *two-way feedback mechanisms*. Reichheld, in his groundbreaking 'Net Promoter Score' (NPS) proposition, posits the notion that companies which are able to measure *positive advocacy* – by subtracting Lickert scale 0–6 'detractor' scores from 9–10 'advocate' scores with regards to a 'product recommendation' question – have created a sustainable service platform which is likely to result in positive performance outcomes. Contributing factors to positive advocacy include factors identified by other commentators such as being *perceived* by customers as being 'easy to do business with', where – in addition to the functional attributes of the offer (price, amenity, product quality, etc.) – 'empowered' service providers do four specific things: deliver the promise, resolve problems 'on the spot' well, provide the personal touch and go the extra mile (Lashley 1997, 1999; Johnston 2001; Fitzimmons and Fitzimmons 2006; Johnston and Clark 2008).

Excellent as this literature is, its empirical foundations are derived predominantly from developed market situations. Services by their very nature are local – they have a high degree of specificity, accounting for cultural sensitivities and preferences – which is made all the more complicated in multi-unit contexts by multiple interactions occurring in remote locations. The international transportation of service operations constructs such as the *service concept* (i.e. the ideology/principles underpinning the service offer), *service delivery system* (i.e. the physical and emotional service provision drivers) and *chain of service/service cycle* (i.e. the end-to-end service process linkages) are likely to be corrupted in international translation. Most likely, firms will have to adapt any element of their service concept, system and/or cycle in order to address both local customer needs and service provider capability. The sections below will deal with this conundrum by considering, first, cultural influences upon customers and service providers, second, the adaptations that international multi-unit enterprises need to make and, lastly, universal service dimensions (such as measurement systems).

5.1.1 CULTURAL INFLUENCES

Several commentators, commonly located within the international marketing services literature, make the observation that – as has been previously stated – due to national sensitivities and idiosyncrasies, service firms cannot transport their front-line service approaches in their entirety into emerging markets. There are two main reasons for this: first, customer competency levels and expectations and, second, service provider conditioning and capability.

5.1.1.1 Customer competency and expectations

There are two interrelated factors in play that companies should consider when addressing emerging markets: first, what are *customer competency* levels (i.e. their grounded experience, knowledge and intelligence relating to what good/bad service actually is) and, second, what expectations they actually have when engaging with a service (i.e. will they be unduly low/high enough to degrade/enhance perceptions?).

- Customer competency – The movement of service provision (within a multi-unit context) from independent to multiple-chain provision brings a promise of consistency, quality, dependability and (possibly) affordability. In emerging markets, new users, lacking education and socialisation, might be demanding insofar as they lack the requisite behaviours to interact with the service delivery system. Previously, service provision from 'independents' might (in spite of all attendant negative factors) have involved behaviours such as bartering and negotiation. Satisfaction was derived not necessarily from quality and consistency, but through means of a complex cost-outcome relationship (i.e. price compensating for quality). In addition, in societies with a high 'masculine' orientation customers might find it difficult to accept service delivery being handled by females. Furthermore, in cultures where there is high 'power distance', customers, lacking hierarchical power within wider society, can abuse their privileged status as customers by treating service providers badly (Waldmeir 2012). Also, with regard to complaining, high levels of emoting – which are acceptable in some societies – can lead to quite extreme behaviours being displayed if customers feel they have been 'cheated'. Overall, customer competency levels remain problematic in markets that are in swift agricultural to industrial/urbanisation transition.
- Customer expectations – In addition, customer expectations in emerging markets can be set unrealistically high due to cultural factors. For instance, in societies with high 'uncertainty avoidance', if customer promises are made by companies, they are taken quite literally by consumers. This means that international companies that have paid virtual lip service to their 'customer charters' in their home territories are wise to not over-promise abroad. In particular, customers that have had experience of subsisting in 'survival' regimes (see below) are likely to hold companies to their product, price and service declarations. Also, given local ethnic values, customs and norms, service cultures and (therefore) customer expectations are likely to differ with regards to issues such as queuing and levels (and types) of service provider 'touches' and interaction. Taken together, the problem that international firms face is that although there are

certain artefacts and behaviours within societies that are observable, implicit basic assumptions, norms and values can remain hidden, making service-systems designs fraught with difficulty.

5.1.1.2 Service provider conditioning and capability

If international multi-unit firms face issues in emerging markets relating to customer behaviour that differs significantly from their home markets, then the same can be said in relation to service providers. Essentially there are two main challenges posed: behavioural *conditioning* that can undermine the ideological essence of the *service concept* and *capability* gaps that threaten execution of the *service delivery system*.

- Service provider conditioning – Several frameworks (i.e. Hall 1976, Hofstede 1980 and Trompenaars 1993, Schwartz 1999, House et al. 2004) provide a template as to how the culture of a national entity can affect its dominant service culture. The cultural conditioning of service providers – due to these embedded influences – can have a profound effect on the viability of a transported *service concept*. In developed market conceptualisations of service discussed above (such as Albrecht and Zemke's 'service management concept', SMC) notions such as autonomous decision-making, participation, two-way communications and feedback exist as a given. In these models excellent service provision is adjudged to have occurred by customers when problems and complaints are resolved at the 'point of interaction' through 'liberated' service providers. This has been consistently proven to be the most powerful force upon 'onward recommendation behaviour'. However, given the empirical observations of the cultural theorists cited above, such behaviour runs contrary to the cultural values and norms of many emerging markets and, hence, the conditioning of those expected to deliver service. Societies that exhibit 'high uncertainty avoidance', 'high power distance' and 'low levels of individualism' do not foster the kinds of autonomous service behaviours that many 'best-practice' western service concepts are designed around. In these environments where service providers have, through intense levels of socialisation, been conditioned to follow rules (to avoid punishment from higher authorities) and demonstrate low levels of discretion (for fear of showing up their fellow workers) western service concepts stressing *participative ingenuity* are unlikely to work unless significant 'reprogramming' occurs at the workplace level.
- Service provider capability – Although education levels are improving in emerging markets, capability gaps remain (as stated above) in relation to appropriate service behaviour. However, where local service providers can be of immense benefit to international multi-unit enterprises is where their linguistic skills, level of cultural sensitivity and local insight can aid *service delivery system* execution. Furrer et al. (2000) in their examination of the interface between homogenised customer segments (*followers, balance seekers, self-confidents, sensory seekers* and *functional analysers*), Hofstede's cultural profiles (*power distance, individualism, masculinity, uncertainty avoidance, long-term orientation*) and Servqual's profile (*reliability, responsiveness, assurance, empathy* and *tangibles*) claimed to find contigual fit, with clear management implications:

For example, for serving followers, who have cultural values of a large power distance and high collectivism (ie more group dependent), service providers should emphasise training their employees to have professional knowledge and to be trustworthy to gain the trust of these customers. To serve the self-confidents who are more individualistic and exhibit low power distance culture, service providers should place emphasis on equipping and empowering the employees so that they are capable of providing dependable, accurate and prompt service to gain the self confidents' appreciation on the high levels of reliability and responsiveness required. (Furrer et al. 2000: 367)

The implications of their research are that managers of service providers in emerging markets increase the capabilities through training mechanisms that, through enhancing knowledge, can increase customer trust levels, thereby improving firm outcomes.

5.1.2 SERVICE ADAPTATION

As stated, during the construction of the service concept and delivery system, firms need to minimise the potential disturbance between corporate and national cultural biases which are reflected in both staff and consumer attitude/behaviours. Thus companies need to analyse the service culture of the national market and adapt the service concept to 'fit' to ensure compatibility and performance. This is a complex process, not least because many internationalising enterprises come from 'dominant' national business systems with a 'one size fits all' paradigmatic approach. Chapter 2 outlined some measure that firms take in terms of 'intra-firm' architecture to ameliorate some of these issues, but what particular aspects of their service systems should companies address/adapt, ensuring optimal 'fit'? Broadly, the literature emphasises three main areas – *temporal, relational* and *functional*:

- Temporal factors – There are various aspects of a service delivery system that relate to time: food production in casual dining environments, customer order fulfilment and/or queuing systems in grocery and the 'chain of service' in knowledge-based transactions, etc. Given that some societies are characterised by 'short' or 'long'-term 'temporal orientations' to life (Kluckhohn and Strodtbeck 1961) it is likely that in some cultural contexts service delivery can be perceived as either too slow or too fast. Also, service providers might be used to working at a certain rhythm or pace based on prior conditioning – unseemly speed, for instance, deemed to be showing undue enthusiasm (therefore showing up others). Hence international companies might have to make adjustments to their service delivery in some contexts to take account of customer and service provider 'temporal dispositions'.
- Emotional factors – Many service operations are dependent for their success upon service providers displaying intentional 'affective' positive emotions. This can be subdivided into two categories:
  - *Emotional labour* – This construct (Hochschild 1983) distinguishes between 'surface' and 'deep' acting. It involves individuals managing their feelings which are translated into observable facial and body displays;
  - *Emotional contagion* – This approach (Hatfield et al. 1994) envisages emotional states being transferred from person to person between an individual and a group or between groups of people. Positive states of contagion are thought to lead to superior service outcomes.

The problem that companies have in stimulating 'affective' emotional behaviour in some contexts is, first, line leadership actions continually undermine the essence of these concepts (see leadership section below) and, second, service providers are incapable (given their bounded cultural contexts) of emoting in such ways. How do you get people to smile and show enthusiasm if they are culturally attuned not to do so. Again, international firms must think carefully about the emotional factors underlying the service concept during their product's transfer into new markets and make critical adaptations to suit.

- Functional factors – The functional factors underpinning the service system are usually referred to as operational systems (see Chapter 3 and below). However, they are typically referred to in terms of supply chain and distribution elements, less typically with regards to in-store back of house (BOH) service 'set-up'. These processes are vital to front of house (FOH) service fulfilment such as unloading deliveries and shelf replenishment. In addition the organisation of merchandising FOH and maintenance of store layouts (including shelf planograms) are important elements of functional service delivery. Issues arise for companies in cultures with high levels of 'masculinity' and extremely low 'gender equality' where 'physical functional' labour is frowned upon for female operatives.

5.1.3 UNIVERSAL SERVICE DIMENSIONS

As previously stated, globalisation theory implies that smart technology, converging capital markets and the increased flows of people across national boundaries (either through economic migration or tourism) are leading to the homogenisation of consumer behaviour. In this paradigm the world can be viewed as a giant 'market place with a market space' for products and offers that adopt a universal positioning. The reality – as the narrative above has argued – is that substantial in-country differentiation persists, particularly with regard to service preferences. But what elements of service-based models are universal? Lovelock and Yip (1996) suggest that, in general, service models can be subdivided in three distinctive ways:

- People processing – This process (i.e. face-to-face business to consumer) is highly context specific requiring multi-domestic, transnational approaches by international companies;
- Information processing – Data transacting (i.e. through banking services) is seen as a universal process that can follow standardised service procedures and is therefore susceptible to global approaches;
- Possession processing – Product movements (i.e. parcel and goods delivery services) are impersonal services which, again, are suitable for global strategies by firms.

In terms of service-delivery systems, the need for people processing adaptability according to indigenous idiosyncrasies seems obvious, given all available evidence. With regards to overall service model adaptability companies such as IKEA allow their country managers a degree of flexibility in selecting a range of merchandise to meet local tastes and preferences. However, group product development is done in Sweden, capital for new openings and refurbishments is deployed out of the Danish HQ and a unitary logistics system transports product bought through central buying systems into stores.

In Toys'R'Us, again, managers are given latitude over running of their business through anticipating local demand patterns (i.e. in China parents want educational toys, in the US TV-induced 'pester power' means that buying trends advertising campaigns). However, whilst there is a degree of local decision-making, store layouts and supply chains remain pre-determined.

Service measurement is sometimes applied universally – particularly in the case of international hotel chains where certain customer segments (i.e. business travellers) are reckoned to have pretty uniform needs. In other contexts, although the measures might be the same, different weightings (according to local preferences) are given to different scores (say speed of service rather than politeness). More recently the NPS concept (detailed above) has gained fairly common currency, meaning that it is applied across different nationalities although some commentators have questioned whether it is culturally acceptable within some contexts to 'recommend' a service or product in case the advocate 'loses face' due to a poor experience. Further issues relate to the meanings people attach to certain questions within particular cultures, the degree of truth they apply when answering (again respondents in some cultures fear surveys as a means of surveillance and/or retribution) and the fact that (universally) most companies are poor at interpreting their data (particularly in alien cultures) to give them meaningful insights that translate into value-added actions. Finally, one facet of service measurement is done universally badly – the measurement of lapsed and non-users, which could aid companies to understand how they extend their serviceable markets.

5.2 International Leadership Style Preferences

One of the main contingencies affecting service delivery (outwith service delivery system blueprint design) is strategic and line leadership. Service contexts such as multi-unit enterprises involve multiple people-centred transactions – the degree to which service providers are motivated and led effectively has an important effect on the speed, quality and consistency of these transactions. But what is leadership and how has it been previously conceptualised? As I elucidated in my previous book leadership is commonly defined as the ability to induce followers to willingly commit to achieving a common goal (Edger 2012:115). To date scholars have researched the domain from *trait* (Kirkpatrick and Locke 1991, Judge et al. 2002), *style* (Blake and Mouton 1985 and Burns 1978), *contingency/situational* (Fiedler 1967, House 1971, Vroom and Yetton 1973, Hersey and Blanchard 1993), *emotional* (Skinner 1976; Goleman 1996, 1998; Autry 2001) and *group/team* (Hemphill 1950 and Belbin 2000a, b) perspectives (see Edger 2012: 115–22). More recently a new leadership genre has also looked at the subject of Leader-Follower contingencies – especially with regard to the dynamics of Leader-Member Exchange (LMX) in 'high distance' situations (see Schyns 2013 for an excellent summary of research to date). The main issue with this body of work – particularly in relation to this book – is its relative anglocentricity. But leadership is *highly culturally contingent* due to differing societal values, therefore any understanding of its nature and effectiveness must take account of its practice within context (House et al. 2004: 5). This has implications for managers who are trying to manage businesses in international situations:

... knowing what is considered to be effective or ineffective leadership in the cultures with which one interacts is likely to facilitate conflict resolution and improve the performance of interacting individuals. Individuals from individual cultures often interact with each other as negotiators, managers, members of joint ventures, or expatriates working in foreign cultures ... we believe that knowledge of each group's culturally endorsed leader behaviours would be beneficial to all individuals involved in substantial inter-cultural interactions. (House et al. 2004: 7)

But which leadership styles work best in which cultures? This section will address this question by, first, examining universal aspects of leadership that can be said to apply to most cultures, second, considering the GLOBE survey (House et al. 2004) – the most significant piece of work to date on divergent international middle-management leadership style preferences – and, third, considering contemporary forces (as measured by the World Values Survey) that are having a profound impact upon changing societal leadership preferences.

5.2.1 UNIVERSAL PREFERENCES

As a construct, leadership is accepted as having a high degree of importance with regards to societal definition, cohesion and symbolism. In most societies (with the exception of Northern European contexts where the notion of the divine right of leaders has been degraded by successive conflicts precipitated by all-powerful despots) leaders occupy an important 'mythical' space in popular imagination, being revered for their status-related charisma and power. In fact, whilst most commentaries on organisational leadership within international contexts stress difference as a start-point to understanding preference, practices and effects, there are some leadership 'principles and laws' that commentators have identified that they believe result in more effective outcomes. As House et al. state:

... in all cultures leader team orientation and the communication of vision, values and confidence in followers are reported to be highly effective leadership behaviours. (2004: 7)

This universal notion of leaders shaping and supervising teams/followers towards common goals, whilst motivating them through expressions of confidence and trust in their abilities, cuts across national boundaries. In a sense such behaviours appeal to the most basic human emotions: the need to feel that there are super-ordinate objectives that justify *existential being*. Problems arise, however, not in universal conceptualisations of what *role* leaders should fulfil, but the *style* in which they should successfully expedite them, according to different societal *norms* and *values*.

5.2.2 NATIONAL DIVERGENCE

The most pertinent study into national leadership style preferences – particularly given the HMUL middle-management focus of this book – is House et al.'s (2004) Global Leadership and Organisational Behaviour Effectiveness (GLOBE) research programme. This ten-year programme was designed to conceptualise, test and validate a cross-cultural integrated theory of the relationship between culture, society and organisational effectiveness, the central proposition being:

... the attributes and entities that differentiate a specified culture are predictive of organisational practices and leader attributes/behaviours that are most frequently enacted and most effective in that culture. (House et al. 2004: 17)

In total, 170 scholars studied societal and organisational culture and the attributes of effective leadership in 62 countries. Seventeen thousand middle managers were surveyed to establish answers to questions such as, what cultural attributes affect societies' susceptibility to leadership influence and to what extent do leadership styles vary in accordance with culturally specific values and expectations?

In terms of cultural attributes House et al. (2004: 30) identified nine constructs (five of which linked back to Hofstede's framework) that they used to measure cultural variation:

- *Power distance* – degree to which members expect power to be distributed equally;
- *Uncertainty avoidance* – extent to which a society relies on rules to ameliorate unpredictability of future events;
- *Humane orientation* – degree to which a society stresses fairness, altruism and caring for one another;
- *Collectivism I (institutional)* – extent to which societies encourage and reward people for being altruistic;
- *Collectivism II (in group cohesion)* – degree to which individuals express pride and loyalty in their organisations or families;
- *Assertiveness* – degree to which people are assertive, confrontational and aggressive with others;
- *Gender egalitarianism* – degree to which a society minimises gender inequality;
- *Future orientation* – extent to which members engage in future-orientated behaviour, i.e. delaying gratification, planning and investing in the future;
- *Performance orientation* – degree to which collective encourages and rewards group members for performance improvement and excellence.

In addition, following grounded research they identified a number of 'culturally endorsed implicit theories of leadership' (CLT) clustered around six broad behavioural categories (House et al. 2004: 14):

- *Charismatic/value-based leadership* – emphasises ability to inspire and motivate high-performance outcomes from followers based on core values. Subsets include: vision, inspiration, self-sacrifice, integrity, decisiveness and performance orientation;
- *Team-orientated leadership* – emphasises effective team-building and implementation of common good amongst team members. Subsets include: collaborative team orientation, team integrator, diplomatic, malevolent (reverse score), administrative competent;
- *Participative leadership* – reflects degree to which managers involve others in making and implementing decisions. Subsets include: non-participative, autocratic (reverse score);
- *Humane-orientated leadership* – emphasises supportive and considerate leadership including compassion and generosity. Subsets include: compassion and generosity;
- *Autonomous leadership* – refers to independent and individualistic leadership attributes. Subsets include: autonomy, individualistic, independence and uniqueness;

- *Self-protected leadership* – focuses on ensuring the safety and security of the individual and group through status enhancement and face-saving behaviour. Subsets include: self-centeredness, status consciousness, conflict inducement, face-saving and procedural.

These cultural and leader attributes were then measured (on a 1–7 scale) across middle managers in ten national clusters denominated as: *Latin America* including Brazil, *Anglo*, *Latin Europe, Nordic Europe, Germanic Europe, Confucian Asia* including China, *Sub-Saharan Africa, Middle East, Southern Asia* including India, *Eastern Europe* including Russia (House et al. 2004: 32, 191). Overall they found that, whilst the general cultural mean was 4/7, measures for 'power distance' and 'collectivism II' *practices* scored highest, whilst 'gender equality' scored lowest, across the board. In terms of difference between stated values and actual practices the largest gap existed within the 'power distance' construct with virtual unanimity prevailing in the 'gender equality' area. With regards to leadership, major divergences existed between national clusters with regards to 'participative', 'autonomous' and 'self-protective leadership' scores (mainly between developed and emerging economies). Figure 5.1 – abstracted by the author from the body of the empirical analysis – demonstrates the most *significant* divergences in leadership styles between developed and emerging markets, illustrating the lowest (highest 'self-protective') ranking societal clusters according to three leader categories, with positively or negatively connected cultural value drivers.

Leader Categories	Cultural Value Drivers	Lowest Ranking Societal Clusters*
Charismatic/value based	+Performance Orientation +Collectivism (II) +Gender Equality -Power Distance	Middle East Confucian Asia Eastern Europe Latin Europe S-S Africa
Participative leadership	+Performance Orientation +Gender Equality +Humane Orientation -Uncertainty Avoidance -Power Distance	Middle East Confucian Asia Southern Asia Eastern Europe S-S Africa
Self-protective	+Power Distance +Uncertainty Avoidance -Gender Equality	**Highest Rankings:** Southern Asia Middle East Confucian Asia Eastern Europe Latin America

* In absolute rank order (i.e. Middle East least participative and values-led, Southern Asia has highest level of self-protection)

Figure 5.1   Model of leader behaviours, cultural value drivers and societal clusters (adapted from House et al: 14, 46–8, 683)

The implications of the empirical findings stated in Figure 5.1 are significant with regards to the focus of this book. First, there is a preponderance of emerging markets that make up the societal clusters that rank lowest with regards to *'value-based'* and *'participative'* leadership and highest in relation to *'self-protective'* leadership. Given the cultural value drivers that are either positively or negatively correlated with these linkages, these societal clusters can be seen to possess low *'performance orientation'*, high *'uncertainty avoidance'*, low *'gender equality'*, high *'in group collectivism'* and – most significantly perhaps given the aforementioned characteristics – high *'power distance'* characteristics. Given that in-country cultural values are deemed (in the views of some scholars) to be 'hard-wired' – possessing high degrees of immutability – these findings and associations make sober reading for organisations expanding into foreign markets that have leadership values/ HRM systems that emphasise participation, involvement, delegation and discretion.

5.2.3 GLOBAL VALUE TRENDS

But are cultural values embedded within societies to the extent that cultural theorists insinuate? Is there hope for western service-based organisations that the *values* of some of their potential *or* existing markets are converging with their own domestic ones, offering up the possibility that the transportation of their product might be made easier? Grounds for optimism can be found in the regularly held World Values Survey (WVS) covering 90 per cent of the global population. Established in 1981 the WVS – widely used by political theorists and governmental agencies – measures individuals' beliefs and values, how these dimensions are changing and what their associated political and social implications might be (Inglehart and Welzel 2005). Analysis of the data has surfaced two dualisms: *traditional* versus *secular rational* values and *survival* versus *self-expression* values, the central components of which are:

- Traditional values – In these societies members are prone to deference to power, high levels of nationalism, religiosity and family ties.
- Secular rational values – Here people have lower levels of religious faith, family values and deference to authority.
- Survival values – In these national contexts undue precedence is given by people to financial and personal security, accompanied by low levels of trust and tolerance.
- Self-expression values – These societies encompass those with more emphasis being given to humanitarian, green and equality issues with greater participation in social, economic and political decision-making.

The Inglehart-Welzel Cultural Map of the World graphically represents 'zonal patterns' where societies are situated on these continuums, with – at the extreme ends – developed 'protestant Europe' and 'English-speaking' societies scoring highly in 'self-expression' and 'secular rational' and 'Africa' and 'South Asia' (including the Middle East) scoring highly in 'traditional' and 'survival' value terms (Inglehart and Welzel 2005).

In addition a number of insights have emerged from analysis of worldwide 'value trends' since its inception, which challenge notions of cultural stasis (Welzel et al. 2003, Inglehart et al. 2010):

- Societal value transition – Societal priorities transmogrify from 'traditional' to 'secular rational' as perceptions of personal and financial safety improve. This is most pronounced in transitioning agricultural to urban/industrial societies. However, the most significant movements occur in industrial to post-industrial/knowledge economies where 'survival' to 'self-expression' value transitioning predominates.
- Dominant variables – The most important drivers in societies experiencing 'value transition' are income, education, age, religion and access to technology.
- Importance of emancipative values – These are a major subset of 'self-expression', incorporating equality, individual autonomy and representative voice, important due to the following factors:
  - The growth of emancipative values in autocratic/despotic regimes (through higher levels of education and exposure to social media) helps instigate democratic movements (such as the 2011 Arab Spring);
  - Emancipative values are correlated to the subjective well-being of people (resulting in commensurate increases in 'wellness' scores).

By implication, movements towards greater 'self-expression' and 'emancipation' in emerging economies should help internationalising companies in terms of product and practice transference. Hence, the notion of culture as an all-embracing, immovable construct is challenged by the WVS which infers that individual preferences and identities are at odds – given their movement in some societies – with the accepted, dominant paradigms.

5.3 International HRM Perspectives

One mechanism which international companies can utilise to shape service and leadership behaviours is HRM policies and practices. What is HRM? For the purposes of this book a pertinent definition is:

> *Human Resource Management refers to all the dedicated activity that an organisation uses to affect the behaviours of the people who work for it … activities include formal employment policies and everyday practices for managing people. (Schuler et al. 2004: 5)*

Multi-unit enterprises are heavily reliant on large numbers of customer-facing employees who can either enhance or degrade the product through their attitudes and behaviours. However, employees are members of firms with distinctive contractual and emotional obligations; the effective management of this symbiotic relationship through HRM can provide organisations with behavioural solutions to the issues posed above. In an international context the application and transfusion of policies across borders is complex – a domain that has been the subject of enquiry by scholars operating in the field of international HRM (IHRM) who have sought to understand and explain

> *how MNCs manage their geographically dispersed workforce in order to leverage their HR resources for both local and global competitive advantage. (Scullion 2005: 5)*

In essence, academics working within the IHRM sphere have sought to investigate how MNCs have achieved HRM coherence across their international portfolios whilst simultaneously ensuring a degree of responsiveness to local demands, values and needs. This section will, first, examine the theoretical perspectives that have been applied to this form of contextual HRM (in contrast to the 'universal' approaches outlined in Edger 2012: 122-6) and, second, elucidate a number of texts that provide us with accounts of IHRM in action.

5.3.1 THEORETICAL PERSPECTIVES

It is important to understand theoretical approaches to HRM because the field is often, mistakenly, believed to be operating in a singular (predominantly US-derived) 'universalistic' genre. But what are the different theoretical approaches that have been applied to the study of HRM within an international setting, how do they differ from normative behavioural accounts and what are their implications?

5.3.1.1 Universal versus contextual

Since the early 1980s, the study of HRM has followed two research traditions: *universal/ strategic* and *contextual/non-strategic* (Wright and McMahon 1992, Brewster 1999, 2002). Scholars operating in the universal/strategic paradigm, adopting nomothetic and deductive social-scientific methodological approaches, have, by building upon the findings of the Human Relations schools of the mid-twentieth century, sought to prove that optimising the vertical and horizontal congruence of specific '*best-practice*' or '*best-fit*' commitment-based HR practices will lead to favourable behavioural and, thus, financial performance outcomes for organisations (Delery and Doty 1996 – see Edger 2012: 122–6, for a full account). Theoretical frameworks that have been used by researchers operating within this domain have mainly relied upon the 'behavioural perspective', although, at times, Resource/Knowledge Based View, agency and systems approaches have also featured (Wright and McMahon 1992).

By contrast, researchers operating within the *contextual/non-strategic* paradigm have studied HRM 'as it is', using an idiographic approach, with inductive methodologies, to note the divergences of HRM at multiple levels both within and between firms (Brewster 1999). Researchers operating within this paradigm have used theoretical perspectives such as *institutional* and *power resource theory* to note differences between practices within different contexts (Wright and McMahon 1992). Elaborating upon the insight that certain theoretical approaches could be labelled 'strategic' or 'non-strategic', Brewster (1999) argued that HRM research and its theoretical foundations could effectively be subdivided according to two dominant paradigms: universal and contextual. Figure 5.2 below, which has been extracted from Brewster's proposition, usefully illustrates not only the differences between HRM research approaches, but also their overarching purpose, focus and dominant narratives:

Admittedly, this figure, which is a rather crude presentation of Brewster's argument, has a few imperfections, such as the joining together of *critical HRM*'s narrative of control and compliance (see Edger 2012: 162–6) with the *institutional* cultural systems approach. Nevertheless, in keeping with Brewster's thesis, this table forcibly demonstrates the

	Universal Paradigm	Contextual Paradigm
Purpose	Improving HRM	Understanding HRM
Social science approach	Nomothetic; testing	Idiographic; generating
Methodology	Deductive	Inductive
Method	Quantitative; surveys	Qualitative; cases
Theory	Behavioural, RBV, systems, agency, transaction (psychology economics and strategic mgmt.	Institutional, power (sociology and political science)
Streams	HRM, SHRM, HPWS	IHRM, comparative HRM, critical HRM
Focus	Managerial/Organisational	Stakeholder
Research base	Manufacturing, high tech. (mainly US)	Service, public sector (mainly Europe)
Narrative	Strategic, matching, congruence commitment, performance	Culture, control, compliance, conflicting interests
Perspective	Convergence	Divergence
Actors	HRD champions	HRD marginalisation
Advantages	Simplicity, coherence, replication, relevance to practitioners	Consideration of external factors & different levels
Disadvantages	Simplistic notion of strategy, dubious lines of causality, narrowness of scope/objectives, inappropriate techniques	Complexity, lack of measurement, replication and generalisability

Figure 5.2 Ideal type paradigms in HRM research (adapted from Brewster 1999)

distinctive differences in approach that have been taken towards studying HRM. Aspects of this model will be touched upon during the discussion of the institutionally-led IHRM perspective below, but Brewster's dominant argument – that studies within the field have largely attempted to understand HRM '*as it should be*' (universal) or '*as it is*' (contextual) – provides a useful outline of our understanding of the approaches that have been taken in this field to date.

5.3.1.2 Institutional perspective

IHRM institutionalist perspectives can be traced back to the 1980s as many scholars, noting the trend towards burgeoning FDI into the UK, tracked the accompanying work systems that were imported by foreign firms, such as Swedish 'socio-technical' systems, Japanese 'lean production' techniques, Italian 'flexible specialisation', US forms of HRM and German 'diversified quality production' (Streeck 1992, Ferner 1997). Scholars began to question whether firms were intent on going global or local with their employment practices (the so-called *'glocal debate'*) and whether strong regional or host country influences were preventing convergence or 'isometric isomorphism' between the subsidiaries of globalising companies and were, in fact, maintaining strong divergent characteristics among firm subsidiaries operating in an MNC context. In a notable contribution to the debate, Warner (2000) concluded in his analysis of evidence of 'hard' and 'soft' forms of divergence and 'convergence' that he could find more evidence of 'soft' than of 'hard' varieties in both cases.

Pertinent to this stream of literature are other texts (such as Weinstein and Kochan 1995; Ferner 1997, 2003; Clark and Almond 2004; Almond et al. 2005) suggesting that there are three possible approaches that an MNC can follow in relation to HRM: to adapt to the environment of the host country (*host country effect*), to introduce country of origin patterns (*country of origin effects*) or to develop their own *hybrid style*. Ferner (2003) argued that, on the balance of available evidence to that particular time, *country of origin effects* remained strong in relation to *payment systems, management development and employee commitment strategies* but that *wage determination, hours of work and forms of job contract* are more likely to be influenced by the *host country environment*.

As previously stated, a contribution to the debate that emerged in the mid-1990s (building on Hofstede's 1980 notions of power distance and of masculine and feminine traits of organisations, dependent on their country of origin) were so-called *dominance effects* (Smith and Meiksins 1995), the idea that dominant or hegemonic states are able to exert organisational, political and technological influence that invites dissemination and adoption of employment practices across the global capitalist system. Research has consistently shown that US-owned MNCs have tended to export the organisational forms and management methods developed indigenously to their subsidiaries elsewhere. They are more likely than those from countries such as Northern Europe to have centralised and formalised systems of human resources and industrial relations management (Almond et al. 2005) and have a tendency, because of strong socio-historical roots (Jacoby 1997), to resist engagement with forms of collective representation. Also, as a result of their market-based norms, US firms have been traditionally keen to export systems of individual appraisal and performance-related pay (Muller 1998).

In addition to this finding, that US MNCs have strong centralising tendencies, Faulkener et al. (2002) also found that within globalising MNCs there were cross-country variations in inter-firm integration ranging from no integration, through partial integration, to full integration, but that firms from the US and UK integrated their subsidiaries to a greater extent than did firms from Germany and France. Through their empirical research into HRM practices (a postal survey of 201 companies and in-depth interviews with 40) they noted that there was some convergence of HRM practices, in that – for example – all countries researched employees' performance-related pay and increased the amount of training in their new subsidiaries.

An extension of this institutional analysis in assessing HRM causality is the *'varieties of capitalism'* approach which states that nations can be divided into two types – liberal market economies (LMEs) and co-ordinated market economies (CMEs) – based on the institutions characterising their financial and labour market systems (Hall and Soskice 2001). LME nations such as the US, UK and Australia are characterised by competitive market arrangements where performance is measured by market value and firms are directly accountable to shareholders. In these countries industrial relations are characterised by open market relationships, collective bargaining is unco-ordinated and takes place at the firm level and firms have the capability to hire and fire with limited constraints. As a consequence, in LMEs, Hall and Soskice assess the applicability and generalisability of 'best-practice' HRM (as defined by Pfeffer 1998 for instance) as being low.

Co-ordinated Market Economies, such as those of the Benelux countries, France and Germany, are characterised by 'stakeholder' capitalist national models where employees, suppliers and customers and financial institutions are part of the overall context in which firms are measured. In these business systems there is an emphasis on non-market relationships: corporate governance does not dictate that firms make public data on issues such as profitability or current returns; minority shareholders are poorly protected in favour of large owners; corporate returns tend to be measured on a long-term basis; and thus, firms can be more long-term orientated and the network of relationships among stakeholders will restrict M&As in a number of ways. The reflective HR environment is such that there is less employer autonomy, hiring and firing choices are restricted, firms are expected to protect employee rights, collective bargaining tends to be co-ordinated, and education and training is closely aligned to the needs of industry. In this environment, 'best-practice' HRM, such as open communications, high wages, job security and employee participation, tends to be institutionalised and common practice.

5.3.1.3 Power resource perspective

Like institutional theory, *power resource* or *resource dependence* theory used by some IHRM scholars focuses on the relationship between an organisation and its external and internal constituencies (most typically in 'owned' asset environments). However, by contrast, this framework emphasises *resource exchanges* as the central feature of these relationships, rather than concerns about *social acceptability* and *legitimacy* (Pfeffer and Cohen 1984). According to this perspective, groups and organisations gain bargaining power over each other by controlling valued resources (Pfeffer and Salancik 1978). Furthermore, HRM activities and processes are assumed to reflect the distribution of power within the system (Conner and Prahalad 1996, Abbott 2006). In the case of acquisitions, the party with the greater bargaining power is the one more likely to shape the HRM activities of the firm (Martinez and Ricks 1991) – usually the acquirer.

The institutional literature on HRM practice dissemination has been questioned for its macro-level, deterministic, structuralist perspective which ignores the reality of micro-level-based politics, conflict and tensions between business units, professional elites and employee classes (Bach and Sisson 2000, Almond et al. 2005). In all three instances, it is argued, access to resources that enhance the power and authority of certain actors and cohorts has an influence on the nature and type of the employment practices that are deployed. The notion that HRM practices are diffused cross-nationally, without any host country managerial input or opposition, is challenged by a *power resource-related* perspective that focuses upon the complex interactions that take place across business unit boundaries in MNCs. Indeed, Ferner et al. (2005), in their research on the diffusion of employment practices within MNC subsidiaries acknowledge that alongside macro-institutional effects, *much of the literature on cross-national employment practice diffusion implicitly adopts a rationalistic, unitary view of the corporation. Transfer takes place where top management see it as a source on international competitive advantage (e.g. Florkowski 1996 and Taylor et al. 1996). In such analyses, the interests and rationale guiding the behaviour of other actors within the MNC are not considered. As a result, there is inadequate exploration of the importance of power relations and conflict in mediating the transfer of policies. (2005: 306)*

This is a point with which Almond et al., in their analysis of practice diffusion from a US MNC in European subsidiaries, agree:

We emphasise that each group of potential effects varies across time and space, both in response to external economic and macro-institutional change, and to the sub-micro strategies adopted by actors at various levels of the organisation ... intra-firm political processes are key elements in the way MNCs operate. (2005: 299)

The importance of power and politics in the HR practice transfer process certainly raises questions about the determinism of institutional theoretical approaches. Clearly, management in the host subsidiary/partnership is subject to rival institutional pressures emanating from at least two normative, cognitive and regulatory frameworks (Powell and DiMaggio 1991), that (directly) of the *local environment* and its *parent company* and that (indirectly) of its *country of origin*. Actors in the subsidiary may derive *power resources* from their being embedded in the local institutional context where they have close relationships with other local actors within prescribed structures, such as collective bargaining machineries or forms of collective employee involvement such as works councils. This may increase the incentive for local managers to resist transfers of practices in case they disrupt existing relationships or breach indigenous laws.

5.3.2 CULTURAL EFFECTS ON HRM

Theoretical perspectives on IHRM suggest that institutional *country of origin* effects (particularly for those companies rooted in 'dominant' systems) and *host country* influences (especially for those with assets in highly regulated external labour markets) have a mediating effect upon the types of HRM that are applied by organisations in an international context. Additionally the degree to which either the owner or partner has access to resources through positional/situational power (possibly derived from their institutional context), will impact levels and types of HRM transfer. But what are the effects of national culture upon HRM diffusion in an international entity? It seems clear that institutional forces determine formal aspects of HRM such as employee/industrial relations policies, contractual relationships (i.e. holidays, redundancy, notice, hours of work, etc.) and rates of pay, but less formal 'best-practice' HRM elements – such as performance management, appraisals, training, communication, performance-related pay , benefits, involvement, etc. – are left up to organisations to decide what is both necessary (given their own modus vivendi) and/or culturally acceptable.

It is widely accepted that international HRM is one of the most complex activities in MNCs – given the need to balance off global consistency with local effectiveness (Laurent 1986). It is made all the more difficult given the fact that as some scholars have observed, some cultures are in transitional stages (see above) and others display more rigid characteristics. For instance, some cultures can be said to exhibit 'tightness or looseness' – with individuals (at a personal or regional level) experiencing higher or lower individual senses of separation from accepted norms (Gelfand et al. 2006). However, where comparisons have been made – largely in comparative rather than in-company analyses – differences have been exposed that have important implications for HRM applications. For instance, a comparison between Indian and UK middle managers showed that there were considerable differences in levels of consultation, involvement and delegation of authority (lower in Indian contexts), posing serious questions as to the transportability of HRM practices such as participation, two-way communications and empowerment (Tayeb 1988). Comparing Chinese and UK managers, a study found that decisions generally taken by junior managers in Britain were referred to higher senior managerial authority in China – again, raising questions around the effectiveness of the transmission of 'best-practice' HRM elements within this context (Easterby-Smith et al. 1995). Additionally, a study of French and Russian management and HRM approaches demonstrated that in Russia staff was wary of any practices that sought to drive autonomous decision-making, empowerment and/or involvement, preferring strong management as a defensive mechanism against potential anarchy. One positive HRM approach in this environment was the generation of trust through promises of job security and direct communication outlining future growth and investment plans (De Vries and Florent-Treacy 2002).

Overall, in line with some of the cultural constructs outlined above, certain HRM practices have been observed by scholars to be affected by specific cultural dependencies (i.e. Sparrow and Hiltrop 1997):

- Selection, training and development – These practices will be affected by embedded cultural values such as 'performance orientation', 'long-termism', and 'power distance' as to what constitutes an effective manager. For instance performance and capability might not be the main determining factor in the recruitment process (rather relationships, loyalty and blood ties) and training and development might be used as a form of reward rather than a form of skills enhancement.
- Communications and participation – Levels of information sharing, face-to-face feedback and involvement will be contingent on levels of societal 'power distance' and 'uncertainty avoidance'. Contexts with high levels of both will have a preference for communications on a 'need to know' basis.
- Performance management – The effectiveness of appraisal systems will be affected by 'power distance' factors which frame the manager/subordinate relationship. An honest and transparent exchange of views is unlikely to occur in societies where people are afraid to 'talk back' for fear of retribution.
- Pay systems – These are likely to be affected by constructs such as distributive justice (particularly with regards to 'gender equality'). Equitable pay and PRP will be affected by societal 'performance orientation' and conceptualisations of fairness.
- HR structures – The power of HR professionals whilst being mediated by factors such as industry sector and company culture, is also affected by extant mindsets regarding the nature and 'place' of strategic power.

Other factors such as age, service, gender, seniority, personality and individuals' own values will affect perceptions of the attractiveness of certain HRM practices in certain societies. Also, as previously stated, organisations might be able to change mindsets and behaviours through training and communications mechanisms. However, embedded societal values remain extremely impervious to change – especially within 'tight cultures', some research demonstrating that up to 75 per cent of HRM practices that will be institutionally and culturally acceptable are predicted by national value sets (Gelfand et al. 2006).

5.4 HMUL Commitment-Based Practices

The previous chapter argued that in order to be successful HMULs must first seek to ensure control across their portfolio of sites. This is due to the fact that in emerging markets where MUEs are, for the most part, in their early stages of development organisations must establish reputations for quality, consistency, safety and reliability. Managers and staff who have not been previously exposed to working in business to consumer (B2C), service-led environments in which frequent transactions occur, require close supervision to provide assured outputs. However, concentrating on control-led practices is not sufficient in businesses that are reliant on the human factor to facilitate functional activities *and* emotional transactions. In 5.2.1 above, reference was made to House et al.'s universal insight that most of the managers they surveyed regarded 'leader team orientation and the communication of vision, values and confidence in followers ... to be highly effective leadership behaviours' (House et al. 2004: 7). Also 5.2.3 highlighted that *self-expression* (i.e. participation in social, economic and political decision-making) and the spread of *emancipative values* (due to education and social media) was beginning to change national value sets in developing markets (Inglehart et al. 2010). Such forces challenge the view that the type of leadership style that is applied in many of these contexts (i.e. Southern Asia, Middle East, Confucian Asia, Eastern Europe and Latin America) – namely *self-protective leadership* which focuses on self-interest, status enhancement and face-saving behaviour – is sustainable (see 5.2.2 above). It is within this shifting, complex terrain that HMULs must motivate and engage their followers by means of a *local vision*, *talent attraction*, *tailored development*, *portfolio teamworking* and *trust and communication*.

5.4.1 LOCAL VISION

House et al.'s (2004) finding that one of the universal leadership attributes preferred by followers, across all cultures, was a strong sense of direction supported by definitive values is the start-point for understanding how effective HMULs generate commitment amongst their teams. All MUEs and, for the most part, their subsidiaries and affiliates, will have a binding long-term vision/view (with a three to five-year horizon most typically) which elucidates a desired future state, where the organisation states *where* it wants to be. This is commonly connected to a mission statement which describes *what* the organisation does, supported by strategy/tactics which say *how* they are going to achieve their aims (often incorporated into a balanced scorecard), underpinned by a value set that outlines the behaviours that members of the firm need to display in order to make it happen (see 4.4.3). These super-ordinate statements, usually crafted by senior policy-makers, are cascaded throughout the organisation through a variety of means and typically form the backbone of internal corporate communication, with core messages from these statements being reinforced at every opportunity through CEO communications, briefings, town hall meetings, etc.

The issue that HMULs have at a local level is that sometimes these high-level statements of intent seem, at best, abstract and detached, at worst, irrelevant. Views relating to the organisation within the portfolio will be dependent upon where sites are within the investment cycle and what support and resources members are receiving from the organisation to expedite the stated objectives. At times members might feel that such super-ordinate statements and goals are rhetoric, warm words that are unsupported by reality. For instance an MUE might say that *what* it exists to do is 'become the leading *x* through constantly delighting its customers', supported by grand pronouncements as to *how* it will achieve it through 'passionate and motivated colleagues', underpinned by values of 'tolerance, respect and integrity' but then act in a totally inconsistent, contrary manner by reducing staffing and maintenance spend to a minimum when it begins to struggle. In cultures where levels of *uncertainty avoidance* are high and workers have taken 'promises' made by the organisation at face value, line management is placed in a precarious predicament. How do they explain that the vision and mission, as it would be understood in developed market terms, is merely a route map or statement of intent that cannot be taken literally *at all times*?

The way in which effective HMULs deal with this ambiguity is to create a sense of purpose and mission pertinent to their particular contexts. HMULs need to create a binding commitment amongst their followers to what they are trying to achieve within their portfolios, in order to guide collective effort and energy. As the HMUL is measured at a portfolio level they must find a means by which every member of their team can articulate *what* they (as a team) are trying to do and *how* they are going to do it. But how do HMULs construct a local vision that drives self-regulating, consensual, collective behaviours?

A start-point will certainly be provided by the organisation's super-ordinate goals and measures, but more likely effective HMULs will attempt to craft a local vision that aims to set them apart from their immediate competitive set, i.e. the other districts in their area or region. To this extent a statement like 'we will consistently be the best-performing district in region *x*' will be backed up by how this will be achieved by an elucidation of key *outputs* such as sales, profit, stock variances/turnaround, standards, health and safety compliance, customer service, etc., supported by *input drivers* such as staff turnover, engagement, absenteeism, service/compliance training, succession, etc. However, *what* the district is trying to achieve and *how* it is going to do it requires significant commitment and buy-in to generate momentum, particularly in circumstances where it seems that the organisation is (perversely) conspiring against its objectives through contra behaviours. Thus, effective HMULs must create a sense of 'teamship' through celebrating success when they achieve their ambitions and *sustain* it through recruiting the right people, training them appropriately in order to work together collegiately in a trusting environment – factors that will be explored more fully below.

Case Study 9 – Local Visioning in Genting Casinos

Paul Willcock is the Managing Director (Provincial) of Genting Casinos UK and sits on the board of the parent organisation. Fifty per cent owned by its Malaysian founders, Genting (with a market capitalisation of over £30 billion) is one of the largest leisure operators in the world with a wide global spread of assets.

The way in which Genting runs its country-based assets is to set an overarching vision, purpose and values, allowing local management to mould and adapt strategy/KPIs according to local conditions. But what are the core elements of their overarching principles that remain immutable? From a vision/mission standpoint (i.e. why do we exist and where do we want to be?) – possibly related to the level of family control and Southern Asian *temporal disposition* – Genting takes a very *long-term view* in the way in which it approaches market planning and resource allocation. Genting is (in a very positive sense) the complete antithesis of other 'quoted' western companies I have worked for, that have broadly taken a very short-termist approach to initiatives and capital investment. In addition, Genting's values such as '*decency*' and '*integrity*' underpin their approach to the way in which they treat all stakeholders; there is almost a '*philanthropic*' thrust to the way in which they do business that I find quite at odds with the CSR 'rhetoric-based' approaches I have seen in some other western corporate contexts! ... The owners and senior leaders of Genting are highly visible in the business, frequently conducting trade visits in the UK, and actively transmit – on a face-to-face basis – what the company stands for and its long-term purpose ... In terms of cultural dynamics it is refreshing to work for an organisation where *strong personal relationships* are valued so highly, although one must always recognise the way in which decisions are made and challenged (in open forums) is distinctly different from Anglo-American contexts ... in meetings due respect must be paid to those in positions of authority ...

With regards to local market strategy, Genting grant a high degree of autonomy to local management. Coming into this job a couple of years ago the challenges I faced were not those posed by the owner, rather the legacy issues posed by previous local management and the casino culture in the UK. What I have been able to do (with full consent of the Malaysian owners) is introduce a balanced scorecard addressing financial metrics, operational excellence, customer satisfaction and employee engagement. We have, for instance, introduced a suite of surveys measuring customer and employee 'inputs' which – certainly in this business – can have a profound impact on operational efficiency and financial performance. I think that the casino business in the UK has been behind many of its leisure counterparts over the past 20 years in the way it has addressed the provision of a stimulating and engaging place for people to work and an exciting, inviting space for customers to 'play'. The industry has been a bit of a 'closed shop', excessively hierarchical (deferential even) and what I have attempted to drive is a more open, 'thriving' culture that is focused upon broadening consumer appeal through a more varied offer ('more than' just gaming) AND higher standards of customer service. In order to do this I have had to sell the message directly at company conferences, meetings and away days ... but I have also had to change the multi-site architecture of the company to drive my vision 'down the line' as well ...

In the past, MULs in the casino business progressed from GM level ... these individuals were steeped in the 'norms' and 'customs' of the industry ... What I have done is hired operations directors that have come from multi-site retail (i.e. Toys'R'Us) and hospitality backgrounds who are well versed in the art and science of MUL ... What do I mean by this? ... Fundamentally, they 'get' operational excellence, can 'manage at a distance' and are well organised and professional (i.e. they prepare properly for on-site strategic, operational and personal development meetings) and understand the necessity of engaging 'hearts and minds' ... Actually what we do is leverage the overarching vision and values of the organisation ('investing for the long term' and 'honesty and respect'), combining it with practical measures, initiatives and (most importantly) behaviours that really bring it alive ... I expect my MULs (as I do hopefully) to set the 'dynamic pace and tone' not just in word but in deed ... Certainly the degree of alignment we now have through definitive measures, accurate business intelligence and 'sharing' best practice/knowledge is allowing the business to take a more homogenous approach ... The point is, this stable long-term parental view/positive 'light touch' cultural environment, is an extremely powerful mixture when combined with a high level of room for manoeuvre on the ground.

5.4.2 TALENT ATTRACTION

As stated, MUEs are people facing businesses where high levels of functional and emotional service levels are required to capture and retain customers. Ideally organisations with good reputations and powerful employment brands should be well placed to attract and retain talent from the external labour market within international contexts. But what do organisations – especially MUEs – mean when they talk about talent? Fundamentally they are not just talking about hiring and retaining high fliers, rather they are seeking to locate and optimise the specific talents of all the staff they attract to 'fit' the diverse capability needs of their business. Furthermore, rather than this function being purely the preserve of the HR department, the process of talent attraction should lie with every manager within the organisation. In the case of MUEs talent attraction applies to all levels of the organisation although for HMULs it relates most importantly to unit manager positions (a major determinant of store success – accounting for a variance of up to 20 per cent in turnover in international premium apparel stores). But what are the issues for

MUEs seeking to attract talent in emerging markets and how do organisations and, more specifically, HMULs overcome them?

There are a number of problems that MUEs face when attempting to attract talent in emerging markets which relate to sectoral, national business system (NBS) and cultural issues. First, negative perceptions of the service sector in many markets provides a formidable rate limiter to recruitment. In societies where the most highly prized jobs have been well-paid government sinecures or professional roles (such as lawyer, doctor, etc.) service sector roles have been shunned by the educated middle classes (Harry 2007). In areas such as the Middle East there has been a large reliance on diaspora labour from Southern Asia – who are granted limited rights and liberties – to fill what are regarded as menial, entry-level jobs – a position that has grave consequences for building a talent pipeline in some contexts. Second, there are NBS effects that also impact the talent architecture of MUEs. Employment legislation might drive either employer (i.e. age, gender and disability discrimination) or employee (i.e. mandatory collective representation) biases. Also, mismatches between the education provision in certain NBSs and corporate requirements (particularly with regards to social and behavioural skills) affect the size of the potential talent pool. Third, from a cultural perspective, *social dependency* aspects that emphasise the merits of 'kith and kin first' lead to nepotism and favouritism – a situation which dilutes rather than bolsters talent reserves within organisations (Ali and Al-Kazemi 2006).

How do MUEs and, more particularly, the HMULs on the ground attempt to overcome some of these issues? From an organisational perspective MUEs will attempt to build their employment brand within local markets by advertising (increasingly upon social media) market-leading pay and conditions (where restrictions apply regarding levels of base pay they will emphasise benefit entitlements such as sickness cover, holidays, pensions, etc.), performance-related pay systems and, most importantly perhaps, in aspirant youthful labour markets, the meritocratic means of development and progression within their organisations. In order to capture the right talent, 'culture fair' curriculum vitae (CV) assessment, interview techniques and psychometric tools are deployed in order to ensure a proper degree of predictive validity.

From a HMUL perspective their job of attracting and retaining talent is obviously made easier (or harder) by how their organisation has positioned its employment brand, particularly against local competition. For the most part, however, effective HMULs will busy themselves with building a high degree of 'bench strength' within their portfolio's internal labour market to ensure there is a sufficient pipeline of talent to fill important positions such as unit, assistant/deputy, section and shift leadership positions. Their starting-point will usually focus upon attitude/motivation (most importantly a 'can do' service-led approach) and then aptitude/abilities (the technical skills to do the job); the former being a trait, the latter being acquired learning. In many contexts HMULs will already have been trained in the judicious application of recruitment and selection techniques in order to obviate any cultural dispositions towards nepotism. The fact that their success lies primarily in the effective performance of their districts should – in most cases – provide enough of a motivation to select according to performance rather than relationship.

Case Study 10 – Local Talent Attraction, Retention and Development in Burberry Plc

Reg Sindall was the Group HRD of Bass Plc 1994–2001 (Intercontinental Hotels, Holiday Inn, Mitchells and Butlers, Bass Brewers, Britvic, etc.), Group HRD of Great Universal Stores 2001–2007 (Argos, Experian, Homebase, Lewis Stores Group, Burberry, etc.) and EVP of Group Resources (encompassing four customer and three employee-facing functions) at Burberry Plc 2007–2012. Reg was also a Non-Executive Director of the international headhunting agency Michael Page (2010–2012).

Attracting and developing local talent has never been easy albeit it has changed noticeably over the past 18 years. First, from an organisational perspective, 20 years ago – when the conglomerate business model was still in fashion – what might be pejoratively termed a *colonial* or *feudal* model towards talent predominated. What I mean by this is that International MUEs (IMUEs) saw talent development as being restricted to a very small cadre at the apex of organisations (largely concentrated on the home country) with expatriates (very much in the same way as in colonial times) being despatched to run outposts of the burgeoning business empire. Today – in a far more enlightened manner in my view – due (largely) to MUEs becoming focused entities around a single industry, brand or identity, *federal* structures of talent attraction and development have emerged. Thus whilst *home-host-home* archetypes of attraction and development might have predominated in the past, today *host-home-host* models are more applicable … Another factor in this development has obviously been the growing economic strength of entities such as the BRIC nations with increasing levels of education/sophistication and also the growth of social media that has opened up a window on the world for previously isolated regions …

Today IMUEs drill down far deeper in order to identify, attract and retain talent – in a sense the 'developed world arrogance' that might have once been a feature of this area in these organisations has now disappeared. In my view successful IMUEs now take what I term a *multi-layered* approach to attracting local talent … What I mean by this is that exemplar IMUEs take an integrated approach, ensuring that all elements of their HRM approaches align with what the brand/company stands for. First – and most importantly – recruitment systems should be aligned with the firm's *core values* (which in the case of Burberry were 'protect, explore, inspire'), which in turn are anchored in the company's purpose (made all the more powerful if it has a strong emotional connection). What does this mean? It requires local recruiters (HR, regionals, store managers, etc.) to, first, have high levels of self-awareness as to what is required to function effectively within the ambient organisational culture and then, second, locate and calibrate appropriate talent that voluntarily *buys into* and *fits* (through attitude, behaviour and disposition) these espoused values … sometimes these values might transcend local ones … but getting local colleagues to believe in and commit to the *why and how* is essential … Upholding and reinforcing these values through constant messaging, communication and modelled behaviours is also key … at Burberry we had transitioned our CEO quarterly webcasts down to monthly ones accompanied by real-time company-wide Facebook interaction ... Second, IMUEs need to pay attention to extrinsic 'glue' mechanisms (although emotional buy-in always precedes this) ... at Burberry every employee was placed in a performance incentive scheme and was a shareholder. Third, extensive training and development systems are required to show that the company is prepared to invest in skills that benefit not only the organisation, but also employees' portability and sense of worth.

Developing local talent is key to sustained IMUE success. In Burberry we were proud of the fact that many of our country managers in the Asian region were of local origin albeit they had developed formidable linguistic, managerial and cultural intelligence skills by attending western universities and/or working in developed country environments ... I think the language point is significant ... idiomatic understanding of what is really meant by home country policy-makers is important in the way in which initiatives, policies and practices are transmitted down the line ... As regards training and development in the field (at regional manager/ store level) the influence of new technology has had a transformative effect ... as the technology underpinning training delivery has changed it is now far easier to communicate to colleagues how stores should be set up, which procedures should be followed, etc. Getting over to sales associates how they should deal with customers through digitalised service delivery training that is constantly reinforced by the behaviours of local management (including regional managers) and embedded by local training teams is essential ... With regards to service training, simplicity and consistency of approach are the most important factors ... The service delivery system at Burberry was called the 'Burberry Experience' which all employees were made conversant with, whatever their level, position, function or location ... interestingly this programme ... which was easily understandable and digestible ... had been developed through empirical analysis of the behaviours of the best sales associates globally and then packaged as a consistent approach to drive *intentional, passionate* and *purposeful* behaviours ...

To what extent is training and development nuanced to take into account local factors? The fact that technology has cut out layers of transmission mechanisms has enabled IMUEs to ensure convergence around common standards and approaches ... Also, due to technology reducing the cost of training, companies like Burberry are able to launch intensive talent management programmes (delivering people, commercial, merchandising, operational skills training, etc.) which in 2012–2013 were planned to cover over one-third of the organisation's employees ... The fact that these programmes had been checked and sanctioned by an executive board (containing leadership representatives from all over the globe) lent weight to these programmes, designed to embed consistent technical and behavioural skills internationally ... In addition these programmes were underpinned by constant endorsement through senior management making frequent international store visits, regular regional conferences and awards ceremonies, where store, call centre and HQ-level service excellence (i.e. politeness, knowledge and quality) was publically recognised and rewarded! ... such events also provided excellent networking opportunities across our international operations ...

5.4.3 TAILORED DEVELOPMENT

A critical function of the HMUL role is to encourage, facilitate and, in some instances, deliver training and development (T&D) which addresses capability gaps within the portfolio. Although development can be viewed as an essential instrument to attract and retain valuable human capital its primary role should be seen as ultimately making employees more productive and profitable through the improvement of technical, behavioural or cognitive skills. In many organisations – particularly those in developed markets that have experienced a severe downturn since 2008 – staff development budgets have been reduced/redeployed as companies have downsized their workforces or sought to deliver training through cheaper means such as web-enabled technology. In growth market contexts many MUEs have continued to invest in development, however, not only because their business performance has made this permissible but also because of the overriding need to upskill labour (particularly management) that, in many instances, lack the requisite supervisory competencies to deliver outstanding performance. What issues do organisations face in devising and delivering T&D in emerging markets and how do they and, more specifically HMULs, overcome them?

Problems relating to T&D in emerging markets can be grouped around operational, cultural and personal capability issues. First, as is the case with MUEs in the developed world, some organisations in developing markets lack the time and resources for T&D, albeit for different reasons. In developed contexts lack of time and resources relates to diminishing levels of revenue investment, whilst in high-growth emerging markets, because of (in many cases) fast roll-out plans and the requirement for people – as one international HRD put it – to 'do the job' rather than 'learn it', there is a temporal squeeze facing T&D. In some cases it is either done quickly in order to satisfy minimum local regulations such as H&S, licensing, etc., or not at all, with staff thrown in at the deep end being expected to learn 'on the job'. Inevitably such approaches prove to be deleterious in the long run as staff leave to join organisations that are willing to make a serious commitment to their learning, development and progression. Second, from a cultural perspective companies that disseminate ubiquitous programmes and modules from the centre without any cultural adaptation, taking into account local behaviours and learning styles, are setting themselves up to fail. For instance several studies have shown that T&D materials that include extensive 'open' group discussions are likely to be of little value in Chinese contexts where the preference is for passive learning in large groups or targeted problem-solving within small teams (Branine 1996, 2005). Third, from a personal capability or absorptive capacity standpoint, organisations need to measure baseline levels of literacy, numeracy and cognitive capability amongst the recipient managerial/employee cohorts before they launch in-house packages that could otherwise (based on preconceived notions of capability) be unfit for purpose.

The best-practice T&D approach that most successful international MUEs adopt naturally involves ensuring that their manuals, programmes and modules have a high degree of cultural specificity, taking into account local laws, norms and preferences. In addition, however, they should consider what types of intrinsic development are most highly sought after by recipients (often outstripping extrinsic reward packages). For instance in Confucian Asia certified managerial development that enhances status and promotional prospects are highly valued (Worm 2001). In-house programmes that have received some type of formal accreditation are also prized, as are on-the-job rotation schemes that improve employees' chances of obtaining general management positions. From the HMUL's point of view, making optimal use of the T&D options and resources on offer from their organisation to benefit the capability and self-efficacy of their people is an obvious thing to do – particularly during appraisals and performance reviews – as it also (potentially) brings huge benefits in terms of reciprocity and exchange.

Outwith Corporate T&D, however, effective HMULs use the resources within their own portfolios to develop 'tailored' skills and capabilities. Organisational programmes are not a panacea – particularly with regard to 'hard' technical operational skills. What successful HMULs are particularly adept at doing is utilising the talents of their wider team to teach and coach core skills. Hence, HMULs might designate certain Unit Managers or Assistants as 'leads' regarding BOH administration, FOH due diligence, service delivery, merchandising, etc. When there are upgrades or changes in these areas the HMUL can deputise their leads in these areas to liaise with company training personnel on an effective roll-out and delivery programme. In cultures where this type of 'distributed delegation' is uncommon due to decisional primacy being accorded to hierarchy and authority, the HMUL must lead by example. Often effective HMULs will become well acquainted with the detail of many of these new approaches (either on a mandatory or voluntary basis) and act as a role model in a 'train the trainer' capacity. In summary, however, most effective HMULs approached T&D in the same way in one major respect: they acted as cheerleaders for T&D at all levels within their portfolios, prioritising time and resources to advance the knowledge, capabilities and, therefore, prospects of their charges without fear or favour.

Case Study 11 – Aligning Talent and Development to a Service-led Culture in IMUEs

Nick Wylde is a Managing Director of Stanton Chase International, a leading global executive search firm. With over 25 years of talent placement experience, Nick has worked extensively for general retailing, leisure, hospitality and travel IMUEs, handling a broad range of head office and 'locally-based' regional/country/field operations assignments. Nick's particular area of talent deployment/development expertise is cross-border service delivery transmission.

IMUEs *must* continually innovate around product and service to ensure they are ahead of the game – especially in high-end 'emotional premium' offers. The major issue they have is how they maintain this 'innovative momentum' across different formats, ownership structures and cultures! It is a complex issue faced by many IMUEs – many of the retail and hospitality organisations I work with are constantly wrestling with the conundrum of service refreshment and improvement whilst being cognisant of challenges posed by local cultural idiosyncrasies (i.e. labour 'mindsets' and skills, customer preferences, market sophistication, etc.) ... One way that they can overcome many of the issues they face in attempting to transport effective service-delivery systems is through the *people factor*; namely, putting the right talent and development mechanisms in at a local level to ensure a greater chance of success ... but what are the specific issues faced by organisations and how do they practically overcome them at a local level? ...

I would subdivide the barriers that IMUEs face in building service-led ethos into three distinct areas: *organisational, 'local' cultural* and *operational* ... First, from an *organisational* point of view, are companies really set up properly to design, deliver and change their service offers? ... in multi-brand organisations, as compared to those with a single brand orientation, discontinuities can occur internationally, if country managers with multiple brand responsibilities fail to understand the service essence of each particular product; i.e. conflating value with mid-market approaches and vice versa ... where it is done well (at Hilton for instance, who run Waldorf Astoria alongside Garden Inn in certain territories) brands are aligned to central marketing teams who have a clear 'line of sight' through the field to the customer ... Matters are further complicated from an organisational standpoint in different ownership configurations: *wholly owned, joint venture* or *franchised* ... the service delivery system can be diluted – particularly in high-end 'premium' environments – if the 'originating' parent does not have full control ... For instance *x*'s concession in a department store concession in New York will not necessarily have the same service standards as its 'own' managed store in the same city! ... Second, *'local' culture* inevitably impinges on the processes of service execution and renewal ... can the values underpinning the organisation's service culture transcend some of the values that threaten to dilute or derail the service promise? ... Third, in connection to the last point, does the organisation have the necessary *operational talent and T&D mechanisms* to overcome transmission issues? ...

This is where the 'local' people factor looms large ... The organisations that I have observed, consulted with and advised (in some cases over a long period of time) have thought long and hard about the capability, competency and *organisational/brand 'fit'* of the local multi-unit operators they appoint ... What stands out for me is the degree to which successful IMUEs measure what I call the *'intrinsic alignment'* of new recruits ... thus, high-end premium apparel companies will relentlessly calibrate whether candidates 'get it' – what the organisation/brand stands for, its ethos and service delivery system requirements, etc. – and are sufficiently emotionally intelligent to meld their behaviours accordingly! ... These organisations will ask themselves whether hires in 'local' markets are prepared to act as *brand ambassadors*, are capable of *living the values* and whether they *fit with the organisational culture*? ... In terms of T&D systems, to reinforce service concept delivery, great IMUEs (such as one I dealt with recently) will have designated senior HR/Operational/Marketing personnel who focus upon driving service improvement ... increasingly these are Third Country National (TCN) 'global' appointments – appointees with a high level of cultural intelligence ... Thus, whilst the central principles of the organisation's service delivery system remain constant, sensitive allowance is granted in relation to the way it is trained out, communicated and explained by 'local leaders' in certain cultures (due to differing preferred learning styles, etc.).

5.4.4 CROSS-PORTFOLIO TEAM-WORKING

Another means by which HMULs gain commitment and buy-in is through the active encouragement of cross-portfolio team-working which yields reciprocity and mutual gain. Given the geographically isolated nature of many of their units (particularly in dispersed urban areas in Confucian Asia, Southern Asia and Latin America), encouraging local team-working which as one HRD put it 'reduces the psychological and physical burden', promises immense dividends in terms of morale and productivity. Effective HMULs recognise that 'the whole is stronger than the sum of the parts': that by getting their team (in particular their unit managers) to work together the general performance of their district will improve. Encouraging high levels of interaction and 'sharing' is desirable particularly with regards to T&D (see 5.4.3 above) and knowledge diffusion and process improvement (see 6.3.3 and 6.3.4 below). However, how do HMULs create effective teams? How do organisations help them to do so and what are the barriers commonly confronted by HMULs?

Starting with barriers, there are three main issues that impede successful team-working across portfolios: architectural imprecision, unit self-interest and cultural aversions to participation and team-working. Architectural imprecision refers to poor structural design of the configuration of districts within organisations. Often, due to secondary segmentation of the property portfolio (where units are split into new formats/old formats, core/non-core, approximations to certain sizes, etc.), HMULs might be designated large territories, overlapping their colleagues. Companies need to judge carefully whether optimal performance is derived from controlling the 'same' type of outlet over a (potentially) vast geography or a 'mixed bag' of units in a tight territory. The downside of the former state is time wasted travelling between units and the difficulties of building a tight team; with the latter, the prospect of handling formats, addressing different channels, that are serviced with different product, promotions, merchandising, customers, etc. Second, the fact that all units are measured independently means that some unit managers might be unwilling to act in a concertive fashion because they believe that by swapping 'soft' or 'hard' assets they might be helping their direct competition. Third, in some *power* cultures where the leader is looked to provide certainty and all the answers members might be insufficiently socialised to work in autonomous teams.

Given these impediments how do MUEs encourage portfolio team-working, and what techniques do HMULs deploy in order to facilitate their success? At an organisational level managing and/or regional directors will pay very close attention to the architecture of their districts to optimise HMUL efficiency and will also keep annual boundary reorganisations to a minimum in order to preserve relationships and tacit local knowledge. In some organisations provision will be made for technology-enabled interfaces/interactions between HMUL-unit manager, unit manager-unit manager (telephone conference facilities, Skype, web-cam, streaming, etc.) to eliminate travel and movement offsite. Other MUEs actively encourage teamwork through PRP mechanisms such as 'contribution' payments (an annual payment of up to 10–20 per cent of base salary) which are based upon the HMUL's assessment of their unit manager's overall value-added to the wider team and general portfolio performance. In terms of team meeting structures some organisations also mandate the numbers and types of meetings that should take place at district (i.e. monthly district meetings with prescribed agendas that fit with normal internal communication/briefings cycles) and unit level (i.e. daily 'buzz' briefings, end-of-shift meetings, weekly action meetings, monthly strategy meetings, etc.).

HMULs, therefore, will probably be prescribed a set team meeting structure and, in some instances, indicative agendas and supporting back-up material and/or visiting technocratic speakers from Head Office. However, ensuring that the team works effectively across the portfolio is an art not a science. Members can dutifully participate within a set framework but how do HMULs ensure that their charges collaborate horizontally? In terms of 'set piece' district meetings HMULs with high degrees of confidence will allow their 'leads' and 'champions' for various business objectives and initiatives time to present, instruct and problem-solve with the wider team. Beneath unit manager level they might also facilitate quarterly meetings amongst their assistant/deputy population in order to encourage cross-portfolio collaboration and 'bring on' emerging talent. But outwith these formal interactions, given the need to bond their team effectively into harmonious units, HMULs will also ensure that time is set aside for socialising where insightful conversations can occur and deeper relationships can be formed between colleagues. From a cultural perspective, certainly within 'high context' environments (Hall 1976), such informal approaches are likely to pay far greater dividends in terms of trust-based team-building. In addition, some HMULs might take a more granular approach, subdividing their districts into what they might term sectors, clusters or 'families' where unit managers (usually situated in tight geographic proximity) work together sharing knowledge and resources. Again however, given the predisposition of managers in certain cultures to exhibit *self-protective* behaviour, effective HMULs must ensure that these teams are assigned clear briefs and expectations and that a code of conduct underpins behaviour between the respective parties.

Case Study 12 – Cross-Portfolio Team-Working in IMUEs

Bob Dignen is a Director of York Associates, an international team and leadership development consultancy founded in 1990 and the author of Communicating Internationally in English. *Bob has worked closely with a large number of IMUE strategic and local leaders over the last 20 years to improve their team/project-working skills, particularly in inter/cross-cultural contexts.*

The term 'teamwork' in itself implies 'work of the team' – a collective body working effectively together to produce a *defined level of performance*. The contingent variables impacting its effectiveness will relate to the way in which *the team is built* (taking into account different personalities, abilities, perspectives, perceptions, etc.) and *the context in which it operates*. Is the environment conducive to high-performance team-working – are the necessary resources provided to ensure optimal outcomes? Having been involved with coaching cross-national and local teams in international situations over the past 20 years I think it is vital that local leaders who want to form great teams take into account three intertwined factors: first, what I call the business *landscape* in which they operate, second, the *success factors* that are pretty universal to high-performance teams, and third, sensitive adaptation to *context*.

With regards to *landscape* local leaders in IMUEs have to deal with four main issues with regards to their own personal mindset/development and that of their teams: uncertainty, complexity, paradox and diversity ... *uncertainty* due to the fact that goals in international contexts can be vague or often change without notice ... *complexity* due to local NBS (the law, institutions, regional government, etc.) effects and the distance from the centre ... *paradox* with regards to the fact that many companies claim to operate in a seamless international fashion but fail to design/allocate appropriate structures, alignment/feedback mechanisms and sufficient budgets/resources for international effectiveness ... *diversity* through different national cultures and traits that (can) lead to misinterpretation, confusion and missteps ... Effective local leaders need to deal with and (if possible) 'close down' many of these issues through resilience and a sophisticated understanding of how they bind together requirements from the centre with local conditions (i.e. controlling the controllables, not blaming themselves or their teams for misconceived or badly timed central initiatives, being adaptable, coming up with creative solutions, etc.) ...

In relation to team-based *success factors*, some pretty *universal* truths apply at local level, not least that effective team-working is based upon: establishing a *clear vision*, fostering adult and *mature relationships*, *supportive behaviours*, clearly *designated roles*, appropriate *support and resources*, a *performance culture* (with planning, measures, quality control and feedback), a strong *communications* approach that satisfies diverse stakeholders throughout the portfolio, ensuring that *diversity is used as a creative strength* rather than as a detractor, *minimising conflict*, etc. ... However, in international multi-site operations the challenge of realising these success factors is made complicated not least by virtue of the fact that the effort required to bond a team whilst 'managing at a distance' is significant, not least when resources are scarce, technology might be unfit for purpose and cultural impediments due to *context specificity* might loom large ...

In terms of *cultural context* the central insight I would make is that the discourses of 'relationship', 'team' and 'leadership' mean different things in different cultures ... often local leaders are operating in 'fuzzy' paradigms in which IMUEs have made a limited effort to adjust their 'managerial systems' to local cultural demands ... the clash between command and control MCS (in spite of the surrounding 'warm people rhetoric') and 'high context' cultures which stress particular aspects of interpersonal interaction, often termed a 'relationship-based approach', is not uncommon ... juxtaposed against this is the difficulty of transposing 'best-practice' HRM (participation, team-working, open communications, etc.) in hierarchical cultures ... it is often said by intercultural commentators that due to 'in-group' collectivism, regions such as the Middle East and Asia might have a preference for a more affiliation-oriented type of team-working ... however in the Middle East, for instance, some western professionals report – supposedly due to huge wealth reserves in some states – a huge tolerance for individual and team underperformance, temporal imprecision and a more relaxed attitude towards detail and implementation ... Similarly, in Asia the concept of 'leader' or 'manager' is reportedly framed by *'content'* notions of expertise and positional primacy rather than facilitation/enabling, *'process notions'* of telling and directing rather than delegating/empowering and *'emotional factors'* such as aggressive power rather than emotional proximity … leading to common perceptions that leadership styles in certain territories are 'old fashioned', itself a manifestation of dangerous levels of cultural dissonance.

How do IMUEs overcome some of these cross-cultural barriers and – indeed – what do local leaders do themselves to engender team-working that ultimately results in positive sales-led service within multi-unit businesses? Some IMUEs will design and communicate a *'coherent logic'* in the way in which they address certain customer groups … IKEA is frequently cited as having been successful in that regard, engendering cross-border coherence through shared values and behaviours backed up by solid systems (i.e. IT, supply chain, SOPs, etc.) … However, convergence and universalism – certainly 'front of house' – is a risk, raising the paradox as to whether or not companies should standardise or localise managerial practices … often there is a lack of clarity about where the balance should fall … but in all honesty perhaps this is the optimal way, albeit living with such 'flux' might appear disturbing both to strategic and local leaders alike! … effective team-building in international operations is both an art and a science!

5.4.5 TRUST AND COMMUNICATION

Thus far, some of the practices elucidated above have cited the need for HMULs to build high levels of trust with their teams in order to create a high-performance environment. There are, however, other important dimensions to building trust that need to be considered independently, particularly in relation to the degree that they communicate openly and honestly with their followers. From a sociological or psychological point of view, trust is an important factor underpinning intra/inter-group relations – generally portrayed as the extent to which one party *believes* that another party will act both *transparently* and *consistently* in a fair, honest and benevolent manner. Its benefits include greater predictability of social life, community cohesion and a more effective working environment that enables members to work together . Breaches of trust can degrade relationships, although they might be forgiven if they arise through a lack of competence or are followed by immediate admission/recovery. Trust builds confidence (House et al. 2004: 7) and followership, with communications between parties forming a key part of the equation. What issues do IMUEs face in building trust, how do they overcome them and how do HMULs create trusting followership in frequently ambiguous and complex circumstances?

The main issue that IMUEs face in building trust in some emerging market contexts is the fact that, due to past experience of the gap between the rhetoric and subsequent behaviour of those in authority, many members are apt to suspend belief in what has been said until they observe actions. In addition, in many societies (particularly those emerging from ex-Communist paradigms) where people have been conditioned to receive information only on a need-to-know basis, members are unused to free-flowing streams of communication; although social media (where it is uncensored), by providing an unfettered 'window on the world', is changing perceptions and expectations in this regard. At a corporate level within IMUEs trust is built (alongside some of the factors mentioned in the sections above) both through the *process, content* and *follow up* of communications. From a *process* perspective senior leaders will attempt to engage *directly* with their management and staff through multiple media, although face-to-face meetings remain the most powerful mechanisms (i.e. 'town hall' meetings, trade visits, conferences etc.). The honesty and transparency of the *content* framed in a jargon-free, simple, consistent manner which is then *followed up* with hard, visible outputs is a vital means of building and sustaining trust throughout IMUEs (Leahy 2012: 275–91). Such approaches serve to underpin the values of the organisation, creating imitative behaviour in cultural contexts where, previously, information and knowledge was deemed to be the sole preserve of those in authority. In some national business systems (NBSs), MUEs are required by law to engage in *indirect* communication with representatives of organised labour and/or regional government officials on business proposals/plans and employment issues; again, successful MUEs are usually honest and upfront about their intentions.

How do HMULs generate trust among their followers? Obviously, operating in an organisational climate where senior members holding privileged positions (at corporate, subsidiary and senior field level) do not abuse their authority helps. But given the levels of interdependency HMULs have with their followers (being measured on virtually the same metrics) and the fact that they are rarely on-site to monitor activities, the necessity to build trusting relationships that result in value-added reciprocity is paramount. Communications and interactions (as detailed above) take place on many levels and it is important that HMULs deport themselves in a balanced, transparent and consistent manner at all times. When they have information they share it and when asked questions they answer them truthfully, which sometimes might involve side-stepping certain issues (with an explanation) rather than outright evasion. During one-to-one interactions with their unit managers either during operational, strategic or performance/development meetings HMULs will seek to be 'straight', seeking truthful dialogue that will 'move the game on'.

For sure, in certain cultures where open feedback is perceived to be confrontational or threatens a 'loss of face' HMULs must patiently socialise their followers to accept useful criticism. One means through which HMULs might achieve this is by demonstrating the *humility* to accept advice and feedback themselves – something that self-protective leaders in some cultures would rarely do. Another means of building trust might be achieved through 'backing rather than sacking' followers for mild misdemeanours or infractions. Thus, HMULs can build their social influence through protecting their followers from punishment (particularly in IMUE contexts where voluminous measures and controls apply) but also delivering on the promises they make. Acting in the role of a 'trouble shooter' – an intermediary between the centre and the unit – the HMUL is well placed to sort out daily irritations and malfunctions. HMULs can gain respect and strong followership by promising to resolve problems and then (quickly) doing so, or – if they are unable to gain resolution – explaining why something cannot be rectified immediately. Finally, an important means of building trust involves the HMULs focus on growth and success within the portfolio, which is a subliminal signal to followers that it is their overriding intention to sustain employment (job security in prized IMUE roles being a prime concern in some contexts) and build the reputations, status and, therefore, promotional prospects of their charges.

Case Study 13 – Communication and Trust in IMUEs in China

Dr Lisa Qixun Siebers (Nottingham Business School), author of Retail Internationalisation in China *(2011), is one of the leading authorities on IMUE expansion in China and Africa. Her sponsors and collaborators include the China Retail Research Centre, Tsinghua University (Beijing), the School of Business Administration, Dongbei University of Finance and Economics (Dalian) and Kenya Overseas Chinese Association.*

From the extensive empirical evidence I have gathered from a number of IMUEs in China (such as Walmart, Carrefour, Metro, B&Q, Tesco, etc.) I would say that the process of transposing 'western' managerial practices such as trust and 'open' communication in Chinese subsidiaries/joint ventures has proved quite challenging in the past due to ownership issues and indigenous cultural affectations ... In what I would term the first wave of IMUE market entry in the 1990s, companies were legally compelled to set up joint venture structures; this inhibited their ability to 'unilaterally' transport practices, although their product/promotional approaches – due in part to their partners' faith in their expertise – were fundamentally ethnocentric ... What has happened as IMUEs have been able to take full control or acquire entities more recently, has brought about an interesting change where companies have taken a more 'country of origin' approach with their managerial/HRM approaches accompanied by a more local 'market-led' approach with their product, format, promotional and marketing mixes (partially driven by increasing local competition) ... The reality is, however, that companies have learnt as they have gone along ... certainly the cultural context within which they operate does not make the transposition of archetypal HRM practices such as trust and communication easy, given 'concepts of managerialism' that exist within Chinese culture ...

Based on my interviews with, and observation of, 'local leader' behaviour (at country, region, city and store level) in Chinese IMUEs I have found/seen that many of these actors feel uncomfortable with some of the values, policies and practices that have flowed from the parent ... In the case of *communications*, although companies like Walmart have tried to implant notions such as a managerial 'open door' policy, Chinese workers are very suspicious of such initiatives ... Managers in China see themselves as fulfilling a more *'transactional'* (i.e. checking, policing, monitoring and punishing) rather than *'transformational'* (i.e. motivational, inspirational and supportive) role ... Also, the idea of *'two-way'* communication seems mystifying to many Chinese given that their social and educational conditioning has been centred upon *'tell and do'* rather than *'ask and contribute'* ... Speaking up in public is not a natural trait; *collectivism* dictates that you should not shame or embarrass your co-workers by demonstrating more knowledge than them or personally *'losing face'* by getting something wrong ... also traditional interviewing techniques fall down often – prospective staff fear communicating any information about themselves due to their worries as to how it 'might be used against them or their families' ... As regards *trust*, one of the main issues is that the word is rather 'light' in Chinese by getting something wrong ... also traditional interviewing techniques fall down often – prospective staff fear communicating any information about themselves due to their worries as to how it 'might be used against them or their families' ... As regards *trust*, one of the main issues is that the word is rather 'light' in Chinese translation, being subsumed by a far more powerful adjective '*guanxi*' which means 'connection', 'ties' or 'relationship' ... no trust can exist unless '*guanxi*' is established first ... what are the implications of this? ... it means that 'ties' must be built through acts such as gifting and exchange ... In a broader context this has caused difficulties for IMUEs who have refused to allow their local managers to build '*guanxi*' through gifting with powerful local officials (i.e. the city MUM with the city mayor) at key calendar events ... this not only threatens to 'hold back' business growth in certain regions (particularly during the recent slowdown and rising rents, wages, product costs, etc.) but is extremely embarrassing for local managers who feel that they have 'lost face' by not showing sufficient respect ... in some cases this is a major reason why local managers might leave and work for local firms ...

In spite of these embedded norms and customs, there is some evidence that *some elements* of leadership/managerial practices are changing and that IMUEs are actually affecting the behaviours and policies of local companies ... Why? ... First, local nationals that have either been educated at western institutions or worked in developed contexts are far more comfortable with so-called 'best-practice' HRM techniques such as open communications and fostering trust through good leadership practice (i.e. putting a high premium on training and development, talent building, performance-related reward, etc.); these managers are able to model behaviours that can be imitated at workplace level ... Second, the 'flexible' managerial approaches used by companies such as Tesco, Carrefour and B&Q are being diffused into the wider system as managers leave and join local companies ... Take meritocratic progression based on performance and know-how rather than status and authority; this concept is certainly gaining traction in certain companies, particularly those in extremely competitive sectors ... Third, due to social media and travel the emerging middle classes are (in part) becoming more used to more 'western' ways of doing business ... indeed, the ritual of 'guanxi' with local officialdom is not accepted as orthodoxy by all businessmen who have observed the practices of some foreign entrants who have steadfastly refused to allow their employees to 'participate' (at least openly!) ... Fourth (and connected to the previous points), there is evidence that Chinese values are beginning to change as a new generation – born after the cultural revolution, in the 1980s and 1990s – demands more transparency and less corruption and bribery by the political elite ... this generation is more willing to challenge perceived inequity and injustice; although bringing about wholesale changes in attitudes and behaviours is made difficult due to entrenched, well-protected, vested interests! ... IMUEs who want to achieve success in China would therefore be well advised to take a 'hybrid' approach ('best of west and east') if they are to be successful.

5.5 Chapter Summary

This chapter has outlined, first, literatures relating to international service operations, international leadership style preferences and IHRM perspectives and, second, the practices which HMULs deploy to generate 'service provider' commitment within their portfolios coupled with how IMUEs develop these skills, behaviours and attributes. With regards to the literature sections, the elements referring to international service operations detailed how different societies and cultures had differing conceptualisations of what constituted 'good service'. Also, service provider capabilities varied according to patterns of economic evolution and cultural predispositions to working within 'service industry' contexts (i.e. in some societies it is perceived as very low-status). In terms of leadership styles, House et al.'s (2004) seminal study was disaggregated by the author to show that societies that showed the highest propensity for 'self-protective' leadership (i.e. displaying high power distance and uncertainty avoidance with low gender equality) were located in many of the emerging markets which provide the context for IMUE expansion. Some solace is provided by the fact that global value trends show movements towards more emancipative and self-expressive norms, suggesting the possibility of 'isometric convergence' of certain leadership values in the medium term (Inglehart et al. 2010). Also, the IHRM literature provides some evidence as to how IMUEs can avoid pitfalls in attempting to overlay individualist HRM practices in diffuse, collectivist environments (Sparrow and Hiltrop 1997, Ferner 2003).

The second part of the chapter elucidated how HMULs attempted to motivate/ engage their followers and the specific development interventions that IMUEs deployed to facilitate this behaviour. The narratives that emerge from these accounts reinforce the fact that the development interventions IMUEs deploy to raise *capability* must be sufficiently *compatible* and 'fit for purpose' (with both aptitude levels *and* cultural predispositions). Based on the evidence provided by the respondents in the Case Studies above, there are a number of solutions to this conundrum, a selection of which includes: offering routes for meritocratic progression (particularly effective in young labour markets), training and development systems which combine 'idiom-friendly' content with 'preferred learning style' delivery mechanisms and HCN manager 'exemplars' that have been exposed to western leadership methods in developed environments (either through placement, rotation or education) that model 'good' leadership behaviour, etc. One outcome of developing better leadership behaviour is to ease the process of implementing change in fast-moving service-based environments, something which is now dealt with in the next chapter.

6 *Implementing Change*

Alongside ensuring control and generating commitment effective HMULs must also implement change. The process of constructing and extending international MUEs involves a high degree of change-based activity, the success of which is dependent upon the executional skills of the middle-management cadre in the field. Also, firms building their international reach through subsidiary/affiliate 'system' growth are subject to external global, regional and national economic, technical, competitive and consumer-related forces. The way in which firms adapt quickly to these changes is, as previous chapters have elucidated, contingent upon their levels of structural and ideological flexibility. Constant change means that MUEs are constantly looking at how they might improve their quality, service and value attributes but, in doing so, will be appraising how they improve work-flow design and behaviours. However, their *responsiveness* is only one dimension of the degree to which they will be able to cope with change, the other being the means through which they *plan* and *implement* change (Jansen et al. 2012). This is made all the more complex in an international context given the distance changes have to travel, with alterations/interventions having to be made to initiatives either at parent or subsidiary/affiliate stages in order to ameliorate failure. There is also a significant adaptive and executional role to be played by field-based personnel given that they are closest to the customer.

Previous commentary highlighted how change is conceived of in the general academic literature through discussing individual and organisational *barriers* to change and how the correct *'climate'* could aid *transformational* and *incremental* approaches (Edger 2012: 183–91). But how is change conceptualised in the international management literature? Fundamentally, there are three streams which relate to its *temporal* dimensions, *process/transmission* and the *absorptive capacity* of subsidiary/affiliates. Commentary with respect to *timing* refers to *when* and *why* organisations initiate change, with texts on *process* and *capacity* relating to *how* they do so. There is scant research into what field-based operatives in international firms do to enact change, most texts assuming an organisational level of analysis. Hence, following this analysis of the literature, this chapter – through outlining some of the change-related findings of the research underpinning this book – will set out what HMULs do in order to implement change in international multi-site situations. It will be argued that although methods vary according to context there are some universal approaches that are adopted in order to ensure effectiveness, including: *shaping mindsets*, building field-level absorptive *capacity, continuous process improvement* and *knowledge diffusion*.

6.1 Temporal Dimensions

Previously, scholars have examined the stages through which organisations need to transition in order to effect change, including the notions of unfreezing, moving and refreezing (Lewin 1951). However, there is another temporal dimension to change which relates to *why* organisations enact change which has been framed according to three phases: anticipatory, reactive and crisis (Carnall 2007). For the purposes of this book the author would argue that on the basis of the extant literature these phases could be redrawn as reimagining, retaliating and rushing. These are outlined below.

- Reimagining – In this paradigm organisations are conceived as being in a constant quest for renewal and reinvention, shaping rather than being shaped by their external environment . Hence firms such as Apple do not follow but lead – in their case by reimagining how stores should sell technology (in their case by application/features rather than product category). Organisations constantly refresh products, structures and behaviours through relentless continuous improvement supported by high levels of internal coherence which transform insights into action. A culture prevails where workers do not fear change but accept it as the norm, a means of competitive advantage that is based upon the *benefits* of constant renewal (i.e. sales and job security) outweighing its costs (i.e. disruption and discretionary effort). The issue for firms choosing to adopt this position are the levels of tangible and intangible resources required for an 'open', integrated culture to sustain the dynamics of ingenuity.
- Retaliating – According to this contingency view organisations are forced to readjust mindsets and behaviours in order to respond to perceived external threats. Hence, the basis for change is framed around arguments that should the firm fail to retaliate to market adjustments, it will be left behind. Often these appeals fail in firms that lack a change culture, especially if the organisation is still performing successfully. Workers who are not conditioned to accept change as 'business as usual' might resist unless the costs of not doing so are communicated effectively. One means by which companies can elicit a behavioural response is to use the so-called 'barbarian at the gates' strategy, although this approach can lose currency if the 'clear and present danger' fails to materialise.
- Rushing – At the extreme end of the curve, organisations confronting extreme crises can use a 'burning platform' position (i.e. declining sales, margins and market share) as a powerful reason to take what might have been viewed previously as unpalatable actions in order to force through changes to systems, structures and behaviours. The problem with this approach is that 'unlearning' old behaviours is extremely difficult and resistance might still be high. In order to effect change quickly, organisations might have to resort to drastic steps such as changing people rather than behaviours.

6.2 Process and Transmission

In a cross-national context whilst the factors alluded to above will have a mediating effect on *when* change is triggered, *how* it is enacted will be complicated by cultural specificity (French 2010). There are two main views in the literature about how change processes should flow effectively, one taking a top-down normative approach, and the other adopting an incremental knowledge-based perspective (with Volberda et al. 2001 integrating both perspectives into their idealised 'model of strategic renewal'). Both of these transmission mechanisms will be outlined below, followed by a section considering the cross-national dimensions of team-working. This is important because whilst the change literature (even in international texts) takes a fairly universal approach to transmission – stressing the importance of participation, involvement and consultation – it is clear that given some of the aforementioned cultural dimensions, different contexts require different applications.

6.2.1 NORMATIVE TOP-DOWN

Many international change frameworks (whether they admit it or not) tend to take their lead from the change guru Kotter, proposing a sequential top-down change process that includes elements such as 'urgency', 'building a guiding team', 'creating visions', 'communicate', 'empower', 'short-term wins', 'don't let up' and 'make change stick' (see Kotter and Cohen 2002 and Edger 2012: 187–8). One of the better constructs is offered by Lane et al.'s 'appraise', 'initiate' and 'reinforce' model which poses a number of useful questions for change makers, acting as a useful checklist for action (2009: 235–50):

- Appraising readiness for change
  - *Visibility* – Which phase are you in (i.e. reactive or rushed)? How do you need to explain changes?
  - *Top support* – How committed are the opinion formers? What is their communications capability?
  - *Change agent appraisal* – Do you have the requisite change skills?
  - *Target group identification* – What is the current ability and motivation of the group targeted by, or involved in, the change?
- Initiating change and adopting new behaviour
  - *Selection and training* – Are the right people in the right place?
  - *Building support for change*:
    i) Road map – Are all stakeholders included?
    ii) Establish need – Are the costs/negative outcomes of previous behaviours clearly stated?
    iii) Obtain commitment – Have you established 'buy-in'?
    iv) Participation – Are people fully involved in the change effort?
  - *Overcoming common roadblocks*:
    i) Poor communication – Are line managers adequately equipped to communicate changes? Is there a need for a third-party intermediary for feedback in different cultures?
    ii) Absence of trust – Are the change makers adequately conducting face-to-face meetings to allay fears?
    iii) Rampant self-interest – Are participants/recipients aware of the upside benefits?
    iv) Scepticism/low change tolerance – Are there too many change initiatives?
  - *Transition devices* – Are the right facilitators (internal or external) in place? Have the appropriate task forces got the right resources?

- *Ongoing honest communications* – Are quick wins being showcased? Is '*victory*' being proclaimed too soon?
- Reinforcing the change
  - *Reward new behaviours* – Are incentives (financial or emotional) fit for purpose?
  - *Align measures* – Do the organisation's KPIs and monitoring/evaluation systems support the new changes?
  - *Benchmark* – Are changes being measured appropriately against previous outcomes (or external best practice)?
  - *Ensure ongoing change readiness*:
    i) People – motivation, skills and abilities;
    ii) Tasks – ensure core tasks are fluid rather than fixed;
    iii) Openness – stay in touch with internal and external environment;
    iv) Organisation – structures (check accountability at all levels), systems (make sure employees are 'connected' to one another) and reward (ensure *person-based* rather than job-based pay).

As outlined previously (Edger 2012: 189), other means of effecting change, if resistance within the core organisation is too high or it lacks the capacity for radical transformation, is to create or buy structures that sit outside the dominant organisational paradigm (Christensen and Overdorf 2000). Some firms have been exceptionally successful (acting in an ambidextrous manner) at creating a 'disruptive space' in which they permit independent agents and structures to evolve, decoupled from the existing entity:

> some companies have actually been quite successful at both exploiting the present and exploring the future, and as we looked more deeply at them we found that they share important characteristics. In particular, they separate their new, exploratory units from their traditional, exploitative ones, allowing for different processes, structures, and cultures; at the same time, they maintain tight links across units at the senior executive level. In other words, they manage organizational separation through a tightly integrated senior team. We call these kinds of companies 'ambidextrous organizations' and we believe they provide a practical and proven model for forward-looking executives seeking to pioneer radical or disruptive innovations while pursuing incremental gains. A business does not have to escape its past, these cases show, to renew itself for the future. (O'Reilly and Tushman 2004: 75)

Thus, decoupled units are granted the autonomy and resources to develop new norms, processes and values outside the constraints of the dominant space (Jansen et al. 2012). As long as these are ring-fenced against interventions from vested interests and politically dominant coalitions within the core, these 'spin outs' can flourish using the resources of the parent. Reverse diffusion might take place, where knowledge, ideas and concepts from this new structure permeate back into the main business. Alternatively, organisations might buy or partner with a firm whose processes, capabilities and values more effectively fit new commercial realities and requirements. Although expensive, this approach can be a fast-track route to achieving more quickly in months what would otherwise have taken years to effect.

6.2.2 KNOWLEDGE TRANSFER/ABSORPTIVE CAPACITY

Previous reference has been made to how firms which sought to generate continuous process improvement utilised systems and frameworks such as TQM (Total Quality Management), EFQM (European Framework for Quality Management), Deming and Six Sigma, the first two stressing content (what to address), the latter concentrating on process (how to address it) (Edger 2012: 190–91). Improvement interventions such as TQM place importance upon the ability of self-managed teams to generate performance improvements at the micro-level of the organisation. Such an approach envisages groups of workers operating in a semi-autonomous environment contributing ideas as to how to make the operation more efficient and effective, formulating best practices which can be disseminated throughout the rest of the organisation. By contrast, EFQM provides a diagnostic model with five interlinked enabling inputs (leadership, people, policy and strategy, partnership and resources and processes) which lead to outputs (people results, customer results, society results and performance). Firms using this model can calibrate where they are and make incremental improvements to identified input areas in order, theoretically, to increase results and performance. By contrast, Deming and Six Sigma concentrate on change process – the former with its 'plan, do, check, act' route map, the latter stressing a 'define, measure, analyse, improve, control' methodology. Also, in-house balanced framework models such as the Tesco Wheel (which has measures attached to customer, people, operations, community and finance) have also been used by organisations as continuous improvement tools.

There are two main issues with these approaches. First, many incremental improvement approaches such as TQM have fallen into disuse and been discredited by lack of management support and their 'stop-start' nature within some contexts. Second, the availability of these frameworks does not mean that they are widely used within multi-unit service environments nor, even where they are applied, that they have any change-making or improvement impact (Van Looy et al. 2003). In 'service shop' contexts (Lashley 1997 and 1999), operational outputs are largely intangible; this is complicated by the fact that process flows (i.e. customer ordering) are intermittent. Controlling all the inputs that feed into service outputs is a complex business, not least due to the primacy of the people factor and the dispersed nature of service outlets. It is for these reasons that co-ordinating and implementing top-down continuous improvement initiatives in service contexts is far more problematic and challenging than in production contexts.

The question therefore remains how change is diffused from the bottom to the top of organisations and vice versa? A stream of literature which I neglected in my previous book, that pertaining to knowledge management, provides some remedies and insights. This body of work has concerned itself with wrestling with the conundrum of how organisations diffuse value-added knowledge throughout their structures for enhanced performance purposes. In the early days of its development the field was dominated by commentators who saw nascent IT systems and technology, which would 'warehouse' knowledge – creating artificial intelligence – as the solution. This approach, however, fell into abeyance when it was noted that although IT provided a platform for 'hard' knowledge collection and dissemination it largely failed (in its early days before web-based applications) to diffuse 'softer', more insightful, knowledge. But what is knowledge and how is its effective diffusion conceptualised by the literature?

In its basest form knowledge can be seen as *data* and *information* (objective facts which are transported around the organisation in multiple forms) which are converted into *insights* (through linkages and attributions), informing action (through a combination of experience, judgement/intuition and values). However, a vital distinction must be made between explicit and tacit knowledge (Polanyi 1957, 1962). *Explicit* knowledge is teachable, articulated, observable, schematic, simple and documented, whilst *tacit* is hidden, unarticulable, hard to teach, rich, complex and undocumented (Winter 1987). Essentially, explicit forms of knowledge can be codified but implicit, tacit forms – developed and 'internalised' over time – are virtually impossible to elucidate in written formats:

> *Knowledge is a fluid mix of framed experience, values, contextual information, and expert insight that provides a framework for evaluating and incorporating new experiences and information*. It originates and is applied in the mind of knowers. *In organisations it often becomes embedded not only in documents or repositories but also in organisational routines, processes, practices and norms. (Davenport and Prusak 2000: 5)*

How is it diffused? Scholars have identified 'open', 'flexible' and 'learning cultures' where organisations view knowledge as a corporate asset, actively encouraging the transfer of knowledge from one unit to another or its external acquisition (Menon and Pfeffer 2003). 'Open' cultures recognise that knowledge can only be created, transferred and transformed through multiple interactions (predominantly *relational*) in order to generate sustainable competitive advantage (Argote 1999, Goh 2002). Issues of size, culture and scale can be overcome by a 'continuous learning' approach where organisations are conceived of as non-hierarchical systems, building and facilitating communities of practice where personal development and 'mastery' are seen as major keys to success (Kolb 1984, Senge 2005).

With respect to the enquiry underpinning this book, a vital contribution is made by Nonaka and Takeuchi (1995) through their *'middle-up-down'* management concept. One of their seven pathways for knowledge creation and diffusion within organisations, this construct conceives senior management setting the vision for the organisation whilst employees confront reality. The gap between both parties is mediated by middle managers (occupying a key intersection point) who synthesise the tacit knowledge flowing from both top and bottom parties into explicit practices and 'ways of doing business'. But how does this conversion from explicit to tacit knowledge take place? In their SECI model of knowledge conversion they frame the transformation process of tacit into explicit knowledge as flowing through a dynamic process where it is converted 'spirally' through the four modes of knowledge conversion: *socialisation* (direct experience), *externalisation* (articulation), *combination* (systemising) and *internalisation* (acquiring new knowledge in practice). Furthermore this tacit knowledge can be subdivided into two categories: technical (know-how) and cognitive (values, beliefs and ideals) (Nonaka and Konno 1998, Nonaka et al. 2000).

Issues arise, however, when internal knowledge markets within firms are hampered by inefficiencies and blockages. Inefficiencies occur when knowledge is hoarded by 'sellers' and there are insufficient mechanisms (such as those encouraging reciprocity) to generate exchange. Also, problems (particularly in international situations) relate to distance and localness where knowledge capture systems tend to be weak or non-existent

Blockages	Solutions
• Lack of trust	• *face-to-face communications*
• Different cultures/languages/frames of reference	• *education, team building, job rotation*
• Lack of time	• *create temporal and physical space*
• Status/Power	• *collapse hierarchies*
• Limited recipient absorptive capacity	• *educate employees for flexibility*
• Knowledge hoarding	• *'ideas more important than status'*
• Error intolerance	• *remove sanctions and retribution*

Figure 6.1   Solutions to knowledge transfer blockages (adapted from Davenport and Prusak 2000: 97)

due to high search costs. Multiple blockages to knowledge diffusion within organisations are common, although some solutions can ameliorate the process:

Several blockages in Figure 6.1 above, relate to behavioural factors which can be addressed through organisational-level cultural and values interventions. In addition many of the solutions involve structured and unstructured strategies for knowledge transfer. Structured solutions (more appropriate for explicit transfer) include manuals, IT hubs, workshops, training, technical reports, assignments, rotation and e-mail. Platforms that encourage a more unstructured approach include face-to-face meetings, social events, knowledge fairs, open forums, 'sitting with Nellie', etc. But which transmission mechanisms are the most effective with regard to codifying and transferring tacit knowledge? The broad conclusion from the literature is that personal interaction (so-called 'social capital') is the most effective form to leverage implicit knowledge, with two aspects relating to *content* and *process* standing out as particularly important:

• Stories and narratives – As humans are programmed to think narratively/emotionally rather than structurally/rationally the best way of conveying 'grounded truths' is through stories and aphorisms which are encoded with meaning. These can be conveyed face to face or, increasingly, through online video and podcast technology.
• Spontaneous interactions – A large body of work stresses the importance of 'unstructured liaisons' such as coffee machine and canteen chats, where individuals exchange insights and knowledge through conversations in unthreatening environments. The obvious issue, in multi-unit contexts, is how these interactions can occur given 'virtual' working arrangements and the fragmented nature of this organisational form. Solutions to this problem include creating 'social space' around structured events such as team meetings, conferences and training sessions.

Whilst knowledge transfer includes creation, transmission and use, it also encompasses absorptive capacity, i.e. 'the ability to recognise the value of new external information, assimilate it and apply it to commercial ends' (Cohen and Levinthal 1990: 128) or 'the capacity of an organisation to purposefully create, extend, or modify its resource base' (Helfat et al. 2007: 4). However, as organisational life is invariably frenetic and managers are hampered by Mintzberg's (2009) conundrum of superficiality (how do you get in deep when there is so much to be done?), issues persist around how organisations create absorptive capacity within their management cadres in order to take on board and transmit important knowledge. In their important article 'MNC knowledge transfer, subsidiary absorptive capacity and HRM', Minbaeva et al. (2003) advance a conceptual model (building upon insights from HRM scholars such as Huselid 1995) that suggests that this can be achieved through building employee *abilities* and *motivations*.

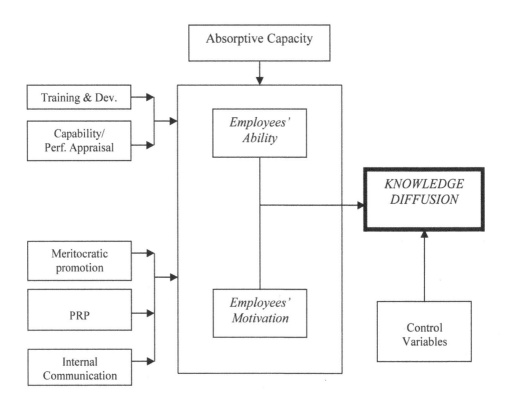

Figure 6.2   Conceptual model of absorptive capacity (adapted from Minbaeva et al 2003: 591)

Effectively what Minbaeva et al. argue is that investment in high-performance HRM work systems (training, appraisals, meritocratic selection, PRP and communications) at a subsidiary level will increase capability and absorptive capacity, leading to more effective knowledge transfer up and down the organisation. Usefully, they also point to a number of control variables as having an impact upon the whole process, not least: *subsidiary age* (older subsidiaries tend to be more autonomous and innovative), *relative size of subsidiary* (larger = more diffusion), *strategic mission* (its clarity helps actors determine which knowledge is most important), *share of expatriates* (greater the number = more knowledge dispersed), *cultural relatedness* (similarities/differences of both source and recipient firms), *home and host country* (differences in economic, political, technological and socio-cultural characteristics of local environments) and *industry* (globalisation cycle).

6.2.3 CROSS-CULTURAL TRANSFUSION

The problem of disseminating change across cultures is addressed in the literature in two ways. First there is the 'geoleader' genre which conceives of culturally adept international managers (developed either through life/work experience and/or training) successfully transfusing change initiatives across borders. The second is the cross-national team literature which examines how teams incorporating members from different cultures should operate. Generally teams are set up with the purpose of generating ideas or solutions to specific business challenges and/or incremental learning. But how should effective teams function? Belbin (2000a, b) stresses the importance of teams having a balance of profiles, a factor that is complicated further within international contexts. According to Snow et al. (1993) the purpose and constitutions of transnational teams can vary according to task, contract and geography:

- Business development (multiple nationalities);
- Regional head offices (several nationalities from a single region);
- Functional (several nationalities from a particular function);
- International joint venture (equal national representatives);
- Corporate head office (a corporate-level team of multiple nationalities).

Task Strategies	Cultural Determinants
Establish Purpose	
mission, goals, measures	Being vs Doing, Task vs Relationship
membership, priorities,	Hierarchy, Low vs High Context
schedules, budget	Individualism vs Collectivism
Task Structure	
agenda, 'engagement rules',	Uncertainty Avoidance
time management, deadlines,	Monochronic vs Polychronic
division of labour	High vs Low Context
Role & Resp. Assignment	
accountabilities, leader role,	Individualism vs Collectivism
facilitator, resource assignment,	Power and Status
attendance, delegation of	Uncertainty and Control
responsibilities (skills and	Task vs Relationship
competencies)	
Reaching Decisions	
whom? (leader or team), how?	Individualism vs Collectivism,
(consensus, vote, compromise)	High vs Low Context, Hierarchy

Figure 6.3 Task strategies and cultural determinants affecting the management of multicultural teams (adapted from Schneider and Barsoux 2003: 221–9)

Issues relate to the fact that, due to differing cultural values and embedded norms, members will have preferences for certain roles, rules and rituals. But what are the task and process strategies for managing multicultural teams, and the culturally-related determinants that can act as a facilitator/barrier to smooth interactions occurring?

Figure 6.3 above considers the types of tasks confronting multicultural teams and the cultural contingencies that will apply. Whilst there will always be initial teething problems with regard to each task, given members' allegiances towards their function, business or country units there are also (potentially) powerful cultural determinants that will shape behaviours. Therefore team members from 'Anglo' cultures are likely to be highly task driven when devising an agenda, whilst colleagues from collectivist cultures are likely to be far more deliberative and consensual. With regard to structuring the task itself individuals from a polychronic background (where time is seen as 'open') are likely to have issues with team members from monochronic cultures (where time is seen as being highly structured and regimented). Comparisons are often made in the literature between German monochronic approaches (need for order and rigid agendas) and French polychronic perspectives (open agendas in pursuance of *la idée*). The question of assigning roles and responsibilities – particularly the team leader role (if one isn't pre-appointed) – is important, not least because different cultures have different views on what a leader should be and do. Germans view authority and legitimacy being connected to technical

Process Strategies	Cultural Determinants
Team Building	
trust establishment, social activities time	Task vs Relationship Monochronic vs Polychronic High vs Low Context
Communication Choice	
language, presentations, conversation, technology	Power, Individualism vs Collectivism High vs Low Context, Monochronic vs Polychronic
Eliciting Participation	
equality, fairness of contribution, listening/interrupting, dynamics of flow	Power Individualism vs Collectivism
Resolving Conflict	
managed, avoided, confronted, accommodated, negotiated, distributive vs integrative outcomes	Task vs Relationship Power, Individualism vs Collectivism
Evaluating Performance	
how (two way)?; direct or indirect (feedback)?	High vs Low Context, Power, Individualism vs Collectivism

Figure 6.4   Process strategies and cultural determinants affecting the management of multicultural teams (adapted from Schneider and Barsoux 2003: 221–2, 229–39)

proficiency, whilst countries with a high power distance appoint on the basis of political power and influence. In terms of reaching decisions, whilst individualist Anglo countries might take a vote for democratic/compromise purposes, members from high context South Asian domains might not put forward a proposal as it is assumed that – given the leader has already decided – universal approval is guaranteed.

In terms of process, strategies for coping with the conduct of meetings also have high cultural contingencies (Figure 6.4). Of particular interest are the means by which teams choose to communicate and the manner in which they do so. Selection of language might confer dominance upon a particular native group, whilst the 'sociolinguistics' of a group helps shape the patterns of team dynamics (Donnelon 1996). For instance members of some cultures (particularly high context) prefer not to interrupt and value silence, whilst individuals from other countries are conditioned to view silence as weakness, preferring 'table tennis' discussions. Also, different cultures have different norms with regards to resolving conflict, those deriving from individualist cultures having a preference for 'zero sum game' distributive solutions, whilst those from collectivist cultures preferring 'mutual gain' integrative justice (at least on the surface). In terms of evaluating team performance, members from heterogeneous Anglo countries have a preference for direct feedback so that differences can be dealt with upfront, whilst members of collectivist homogenous cultures prefer giving feedback in less public situations for fear of upsetting authority or co-workers.

6.3 HMUL Change-Based Practices

The literature above referred to the desirability of transformational change being promulgated within organisations in a 'reimagining' rather than a 'retaliative' or 'rushed' manner, and successful 'knowledge-based' organisations following a 'middle-up-down' form of incrementalism (Nonaka and Takeuchi 1995). Successful organisations are also deemed to act in an 'ambidextrous' fashion, creating space for innovative structures to flourish alongside the operational core (O'Reilly and Tushman 2004). In international contexts teams working on top-down change initiatives and projects, which include members from disparate cultures, need to be formed, run and measured sensitively, taking account of idiosyncratic cultural preferences and dispositions for optimal outputs (Schneider and Barsoux 2003). However, organisations should recognise that 'social capital' rather than structured channels of information exchange are more effective means of transferring 'tacit' knowledge given the way that humans process information in narrative/emotional rather rational/functional terms (Polanyi 1957, 1962). Also, the successful transfusion of change in international organisations is contingent upon the 'absorptive capacity' (i.e. ability and motivation) of recipients within the subsidiary, something that can be accelerated through high-performance HRM interventions (Minbaeva et al. 2003). However, to what extent do any of these insights apply to the IMUEs considered during the research for this book, and, more pertinently, how do HMULs enact change within their portfolios in international corporate contexts?

With regards to the former question, many aspects of the best practice approaches outlined in the sections above were evidenced amongst some of the organisations examined during the course of this research. Care was taken to construct and facilitate multicultural team-working (often with external consultant guidance), and organisations, for the most part, attempted 'pre-emptive' change either through existing or specially constructed structures. However two things were particularly striking. First, the speed of technological change heralded by wireless, cloud and web-enabled technology, fundamentally altering consumer purchasing behaviour (i.e. searching, choosing, buying, collecting, etc.), meant that many firms were being forced to *adjust* their ways of communicating and transacting with customers at an exceptionally rapid rate. In some cases technological innovation around customer order capture and payment was beginning to outstrip resources and capability (with regards to both conception and implementation) in some IMUEs. Second, at an organisational level, due to the costs associated with encouraging tacit, social capital-based knowledge exchanges (i.e. through rotations, conferences, events, social gatherings, etc.) and the fact that many organisations continued to believe in 'rational' (i.e. written) rather than 'relational' forms of diffusion, important insights remained buried within organisations. Indeed, few organisations either encouraged or utilised the types of 'middle-up-down' processes of knowledge dissemination advanced by scholars. However, given the enquiry of this book, how did effective HMULs, first, implement change when they were asked to by the organisation and, second, how did they seek to continuously improve activities and processes within their portfolios? In the case of the former, as the sections below will elucidate, they concentrated upon *adjusting mindsets* and *creating capacity* to take on board change; in the case of the latter, they were adept at fostering *continuous process improvements* and *knowledge diffusion* within their portfolio. These will now be considered in turn.

6.3.1 ADJUSTING MINDSETS

Change is an unremitting feature of organisational life. External forces such as the macro-economic environment, competitor activity (particularly local champions in IMUE contexts), government intervention, technological innovation and enhanced consumer expectations increase the pressure upon IMUEs to evolve their formats, product quality, pricing and means of service delivery. In response to these pressures organisations have to constantly review, adapt and modify their business models to ensure that they maintain efficiency and effectiveness. Change programmes are promulgated – either at a global or local subsidiary/affiliate level – in an attempt to anticipate or react to these dynamics, with emphasis being given to improving operational/technological capabilities and associated behaviours. However, the *process* of implementing change is dependent on creating an environment where recipients are in a state of 'readiness' with mindsets that are adjusted to embrace rather than resist. If the definition of mindset is a *'cognitive bias'* – a set of established assumptions held by individuals or groups that inform behaviours and choices that can create 'mental inertia' through 'groupthink' (Janis 1972) – organisations have a major task in ensuring that their people maintain a high degree of open-mindedness and flexibility in order to absorb and enact vital initiatives. What are the main issues that IMUEs face in adjusting mindsets, how do they do it and what part do HMULs have to play?

IMUEs face operational and cultural issues in attempting to inculcate a 'change acceptance' mindset within their organisations. From an *operational* perspective, problems relating to relevance and distance impinge heavily. Are changes originating from the parent 'fit for purpose' in foreign contexts? For instance, changes to work systems, tasks and process flows that are deemed appropriate in one context are not necessarily applicable in others unless levels of resources, capability and expertise are sufficiently factored into programmes. Also, organisations must always take account of the fact that whilst change seems rational from a corporate perspective, the fact that in the past its benefits have been overstated in comparison to personal costs (job security, time, effort, disruption, etc.) means that initiatives might be met with scepticism, resistance and/or sabotage. In many cases, from an operational point of view, the field will often apply its own 'patch ups' and 'workarounds' in order that the ends of the initiative are fulfilled without resort to (defective) means of implementation (Edger 2012: 203–6). The degree to which the organisation actively learns from these interventions/inputs by providing feedback loops to incrementally improve change initiatives has a high contingent effect on their long-term sustainability and success – something that is not made easy given issues pertaining to distance, time and space for IMUEs. Also – from a *cultural* perspective – problems of 'cognitive bias' are particularly pertinent with regards to the issue of adjusting mindsets. Change implies 'resetting' assumptions, actions and behaviours, but how is this possible in developing market cultures that might display some or all of the following characteristics noted by scholars: an aversion to interventions from *outsiders*, a *temporal* disposition that militates against rapidity, a preference for *fatalistic submission* rather than forced progress and low levels of *achievement orientation* in terms of goal attainment?

How do IMUEs adjust mindsets amongst their people to accept change as an imperative and what part do HMULs have to play within their own teams? Substantial reference in this book has already been made to the ways in which organisations '*socialise*' members to accept new values and ways of working through immersion programmes, educational interventions and role models (i.e. senior staff and expatriates) who set the 'benchmark' for desired behaviour. In addition the fact that many of the values in emerging economies are transitioning towards more secular 'developed' paradigms (i.e. equality, participation and self-expression) is of assistance (Inglehart et al. 2010). But given the relatively fixed and embedded nature of many cultural traits (due to religion and/or national business systems), organisations cannot afford to let up in both extrinsic and intrinsically-based efforts to ensure adaptability and flexibility, especially at the point of implementation.

At middle-management level, HMULs, sandwiched between the architects of change and its execution on the ground, play a vital role in the change process being successful. How do they cope both personally and managerially? In order to become part of the solution rather than the problem they must firstly address and adjust their own 'cognitive bias' and prejudices (Edger 2012: 194). Contra behaviours (i.e. resistance, 'bad mouthing', despondency, etc.) will be imitated by their charges. They must 'buy into' and transmit the fact that stasis is not an option given the challenges faced by the organisation – complacency, when the company seems to be performing well, is the harbinger of future failure. To this extent 'upselling' (without inflating) the benefits to compensate for the costs that will be incurred during the change process, is a particularly important leadership role fulfilled by the HMUL. Alongside mental and behavioural preparedness, however, HMULs must possess significant managerial nous in order to implement change successfully at a local level, organising their human and physical resources effectively to create 'capacity' to take on board and enact change, a process that is examined in the section below.

Case Study 14 – Upselling Change into an IMUE Indian Subsidiary

Robin Jarvis is the International Operations Director for Anglo-American, Inc. (AAI) – all pseudonyms – a multi-site wholesaler that has attempted to obtain a foothold in the Indian market through greenfield site acquisition and organic growth.

The first thing to say about the Indian market is that it is not homogenous – the greater Mumbai market differs completely from other conurbations, especially in the South. Dialects, the level of infrastructure, access to well-appointed land and real estate, skill levels and degrees of retail 'sophistication' are variable to a degree that I have found in few other growth markets ... factors in themselves that make growing a multi-site wholesale network more difficult and complicated than almost anywhere else ... With regards to 'upselling change' and embedding it there are a number of issues we have encountered in our Indian operation and some specific interventions we have applied in order to facilitate their transmission and adoption ...

The first thing to say about this market is that it is very *hierarchical* ... people are very conscious of their positions and what 'is' and 'isn't' their responsibility ... for instance, in one of our US sites if a manager sees any garbage or litter on the floor they will just pick it up ... in India, managers will get somebody else to do it! ... In this society the *caste system* plays a major part in people's preconceptions of what 'they' and 'others' should do ... Also from an *employment law* perspective there are particular rules regarding workers' rights and you tend to find that a lot of staff are recruited on a temporary basis first ... In addition the *unions* can be very 'difficult' ... to give you an example in one city a particular union insists that we employ 'their people' to unload freight! ... Basically you have to understand employment law peculiarities both at national and regional level to calibrate your levels of flexibility and 'room for manoeuvre' ... Obviously such cultural and legal characteristics can act as inhibiters to introducing things like new service programmes and notions of multiple-tasking/demarcation removal ... people will have the mindset that it isn't their place to do certain tasks and/or say that changing/introducing certain practices and systems isn't possible due to the law! ... The question is how we have overcome this?! ...

The way in which we have overcome resistance to change is, first, through the decision we took to develop the business in an organic rather than acquisitive manner ... this has meant that we have avoided some of the legacy organisational culture issues that we might have encountered – even though it has meant that growth has been slower ... Second, we appointed a US manager of Indian parentage to run the operation (even though he had been born and raised in the US he spoke the dialect of the first territory we penetrated and had family in the area) ... this meant we had somebody conversant with the way in which we did things but also sensitive to the cultural values of the context we were going into ... Third, for the first unit we opened, we seconded managers out of our US and UK operations to 'set it up right' with locally appointed management ... this set the template for the way in which we wanted the operation to be run ... Fourth, we recruited well-educated 'local managers' who 'wanted to get on' and trained them in AAI systems and standards ... we actually sent out two supervisors (both Indians who could speak the local language) to train in the customer service system levels required: how teams should work together (for instance when queues built up at the tills) and the values we held dear as regards customer service (which are contained in a simple four-step programme) ... our ethical standards were also incorporated into the operation (i.e. no bullying, firm but fair, treating people with respect, etc.) in written, taught and modelled form ...

We believe that as we have patiently built the business up from one unit we have actually *built a culture* that is pretty accepting of change – highly necessary because as we have rolled out more sites changes have inevitably been needed ... But as we have also worked upon being a *'nice place to work'* with good wages (including the same bonus system as the US/UK) and conditions, we have found that our turnover is pretty low (some managers that have left have even come back!) ... We also have a management trainee scheme in place to ensure that as sites become vacant we put well-equipped managers in place who are able to lead large teams; because India is no different in many respects to anywhere else – the right manager in the right unit pays enormous dividends! ... In particular they are capable of explaining why change is needed both to the staff and union representatives so that they can attempt flawless execution.

6.3.2 CREATING CAPACITY

Derived from economics, the notion of capacity – in behavioural terms – refers to the extent to which individuals can use their 'installed productive capacity' (i.e. abilities and motivation) in order to optimise outputs. However, there is a relationship between capacity and outputs. If demands upon individuals grow, increasing capacity is utilised, placing limitations upon output quality and performance. Hence, organisations should both measure *and* work within their capacity constraints, or increase levels of absorptive capacity amongst their staff in order to provide a degree of output surety. Doing the day job *or* concentrating upon implementing change cannot be a binary choice for employees in MUEs – they must do both. The challenge is how organisations manage both complementary processes, ensuring that neither is degraded by the other. What operational and cultural challenges do organisations face creating capacity, how do they solve them and what part do HMULs play at field level?

The main issue that IMUEs face, given their requirement for unrelenting change in the face of rapidly changing external conditions (wrought by economic, technological and consumer forces), is the scale, rate and complexity that confronts them both in terms of the content and process of change. Simply put, there is too much to do, with too little time available. Added to which, in emerging markets due (in some cases) to external labour markets being mismatched with corporate needs, capability issues place real constraints on their ability to effect transformation quickly. The way in which they resolve this conundrum is, first, create subsidiaries/affiliates with the requisite absorptive capacity through carefully designed HRM systems that ensure that ability and motivation levels are 'fit for purpose' (see 6.2.2 above). Second, they pay due regard to scheduling and processes, ensuring that enough 'bandwidth' exists (i.e. time to complete allotted 'fixed' and 'variable' tasks with allotted resources). Often this activity is regulated by enterprise resource planning (ERP) systems or deputed 'gatekeepers' or 'filters' such as operational planning executives (OPEs) that sit between the corporate technocracy and the line. Third, organisations will ensure that operatives – expected to implement changes – already have the right 'tools to do the job' (i.e. machinery, technology, information, staff, etc.) so they are not distracted 'fixing' one defective process whilst being exhorted to change another. Fourth, changes (and the standing orders underpinning them) require simplicity for executional purposes, so that they can be understood and embedded as an 'everyday way of life' as quickly as possible.

How do HMULs create capacity at field level? Mimicking central approaches, they adopt 'local' organisational and HRM approaches to creating capacity in the context of implementing change. To be sure, wave after wave of unremitting change (especially when it is ill-conceived, communicated and implemented) can cause issues such as stress, paralysis, burn-out and disillusionment at field level within MUEs. The originators of top-down initiatives – be they the corporate centre or subsidiary head office – can become despised and ridiculed, with operatives adopting (at best) an ambivalent attitude to the latest 'fashion' or 'fad'. As stated in 6.3.1 above, effective HMULs will attempt to adjust mindsets to accept the principle and necessity of change but might be constantly undermined by some of their (to put it politely) inexactitudes. From a 'local' organisational standpoint, in order to ease the process of implementing change, effective HMULs will create capacity within their districts in three ways. First, they will appoint 'leads' or 'change champions' with the requisite skills, knowledge and energy that act as 'point people' for the portfolio on initiatives and upgrades. This serves the dual purpose of preserving their own capacity for action whilst devolving responsibility (if not accountability) to line level where the 'rubber hits the road'. Second, relatedly, given that those directly responsible for implementing changes at store level become acquainted with the nuances and detail of the changes, they are best placed to suggest 'patch ups' and 'workarounds' that might ease their implementation, freeing up valuable capacity for other imperatives to be satisfied. Third, HMULs will draw down resources and support from all their 'enabling networks' within the wider organisation (i.e. trainers, functional experts, peers, etc.) to help them successfully 'bed in' changes (Edger 2012: 170–73). From a 'local' HRM perspective effective HMULs will increase capacity/ discretionary effort in order to drive productive output through selection and training interventions (ramping up skill levels) and reward, public recognition, 'treats' and promotional mechanisms which provide extra motivational stimulus. What they don't do is adopt a *self-protective* leadership position in which they abandon all accountability to their charges in a self-serving 'pass the buck' manner. Such behaviour undermines two fundamental requirements of leadership whatever the cultural context, namely, follower trust and confidence (House et al. 2004).

Case Study 15 – Creating Capacity in Emerging Market Local Leaders

Dr Nollaig Heffernan, Chartered Psychologist, teaches resilience, leadership and change management to multi-site leaders in emerging markets (particularly the Middle Eastern Gulf States). Designer of the ILM 72 psychometric test, she teaches at the EHL (Ecole Hotelier Lausanne), is a visiting lecturer on the MSc in Multi-Unit Leadership at BCBS and is employed as a consultant and coach by many major international corporations. Dr Heffernan has assessed and coached numerous cohorts of emerging market multi-unit leaders with the aid of the MTQ48 personality profiling questionnaire.

It's interesting to look at some academic texts on change in emerging markets and see that some eminent scholars remark upon how – due to so-called *uncertainty avoidance* and *temporal factors* – change is hard to drive through at ground level. My experience training multi-site leaders in emerging markets is slightly different!! What I have found is that the *receptiveness* and *acceptance of change* is very *high* but it is the *managerial capability* to implement successful change that is (sometimes) *low*. During the change management courses that I run with multi-site managers it is not their psychological disposition to the '*why*' that is necessarily an impediment, rather the '*how*'! The real question is how local leaders can create capacity within themselves and their wider team to make change happen?

With regards to the multi-site managers in the emerging markets I teach and train – *change receptiveness* is high. (*Why*?) Fundamentally the emerging countries in which I teach middle managers have had an exponential rate of change that is unimaginable within the developed world. I have literally had senior managers in the room that have recounted stories about how they walked for days across deserts to get resources for their villages and now inhabit ultra-modern metropolis with all the latest mod cons! In many ways they are receptive to the notion of change because they see the economic and social benefit it has brought them and their families. Also, due to the ambient wealth of their countries there is an expectation that fast-paced change and innovation in their countries will continue, the effects being perceived as largely beneficial – a source of great national pride – rather than a threat (as in the case of many inert cash-strapped developed economies). Really the problem relates to how much change these societies can take on board – at times it seems that their propensity to 'go for it' and try things is too ambitious and dangerous, especially when they might lack the ambient capacity to cope.

It is their *capability and capacity* to implement change that is an inhibiter. (*In what way?*) The major insight is that although emerging economies have a burgeoning number of specialist experts who can make vast and grandiose projects happen, they lack *grounded managerial and leadership skills* to ensure flawless execution. Basic managerial skills such as communications (selling the 'benefits' and 'outcomes' to stakeholders and recipients), delegation/empowerment, project management, risk assessment and monitoring are essential skills that underpin the 'human dimensions' that determine whether or not certain initiatives, projects and plans are ultimately successful. This proves fertile ground for many western training consultancies; for instance in country *x* there are over 5,000 training providers peddling 'how to' managerial solutions. Courses such as situational leadership, personality profiling and psychometric testing are particularly popular as local managers want to understand the concepts of 'difference, adaptive style and performance outcomes'. The dangers inherent in this are the degree to which highly educated specialists in emerging markets take courses because they regard them as 'fashionable' or a 'nice to have' on the CV rather than as a practical tool for help!

In the case of multi-site managers, I have come across many dynamic change agents through the courses I teach who measure (on psychometric testing) as favourably as any high-performance managers in the 'west'. Their one distinguishing characteristic is that – broadly speaking – they have already received *practical training and insight* (either by the organisations/expatriates they work for or through acquired experience through international *rotations, placements and assignments*) that has granted them the capability to not just be receptive to change, but to also make it happen!

6.3.3 CONTINUOUS PROCESS IMPROVEMENT

Whilst effecting the global centre or local head office's demands for transformational change programmes and/or top-down initiatives is important, HMULs must also lead and encourage the practice of continuous process improvement at portfolio and unit level. In most MUEs every site is different. Due to footprint constraints (imposed by landlords and/or legacy real estate) and locational differentials that impinge upon the rhythm of the business (i.e. demographic profile, high street versus mall, etc.), the HMUL has ample opportunity to make improvements to the FOH process flows within each site. In addition, rather than accepting BOH standards and procedures as a 'fait accompli', HMUL and their teams have ample opportunity to make *value-added* adaptations that fit with the operational needs of the business (Chang and Harrington 2000). What HMULs should seek to do, when assessing improvements, is examine a process (which can be defined as the movement of 'transformed inputs' consisting of customers, information or materials from one stage to another), and assess whether or not they can make improvements to its speed, cost, dependability, flexibility, quality or safety. Can they eliminate non-value-added activity stages, time-wasting decision points or blockages/pinchpoints? In normative terms process effectiveness is derived from staff, technology, machinery and facilities (the 'transforming inputs') being applied and aligned efficiently to processing aforementioned 'transformed inputs' (Slack et al. 2009). Productivity gains arise when the effort and expense of the 'transforming inputs' are reduced whilst producing a greater volume and quality of outputs. Clearly, at outlet level great advances in efficiencies can be made by organisations that instigate (piloted and proof-tested) process improvements – however, the capacity of individual units (assisted by HMULs and their peers) to make significant differences in operational capability should not be underestimated. However, what issues do HMULs face in attempting to encourage portfolio-wide process improvements and how do they overcome them?

The issues that HMULs face in attempting to encourage a continuous process improvement mentality, are derived from both operational and cultural sources. From an operational point of view HMULs might report to line managers who (due to their own self-protective instincts) go by the dictum 'do it the company way, or the highway!' Although it might offend common sense to think those senior actors and, indeed, some technocrats, would oppose micro-improvements that could benefit operational efficiency it would be a mistake to ignore the 'not invented here' syndrome. In some businesses – such as Walmart when it was run by Sam Walton – 'local leaders' (i.e. regional VPs, unit managers, section managers, etc.) are encouraged to run their parts of the business as if they owned them. Some strategic leaders are constantly exhorting their middle and junior managers to come up with and apply improvements that (if they work) can be diffused throughout the rest of the business (see 6.3.4 below). However, in cultures that are characterised by *high power distance* (i.e. hierarchical and 'stratified') with high levels of *uncertainty avoidance* (i.e. all decisions are deferred to a higher authority), inculcating junior levels of management with the courage and imagination to embark on process improvement is naturally difficult. How do HMULs in exacting cultural multi-site situations overcome these behavioural impediments?

As most HMULs have been unit managers, the first thing that needs to be said is that they have probably been promoted (amongst other reasons) for their ingenuity and proactivity. That is to say, many HMULs in IMUEs have already proved site-level adeptness for initiating micro-process improvements. They will also have a high degree of *curiosity* having garnered a number of insights from a variety of sources such as competitor site visits and observations from other units within the MUE's regional business (or even home country). Now they need to lead by example by, first, making an assessment of the process efficiency of their units and, second, cheerleading and rewarding best practice behaviour. As to the former, HMULs will become acquainted with their individual sites and, whilst doing so, will ask themselves the following questions:

- *Location* – How good is this location? How visible is it? What is its footfall? How can we attract more attention?
- *Car parking* – What is the car parking capacity? How safe and secure is it? Is it used solely by our customers?
- *Layout* – What is the size and layout of the unit? What are the FOH and BOH blockages?
- *Service cycle* – What is the customer journey from entry to exit? How smooth is the experience? What are the *functional* blockages?
- *Experience* – What senses are stimulated positively by the visit? How effective are the *emotional* stimulants?
- *Product and promotion* – Does the range address the local market? Are the promotional mechanics fit for purpose?

Along with their units, HMULs will have a degree of human, physical and financial resources (or sleeve) which they can judiciously deploy (sometimes nefariously) in order to make significant improvements. Also, during a refit the HMUL and his team have a major opportunity to make the store more efficient and attractive (both for themselves and customers) if they work closely with the refit team (i.e. project managers, building managers, architects, store improvement leads, etc.). By and large, however – given that sparkles or refits rarely occur within a four-year cycle in most MUEs – the HMUL is required to rely upon extant resources and latent ingenuity to promulgate process improvements. Effective HMULs are also more likely to stimulate unsolicited, spontaneous behaviour not only through setting an example by doing it themselves but also by rewarding and recognising exemplar improvement behaviours at all levels in their portfolio, fostering a culture of continuous process improvement. As failure is a required feature of improvement and innovation – and therefore might be rejected in cultural environments where rule adherence and obedience are obligatory – HMULs might *transfer risk* from individuals to 'collaborative teams' where increased risk-taking and experimentation is deemed 'safer'. How this knowledge is transmitted across the portfolio and wider organisation is also important and will be the next behaviourally-based change practice to be discussed in the section below.

Case Study 16 – Local Agility and Adaptability in Services-Led IMUEs

The excerpts below are derived from 'services-led' IMUE senior practitioners who were asked to comment and reflect on the degree to which growth market 'host country' field-based personnel (such as area/regional managers/directors) were accountable for driving improvement and innovation at 'micro-levels' within the organisation.

We are a service-based company that delivers optimal solutions for both clients and candidates ... given differences in local labour markets, languages and employment laws we don't look to recruit English speakers as consultants, rather we look for excellent communications and problem-solving skills on the ground ... we want entrepreneurialism albeit within a broad strategic framework ... consultants have to 'pull and chase' ... they have to be agile ... our area managers are there to encourage entrepreneurial behaviours – creating the right solutions for clients ... how do we develop this? ... First, we don't 'force our way'; for instance when we buy a business we generally keep the local leadership who – given they have set up the business – have high levels of innovation anyway ... Second, most of our multi-site personnel are inducted into this 'mindset' of working, having mainly started at consultant level ... Third, we do not penalise people that take the initiative and fail; at some point they will succeed. (Mara Swan, EVP Strategy and Talent, ManpowerGroup)

In our emerging market 'early years business' three things dictate that we require innovative and adaptive thinking in the field – the site/lease, external regulation and individual parent/child requirements ... (*Site*) In one Southern Asian territory, due to land scarcity, the government only guarantees three-year leases for our businesses which requires a fair degree of adaptability and creative thinking among our multi-site managers ... (*Regulation*) Different regulations in different territories mean we have to adapt our practices; in one territory for instance it is necessary for all visitors to the site (children, parents and outsiders) to have their temperatures taken aurally before entering the nursery to prevent the spread of illnesses ... (*Child/ Parent*) Every child is different, as are the levels of parental expectations ... in order to 'forge a bond' with the parents – to ensure we retain happy customers! – we must establish what they want … in Asia this can mean teaching English from a very early age … the point is this – our single and multi-site management must be adaptive and responsive to both local and individual demands, making sure the processes and resources are in place to deliver … how do we encourage this? … by providing our multi-site operators with the systems to drive occupancy *and* ensure safety/consistency but also by empowering them to fulfil customer needs … (John Woodward, EVP KUE Inc., Singapore)

In highly 'intangible' businesses such as 'on-site services' the service solution is really about people … therefore solutions really have to be driven at a local level … In spite of moving to a global sector structure to provide better integrated services to global MNCs, local managers must – due to local requirements – provide discrete service solutions … Within certain territories there will also be a difference in business mix – in the US the emphasis is upon concessions whilst in Poland it revolves around 'technical' facilities management … actually multi-site managers who are entrepreneurial can bring a lot to the party at a local level as there is a different balance of 'pure service' requirements in different territories … (Andy Vaughan, SSD, Sodexo)

In our emerging markets business in Asia (i.e. China, India, Malaysia, Indonesia, Philippines, Vietnam, etc.) we grant a fair amount of autonomy to our Local MDs (typically responsible for up to 15 branches) and our branch managers who really (given the size of their regional/city markets) can be described as 'mini-MDs'. Thus – whilst we have quite standardised global BOH systems (IT, auditing procedures and KPI measures) coupled with a product range that is increasingly becoming generic in nature (product innovation processes have been centralised over the past two years) – local MDs have a fair degree of flexibility and autonomy regarding price/ key account handling and selecting product offer/ranges (from our global category experts). Why? First, each territory has different pest/hygiene problems which need to be dealt with in different ways (due to climate and infrastructure). Second, markets are at different stages in development – particularly with regards to 'hygiene solutions'; in one territory we might be required to get rid of an odour, whilst in others our field-based technicians are required to tackle the source. In order to tailor our services to fit local idiosyncrasies we require local managers who are agile, flexible and innovative, matching product/price/service to their local micro-market needs. The best local MDs and 'mini-MDs' will understand the nuances (*both existing and changing*) of their local markets and customise solutions to achieve optimal 'fit' – without abusing their authority through 'gorging' and/or under-charging … (Jeremy Townsend, CFO, Rentokil-Initial).

6.3.4 KNOWLEDGE DIFFUSION

Whilst it is a fact that most sites have their own positional and operational idiosyncrasies, there are transferable insights that can add significant value both within the HMUL's portfolio and in the wider organisation. The basic premise of this book is that effective

MULs act as 'local leaders in multi-site situations' because, contrary to the view that standardised chain formats are optimally efficient if 100 per cent of their operations are replicated throughout the whole estate, it is the author's belief through a process of intense empirical observation and analysis that the most successful operations – whilst fixing certain immutable facets of their operation (usually BOH standard operating procedures) – adapt themselves to the peculiarities of their local environs. This cannot be done solely on a 'top-down' basis through head office 'guessology', operating as they might hundreds or even thousands of miles from the theatre of operations. How do organisations capture valuable insights in a 'bottom up' manner that can be recycled into general performance-enhancing improvements? The literature above (see 6.2.2 above) referred to barriers that exist during the process of 'upwards' knowledge creation and dissemination within organisations – blockages that can be exacerbated by distance, cultural and micro-political forces between entities in MUEs. How do organisations overcome these problems? Additionally how do HMULs act as a 'middle-up-down' interface within this process and, more specifically – given the nature and focus of their roles – how do they facilitate the transmission of knowledge from one area of their portfolios to another?

In terms of encouraging 'bottom up' knowledge diffusion, which can then be diffused organisation-wide, as has already been mentioned, mechanisms such as senior field visits/'back to the floor' weeks, managerial rotation and active feedback loops (i.e. daily/weekly collection of insights by head office from front-line operators either by telephone conference calls or webinars) can be exceptionally successful in fostering transference. Also conferences, events, post-meeting meals, etc. can encourage 'social capital' interfaces where deep tacit knowledge on how things *should* actually be done in practice, given the shifting dynamics of consumer behaviour, can be productive. A major issue, however, relates to phenomena such as knowledge 'hoarding'; namely, the belief that sharing valuable insights will improve operations against which the possessors of critical insights compete on a daily, weekly and yearly basis. For, whilst organisations compete externally in markets, in most MUEs – given the plethora of league tables, budget measures and targets – strategic business units are also competing against *one another* (region versus region, country versus country, area versus area, district versus district, unit versus district and external markets, etc.). Smart companies will recognise this conundrum by encouraging benefit-based reciprocity systems. 'Sellers' of knowledge will be compensated if they transact with 'buyers' through 'hard' or 'soft' forms of reward and recognition.

But how do HMULs encourage knowledge diffusion across their portfolios? Reference has already been made to the fact that effective HMULs adopt an architectural solution to sharing tangible and intangible resources by splitting their portfolios into geographical 'clusters', 'families' and/or a 'hub and spoke' format where primacy (at the 'hub') is accorded to a 'house of excellence' or unit manager 'lead'. In addition to this structural solution, HMULs will apply relational interventions by leveraging district meetings, away days, training sessions and conferences to allow insights and knowledge to flow between parties informally. In practical terms rotating unit managers or facilitating best-practice visits by unit managers (and sometimes their teams) to exemplar operations (either company owned or competitor) are other means of ensuring knowledge acquisition. This is particularly useful with regards to understanding visible processes such as service cycle efficiency and service provider behaviour. Where practicable, effective HMULs will also engage, horizontally, with their peers and, vertically, with superiors and head office in order to garner valuable insights that they can transfer back into their units.

However, in order to embed knowledge exchange as a sustainable 'day-to-day' activity, the effective HMUL must actively demonstrate that s(he) highly values such practices by visibly recognising 'sellers' who provide beneficiaries (including the HMUL measured at a portfolio level) with – in some instances – major performance improvements.

Case Study 17 – Sharing Best Practice at Haagen Dazs International

Clive Chesser was International Operations Manager for Haagen Dazs (owned by General Mills), responsible for the operations of 680 café stores in 56 countries; one-third company owned, two-thirds run by joint ventures, master and individual franchisees. Here he recalls the process of designing, piloting, capturing best-practice process/content insights and rolling out an international branded service experience internationally.

It had become clear to us that the in-store Haagen Dazs 'brand service experience' (BSE) was not delivering the emotional connection that befitted a brand based around 'indulgence'; there was a mismatch between what the brand stood for in grocery channels and what consumers said that they experienced in our store cafés. In many ways it was worse in mature brand lifecycle markets (such as France, Spain, UK and US) than elsewhere, although developing markets required attention due to cultural issues ... What did I do? ... First, I constructed a major stakeholder map comprising internal (regional VPs, store directors, support functions; HR and marketing) and external stakeholders (master/individual franchisees, and joint venture partners). Then I went out around the world and sold the project ... There was more resistance to the idea of revamping service in markets such as China (positional power factors) and France (brand life cycle) where, culturally, they were not necessarily attuned to the benefits of such a project. In Japan I needed 'four yeses' before I got a real yes! Third, having got broad support and money we engaged consultants and really dug deep to understand the customer journey and the various service touch points. Fourth, we constructed a model for a pilot in four territories; this comprised a completely new service concept 'bringing the brand to life' backed up by intensive interactive training programmes that were adapted to local nuances (although the overall measures for the pilot – sales/customer loyalty/ customer satisfaction) were the same for all. Fifth, we trained out the new 12-step programme with desired behaviours in a 'train the trainer' fashion – top to bottom. So ... making people feel welcome, bringing the brand to life through offering free samples, demonstrating product knowledge, identifying needs, speedy service, fun check backs, etc.

Although the line were absolutely critical in helping us land this project (i.e. in Spain – which accounted for 10 per cent of the estate – the store director was totally enlightened and on board), support was patchy at first. One crucial enabler to the success of the whole project was the regional training directors (particularly the three 'bright and progressive' RTDs representing Latin America, Latin Europe and Southern Asia). Prior to this project these RTDs had not really interacted on an international basis (global HR being run on a devolved regional basis) but this project brought them together. We held a number of formal and informal meetings/calls either as a group or individually ... as the project progressed they were able to share insights and best practice both in relation to what was working in certain markets and also how best to co-opt the operational line (upselling commercial/performance benefits) ... in addition they were pivotal in mobilising their field-based trainers who interacted with local operators to ensure translated materials reflected both the original intentions and central principles of the BSE and local needs/preference ... language was important ... although I was fairly relaxed about local 'iterations', I was reliant on the global training team to ensure a high degree of consistency of interpretation and execution (my Mandarin for instance isn't very good!) ...

Overall the pilot was a huge success with sales increasing by 13 per cent and loyal customers (those likely to repurchase and recommend) increasing from 30 per cent to 43 per cent. Another consultancy engaged purely to measure outputs also reported very positive variances on ROI, other customer satisfaction indices, employee engagement and retention. During roll-out the success of the new service concept continued. Each training and implementation package was customised for the local market (what was permissible in Saudi Arabia for instance was different to Brazil). However, the customer measures remained the same across the world, allowing like-for-like comparisons. I believe the best practice and insights shared amongst the RTDs and their teams was crucial to this project's success ... Also, where the store directors were either culturally or personally tuned into the programme (often through RTD influence), it was a major success as they influenced their franchisees or store managers positively. As a major transformational change programme, the role of the RTDs in capturing, sharing and training out best practice both in *process* and *content* terms, through their close liaison with field operations was pivotal.

6.4 Chapter Summary

This chapter has concerned itself with understanding how internationalising organisations generate change/transfer knowledge in terms of top-down, bottom-up and middle-up-down processes. The first half of the chapter addressed some of the extant literature on these areas, making the observations that due to polychromic 'temporal' frames of reference, high degrees of 'uncertainty avoidance' and an aversion to showing initiative – causing oneself or others to lose face – there might be issues with either generating change and/or diffusing knowledge within certain developing market contexts. Indeed, the narrative themes derived from both the academic texts and *some* of the Case Study evidence suggest that IMUEs are hampered in these areas by a lack of individual 'installed' *capacity* (i.e. abilities and motivations) which, in turn, hampers degrees of *collaboration*. However, some cause for optimism exists, when one dissects respondent accounts relating to HMUL practices and IMUE development interventions. These show that mindsets with regard to top-down change can be re-set through benefit upselling (Case Study 14) and by teaching managers how to create capacity for change initiatives through *basic* managerial training (Case Study 15).

With respect to bottom-up and middle-up-down improvement and best practice knowledge diffusion, solutions are advanced by practitioners (Case Study 16), where 'agile', 'entrepreneurial' and 'flexible' behaviours are fostered in 'pure service' environments through entry-level immersion conditioning and explicit encouragement/ endorsement by IMUEs (i.e. lack of sanctions for failure and good exemplar behaviour). Indeed, one of the contributions that is made by this study (see concluding Chapter 8) – when one triangulates the accounts of practitioners from 'intangible' service-led IMUEs – is the degree to which they permit their local field-based personnel (for sound economic reasons) to customise their offers to local demand to a far greater extent than firms with a higher goods/service mix. In terms of organisational interventions to encourage best practice diffusion reference has previously been made to the creation of forums where social capital can be traded, and the utility of activist central and regional technocrats (see Case Study 17). Also specifically with regard to HMUL portfolios, best practice sharing can be facilitated through well-planned district meetings, social events and architecture (i.e. supportive 'communities of exchange and practice' such as clusters, families and 'hub and spoke' mechanisms).

But, given the specific practices that HMULs are expected to expedite in this, and previous chapters, what are the personal characteristics they must possess in order to have some chance of success? More importantly – examining the empirical evidence provided thus far – what are the development interventions that IMUEs can deploy to elevate the technical/cognitive skills and behaviours of this vital cadre of local leaders?

7 *Characteristics and Development*

The previous chapters outlined the performance factors that influence IMUEs at both parent/owner and subsidiary/partner level, followed by consideration of the activities and practices of field-based local leaders. Understanding what local leaders should do in IMUEs is important, but this book would be incomplete without addressing the skills-based, behavioural and cognitive *personal characteristics* that IMUEs require from this vital cohort to expedite key operational imperatives. More importantly, how do they *develop* these characteristics?

Local leaders in IMUEs – such as HMULs – are instrumental in ensuring that strategic objectives are achieved through precise operational implementation and/or imaginative adaptation. Their importance to organisations is crucial, not least because the approaches of IMUEs to international expansion in terms of human capital deployment and optimisation have changed significantly over the past 20 years, as Reg Sindall noted in Case Study 10:

> ... *from an organisational perspective, 20 years ago – when the conglomerate business model was still in fashion – what might be pejoratively termed a* colonial *or* feudal *model towards talent predominated. What I mean by this is that International MUEs (IMUEs) saw talent development as being restricted to a very small cadre at the apex of organisations (largely concentrated on the home country) with expatriates (very much in the same way as in colonial times) being despatched to run outposts of the burgeoning business empire. Today ... due (largely) to MUEs becoming focused entities around a single industry, brand or identity,* federal *structures of talent attraction and development have emerged. Thus whilst* home-host-home *archetypes of attraction and development might have predominated in the past, today* host-home-host *models are more applicable. (Reg Sindall, EVP Group Resources, Burberry Plc [Case Study 10])*

As regards leadership styles, House et al. (2004) – in the most comprehensive analysis of international middle-management leadership to date (see sections 5.1.2 and 5.1.3 above) – noted that there were certain universal characteristics of effective leaders:

> ... *in all cultures leader team orientation and the communication of vision, values and confidence in followers are reported to be highly effective leadership behaviours. (House et al. 2004: 7)*

Juxtaposed against this finding, however, were their empirical observations that in developing/growth market contexts 'ideal' leadership types (i.e. charismatic, values, team-orientated, participative, humane and autonomous) were not the dominant forms of practice. For instance, 'charismatic/value-based' leadership styles predominated *least* in the Middle East, Confucian Asia, Eastern Europe, Latin Europe and Sub-Saharan Africa contexts; 'participative leadership' was in evidence *less* in the Middle East, Confucian Asia, Southern Asia, Eastern Europe and Sub-Saharan Africa regions; whilst 'self-protective leadership' master/servant styles were *most* prevalent in Southern Asia, Middle East, Confucian Asia, Eastern Europe and Latin America.

Thus, such leadership styles would seem contrary to the principles and practices that many 'western' IMUEs espouse. Given their levels of actual growth and ambition, how do IMUEs expanding into these territories overcome this problem?

The previous three chapters (on control, commitment and change) provided significant evidence and commentary as to how IMUEs sought to resolve this conundrum; namely, how they could transfuse 'western' managerial practice into 'divergent' territories with cultural customs and systems that – because of their social, political and historical antecedents and predispositions – militated against adoption. *But*, whilst there was some evidence of 'convergence' through changing value systems brought about through best-practice transfusion, socio-economic factors, increasing levels of education and the spread of social media, issues – as the numerous Case Studies illustrated in the previous four chapters – still remain. For, in addition to NBS and cultural forces, IMUEs' failed attempts to 'meld' local leader behaviours were compounded by the major obstacle of structural, physical and emotional distance. In essence local leaders were – in many instances – at the end of a very long chain of command which differed according to a complex, and sometimes confusing, matrix of ownership types/structures. *Direct ownership* types might be structured according to subsidiary country management or brand sector principles; *alliance structures* might include a country management hierarchy overseen by two (competing) 'partners'; *market contracting* might involve direct 'supervision' by the owner through the form of 'master franchisee' agreements or indirect control through 'sub-franchising', licensing and concessions. All these configurations pose particular problems to IMUEs attempting to drive 'product system' conformity, consistency and quality through their field-based local leadership cadres.

One means by which IMUEs can obtain greater 'outcome assurance' is to select and develop local leaders against a verified set of skill-based, behavioural and cognitive characteristics. But what should these characteristics be? Previous commentary (Edger 2012: 217–45) highlighted the personal characteristics of effective local leaders in developed market 'multi-site' situations. However, whilst – in positional terms at least – local leaders in IMUEs are faced by the same issues (i.e. leading at a distance) the cultural contexts within which they operate, as has been outlined in detail in previous chapters, are significantly different. Fortunately, the empirical evidence provided by the experts (i.e. practitioners, consultants and academics) interviewed for this book provided a number of insights which can give us some indication as to what personal characteristics IMUEs seek from their local leadership cadres in order to secure operational efficiency and effectiveness. In addition these respondents also provided plenty of 'grounded solutions' – based on practical observation and experience – with regard to the development interventions that are likely to have the greatest chance of success of melding appropriate skills, behaviours and 'thinking' styles. Indeed, following the codification and triangulation of the data they provided, a number of broad 'characteristic requirements' emerged around the areas of *expertise, emotional intelligence, energy* and *ethics*. A number of dimensions were associated with each cluster: expertise incorporating *knowledge (explicit technical and local tacit)* and *judgement, courage and adaptability*; emotional intelligence including *self-awareness and humility, awareness of others and respect* and *relationship and conflict management*; energy and ethics including *passion, pace* and *morals*. These will now be considered in turn.

7.1 Expertise

In the academic literature there are two main approaches to understanding expertise: first, the *communities of practice* and, second, the *individual expert capacity* view. The former sees expertise as a socially constructed phenomenon where narratives and bias for action are shaped by groups, enabling members to codify, transfer and enact expertise within specific domains (Goldman 1999). Problems pointed out by this domain relate to the emergence of 'groupthink' and isometric convergence that stifles original thinking (Janis 1972). The latter defines expertise as an innate characteristic of individuals which is formed as a result of absorptive capacity, environmental context and continuous and deliberate practice (Chase and Simon 1973, Ericsson 2000, Gladwell 2008). With regard to local leaders in IMUEs the fact that individuals from host country origins possess 'experiential expertise' in their local national business system and cultural contexts provides an advantage to companies that are attempting to grow their businesses in these unfamiliar environments. However, the downside to locally recruiting relates to the fact that putative employees might be deficient in IMUE 'ways of working' from both a technical skills and behavioural point of view. So what are the specific facets of expertise required by IMUEs from local leaders and – if lacking – how are they developed?

7.1.1 KNOWLEDGE

To academics knowledge is a familiarity or understanding of something such as information or skills that are gained through experiential or taught processes (Polanyi 1962). Within organisations, knowledge manifests itself in both explicit and tacit form (Nonaka and Takeuchi 1995). *Explicit knowledge* is expressed formally, being transferred through mechanisms such as written instruction and/or verbal communication. By contrast, *tacit knowledge* is difficult to transfer as it comprises informal habits and cultural idiosyncrasies that people and organisations are often unaware they possess, or are unaware of how it provides inimitable added value (see section 6.3.4 above). The process of transforming tacit knowledge into an explicit form is regarded as possible in some instances, through codification, articulation or specification. Field-based local leaders in IMUEs need both technical explicit knowledge and tacit knowledge; the former in order to expedite the organisation's operational requirements, the latter in order to perform effectively within a specific NBS and cultural context.

With regard to explicit technical knowledge, two dimensions become apparent from an analysis of the empirical data. First, local leaders should understand and master the standard operating procedures and systems that underpin the product concept:

Getting the local leadership (i.e. regional, territory and store managers) to understand, buy into and execute the 'basics' – the core operating standards – is a hygiene factor for most businesses. (Kevin Todd, CEO Rosinter Russia [Case Study 5])

In order to do this, local leaders should be equipped with the necessary managerial planning , organising and prioritisation skills in order to maintain an *'operational grip'* on their businesses and free up *capacity* in order to lead their people:

... area and unit managers have to do two things well – run a strong P&L whilst ensuring that the educational/duty of care needs of their charges are attended to. (John Woodward, EVP KUE Inc. Singapore [Case Study 8])

With regards to local tacit knowledge, local leaders in growth markets are frequently called upon to interact judiciously with local officials, authorities and agencies, understand and comply with local industrial relations policies and employment laws *and* assess, monitor and (possibly) respond to competitor activity in local micro-markets. Most importantly they are expected to act as a bridge between the centre and units, often acting as a critical 'linguistic filter' between policy-makers and implementers:

I think the language point is significant ... idiomatic understanding of what is really meant by home country policy-makers is important in the way in which initiatives, policies and practices are transmitted down the line. (Reg Sindall, EVP Group Resources, Burberry Plc [Case Study 10])

However, powerful counter-forces threaten to dilute and derail both forms of knowledge deployment. First, due to extant cultural concepts of managerialism and a lack of skills training:

... [local leaders in growth markets] lack grounded managerial and leadership skills to ensure flawless execution ... skills such as communications (selling the 'benefits' and 'outcomes' to stakeholders and recipients), delegation/empowerment, project management, risk assessment and monitoring are essential skills that underpin the 'human dimensions' that determine whether or not certain initiatives, projects and plans are ultimately successful. (Dr Nollaig Heffernan, Ecole Hotelier Lausanne [Case Study 15])

... the issue is, however, there is a short supply of 'local' talent, conversant with 'western business practice' and discourse (either through immersion or education) and very often a 'bidding war' ensues for the best talent, which has a propensity – due to the large number of opportunities – to move frequently. (James Hyde, Senior Partner, Korn Ferry International [Case Study 2])

Second, IMUEs themselves make it difficult to ensure that they develop, align and harness both forms of knowledge because of their own architectural imprecision:

Ramping up this complexity, the 'regionals' (HMULs) as we call them have different job titles, job descriptions and objectives in every region! ... As such we do not have any formal development programme for our MULs, many of whom originated from store management level. (Chief People Officer, PremCo [Case Study 4])

To be sure – even within certain denominated geographical territories – geographical distance issues constantly threaten to disable attempts to ensure consistency and dependability:

> … *[ensuring operational excellence] is highly complex in diffuse international contexts due to distance, capability, language and cultural disposition. How do you ensure that the standards and service promise in one of our branded restaurants in St Petersburg is exactly the same as in Kazakhstan? (Kevin Todd, CEO Rosinter Russia [Case Study 5])*

How do IMUEs overcome such issues in order to ensure proper deployment and development of explicit (technical) and tacit (cultural and NBS) knowledge? The answer is that they achieve it in three ways: through structural congruence, extrinsic KPIs and reward systems and intrinsic training and development mechanisms:

1. *Structural congruence* – The start-point to understanding how IMUEs ensure operational excellence is through configuration (see the EVP Burberry Plc's comments at the beginning of this chapter). Increasingly, multi-brand firms are taking a branded/channel approach rather than country-based one in order to ensure alignment of purpose, policies and practices:

> Global sector directors *are now hard-lined into direct reports in each territory, with the view being taken that technical expertise needs to be shared 'within sector' … [and] managed on a global basis allowing better line of sight (in terms of ROI, P&L, etc.) and more focus on growth sectors within given markets. (Andy Vaughan, SSD Sodexo [Case Study 3])*

> *In Rosinter we have just changed the operational architecture to focus more around* single rather than *multi-brand sites, which in turn creates a sense of purpose, identity and (most importantly)* autonomous know-how *(i.e. how to* slightly adapt the format and product sales mix to add value in distinctive micro-markets) … *in addition, monitoring systems, metrics and reward can also be adapted to be fit for purpose, ensuring people have 'skin in the right* game!' *to perform. (Kevin Todd, CEO Rosinter Russia [Case Study 5])*

2. *Extrinsic systems* – As Kevin Todd commented above, such a degree of structural congruence generates focus, particularly when it is backed up with extrinsic KPIs and incentives. This is a position endorsed by other respondents who saw KPI-linked reward not only as being important from a 'line of sight' perspective but as being of high value (whether individually or team-based) to managers located in growth markets who – perhaps in comparison to their 'developed' market compatriots – place a high premium on extrinsic 'hygiene' cash motivators:

> … *most importantly, we have a set of KPIs for Zone Area Managers that pretty much run vertically throughout our entire multi-unit dealer/showroom operation which consist of four fundamental metrics: volume, market share, profit and quality. These will be measured, on a weekly and monthly basis … the data gives the organisation 'line of sight' on how units are performing, be they owned, 'master franchisee', 'franchisee', etc. (Bryn Thomas, Finance Director, PSA Peugeot Citroen [Case Study 1])*

Another approach adopted by MUEs has been through reward systems (whether individually or collectivist). This is a developing area although my feeling is that bonus and incentive systems that are linked to certain outcome metrics are more powerful (given 'hygiene' level socio-economic circumstances) in some markets than they are in others. (Professor Paul Turner, BCBS [Case Study 6])

3. *Intrinsic systems* – In order to get field-based local leaders in IMUEs to act and behave appropriately, intrinsic approaches (which bear a close resemblance to so-called best-practice HRM mechanisms; see Edger 2012: 125–6), such as creating an attractive working environment and training programmes, which increase levels of technical/managerial expertise, are also important factors in aiding development:

... as we have also worked upon being a 'nice place to work' with good wages (including the same bonus system as the US/UK) and conditions, we have found that our turnover is pretty low (some managers that have left have even come back!) ... We also have a management trainee scheme in place to ensure that as sites become vacant we put well-equipped managers in place who are able to lead large teams; because India is no different in many respects to anywhere else – the right manager in the right unit pays enormous dividends! (Robin Jarvis, AAI India [Case Study 14])

However, getting regional operators to buy into best-practice training is difficult in some organisations as there might in some cases be a 'try before people buy [approach]... [due] to the power and authority of ... International Regional Company MDs ...' (Chief People Officer, PremCo, Case Study 4). Solutions to this in IMUEs reside in having coherent and effective 'top-to-bottom' training structures and utilising digital/electronic platforms to 'get directly' to highly dispersed field-based personnel:

I was reliant on the global training team to ensure a high degree of consistency of interpretation and execution (my Mandarin for instance isn't very good!) ... the role of the RTDs in capturing, sharing and training out best practice both in process and content terms, through their close liaison with field operations was pivotal. (Clive Chesser, Operations Manager, Haagen Dazs International [Case Study 17])

As regards training and development in the field (at regional manager/store level) the influence of new technology has had a transformative effect ... as the technology underpinning training delivery has changed it is now far easier to communicate to colleagues how stores should be set up, which procedures should be followed, etc. Getting over to sales associates how they should deal with customers through digitalised service delivery training that is constantly reinforced by the behaviours of local management (including regional managers) and embedded by local training teams is essential. (Reg Sindall, EVP Group Resources, Burberry Plc [Case Study 10])

Such approaches to field-based training in IMUEs are made all the more effective if the materials fit *cultural learning preferences* (i.e. team-based action learning/problem-solving in Confucian Asia), the content is kept *simple and made memorable* (due to field-based time pressures) and, ideally, forms some part of an *accredited programme* (thereby increasing its transactional value for recipients).

7.1.2 JUDGEMENT AND COURAGE

Allied to this requirement for explicit and tacit knowledge is the need for judgement (which is certainly aided by sound knowledge) and a courageous approach to apply it without continually deferring to higher authorities. To academics *judgement* is viewed in two ways: first, as a *cognitive capability* to effectively evaluate evidence prior to making a decision and, second, as the capacity for *wisdom and discernment* (Tichy and Bennis 2007, Nonaka and Takeuchi 2011). With regards to the former, the possession of key *cognitive* (i.e. *thinking and sense making*) capabilities which enable managers to make associations, connections and linkages – disaggregating data and information to provide valuable insights – is an essential feature of effective leaders. As regards the latter – practical wisdom or an ability to apply adjudication or discernment – this is judged as being particularly important for leaders with regards to three specific domains: people, strategy and crisis – with people being highlighted by them as the most important 'judgement call' (Tichy and Bennis 2007, Nonanka and Takeuchi 2011). With respect to *courage* – cited by ancient and mediaeval philosophers as being one of the four main virtues alongside prudence, justice and temperance – the ability to act 'rightly' in the face of opposition or opprobrium is judged to be one of the key attributes of effective leaders (Treasurer and Shriver 2011).

The *requirement* for judgement amongst HMULs stems from the many 'calls' that they have to make on a day-to-day basis that cannot possibly be resolved by constantly checking with higher authorities. Previous chapters highlighted a number of functions and activities that HMULs undertake that require some form of adjudication, not least selecting the 'right unit manager for the right site', selecting appropriate development interventions for their people, balancing the talents and personalities of a team, setting a local vision, prioritising certain objectives above others and – due to the fact that every site is likely to have slightly different characteristics (i.e. flow, position, facilities, capital and human resources, competitive set, etc.) – continuously making value-added process improvements at unit level. In addition, HMULs might be required to make '*local calls*' with regards to relationships with officials that might prove fruitful in the future and local product promotions that 'fit' with consumer preferences:

> *... field operations (particularly zone area managers) will have some flexibility as to what incentives can be deployed for the dealers themselves (i.e. extrinsic cash or intrinsic treats) or the end-consumer (i.e. cash off, free 'add-ons' or finance-based offers). The point is that 'one size does not fit all'; local field operations can choose from a menu of items to 'animate' either the dealer or the consumer. A finance offer might work in one territory whilst a loyalty/service-based offer might work in another – it is a matter of local judgement as to what will work and why! (Bryn Thomas, PSA [Case Study 1])*

In order to apply a degree of judgement, courage on the part of the HMUL is required not least because the way in which they manage and despatch tasks might cut against orthodoxies held dear either at the centre or locally. This is where they need to apply discretion, adopting a 'best of each approach' that has not necessarily been prescribed in any manual or 'standing orders':

... [local leaders] bring a level of what I term 'fusion'; for instance in US-owned IMUEs, blending meritocratic, 'individualistic', performance-based cultural approaches with local cultures (especially in Asia) that favour more 'collectivist' loyalty, relationship, 'longevity' and trust-based approaches ... 'local leaders' are appointed on the basis that they have the courage and 'nous' to adopt a hybridised 'best of each' approach. (James Hyde, Senior Partner, Korn Ferry International [Case Study 2])

But what are the *issues* faced by HMULs that might ameliorate these important characteristics? First, from a cultural standpoint, HMULs might be working in contexts where the values espoused by the parent – particularly with regard to service – are undermined by local behaviours and capability:

Second, 'local' culture inevitably impinges on the processes of service execution and renewal ... can the values underpinning the organisation's service culture transcend some of the values that threaten to dilute or derail the service promise? (Nick Wylde, Managing Director, Stanton Chase International [Case Study 11])

Second, HMULs themselves have been conditioned through parenting, education and socialisation to behave in ways which are consistent with societal norms. Received wisdom might dictate that managers are only seen as effective if they maintain a 'high distance' with their followers, act in 'self-protective' ways and punish 'miscreants' who fail to 'do what they are told':

Managers in China see themselves as fulfilling a more 'transactional' (i.e. checking, policing, monitoring and punishing) rather than 'transformational' (i.e. motivational, inspirational and supportive) role ... Also, the idea of 'two-way' communication seems mystifying to many Chinese given that their social and educational conditioning has been centred upon 'tell and do' rather than 'ask and contribute' ... Speaking up in public is not a natural trait; collectivism dictates that you should not shame or embarrass your co-workers by demonstrating more knowledge than them or personally 'losing face' by getting something wrong. (Dr Lisa Qixun Siebers, NBS [Case Study 13])

Positional authority in some cultures might potentially reduce the capacity of managers to act courageously (i.e. autonomously, innovatively or on impulse) due to notions of primacy:

... one must always recognise the way in which decisions are made and challenged (in open forums) is distinctly different from Anglo-American contexts ... in meetings due respect must be paid to those in positions of authority. (Paul Willcock, Managing Director, Genting [Case Study 9])

If there is a requirement for HMULs to display some form of judgement (backed up by fortitude), how do IMUEs develop such characteristics in contexts where individual initiative and action is at best frowned upon, at worst punished? The answer to this is that IMUEs can intervene in three ways to elicit and encourage these characteristics through *modelling*, enshrining *empowerment* (removing sanctions) and *rotating* personnel:

1. *Modelling behaviours* – At the 'start-up' phase of the operation IMUEs are likely to use (talented) expatriates – or in some cases credible ex-HCNs – to demonstrate required behaviours:

   ... for the first unit we opened, we seconded [ex-HCN] managers out of our US and UK operations to 'set it up right' with locally appointed management ... this set the template for the way in which we wanted the operation to be run. (Robin Jarvis, International Operations Director, AAI Inc. India [Case Study 14])

   As the operation becomes more established senior personnel both from the centre and subsidiary/partner level need to actively demonstrate what 'good looks like' through being highly visible and maintaining best-practice facilities that 'showcase' required skills and behaviours:

   ... best-practice behaviours need to be modelled by senior management, *supported by an* operational architecture *which shows what good looks like (i.e. exemplar stores), and by local leaders with clearly defined/appropriate skills, roles and responsibilities, resources and a clear line of sight ... In international contexts where (some) 'hierarchies' have 'outsourced' blueprint accountability – 'swooping down' to apply sanctions and penalties only when it goes wrong – you have an inappropriate culture that leaves people demoralized and fearful on the front-line. Senior executives need to model good behaviours because it sets the tone and desired standard down the line ... throughout my career, and also here at Rosinter, I have always believed in having 'Centres of Excellence' that are beacons of good practice, spread out across the organization to diffuse best practice. (Kevin Todd, CEO Rosinter Russia [Case Study 5])*

2. *Enshrining empowerment* – The second way in which IMUEs can encourage field-based operatives to demonstrate initiative – a particularly important trait given the need to instantly resolve and rectify service breakdowns – is not only for senior managers to model desired behaviours but also (as was hinted at by Kevin Todd above) to actively encourage empowerment through removing the threat of sanctions (other than in the case of serious managerial breakdowns). Allowing managers to experiment and make mistakes so that they are able to build their levels of confidence is key:

   Through empowering managers on-site (in the same way we do in the UK) ... by giving them the training and the systems that give them the courage and confidence to provide a great service that they could take pride *in ... any serious problems that arise are resolved by virtue of the fact that local leadership (i.e. area, regional and board level) are close to the businesses – regularly out in the field and/or easily accessible to* generate *confidence ... to help rather than punish ... By employing highly competent people whom we invest heavily in, backed up by leaders who* listen *rather than just monitor and pounce ... we believe things are rarely hidden from view (no more so than the UK). (John Woodward, EVP KUE Inc. Singapore [Case Study 8])*

Case Study 18 – Local Leader Expertise in IMUEs

Kevin Todd is the President and CEO of Rosinter Restaurant Holdings, Russia's largest multi-brand casual dining chain (approximately 460 units – one-third franchised – and 11 brands, including Il Patio, Planet Sushi, Costa Coffee, McDonalds and TGI Friday) operating in 10 countries, spread across 44 cities. Over a successful 30-year career, Kevin held several senior executive roles in the restaurant industry and was MD of the franchise arm of Volvo, Europe. A Visiting Professor at BCU, Kevin is also a Council Member of the EFSF (European Food Service Forum).

In my view successful regional and territory managers in international contexts have three particular traits with regards to *expertise* … First, they possess *domain knowledge* of the 'art and science' of MUL and they have mastered the *craft skills* necessary to ensure (particularly in hospitality) that a quality product and experience is delivered in their units time after time … with regards to *domain knowledge* they know that in order to release time to manage at a distance effectively, they need to *create capacity for action* by being well organized: judiciously delegating and, having a prioritized plan of action (based on their own portfolio's balanced scorecard), driving performance both for the short and long term … but this alone is not enough … in order to gain *credibility* at unit level they require in-depth industrial knowledge of what it is that is being produced and delivered … in hospitality (unlike retail) where product is being manufactured on-site and then being delivered through a defined service 'concept' or 'system' it is essential that HMULs get the 'nuts' and 'bolts' of volume and capacity management: pre-session set-up, in-session throughput management, customer rhythm, etc. … they need to get on top of the science as well as the art of MUL … in international contexts where 'self-protective' concepts of managerialism might involve 'power-based telling' rather than 'modelling', 'coaching' or 'training best practice' this becomes problematic … it is therefore necessary that the importance of holding, demonstrating and diffusing craft knowledge (rather than hoarding it) *runs from the top to the bottom of the operational line* … I would also add that in highly ambiguous local markets where getting things done (i.e. maintenance, refurbishments, new openings, operational certification, etc.) is highly contingent on local authorities and services, HMULs need strong *local networks* to get things done on time and to the required standard … *time* is the enemy of business; great MULs are *'fixers'* – getting things done by *mobilizing enabling parties* (getting the right 'stamps' on documents and having the correct paperwork is particularly important in Russia for instance) …

The second trait is *judgement* – particularly around *people*. Customers are purchasing both product and an emotional experience (which can differ according to occasionality), which require service providers to behave in an appropriate manner … the individual who sets the tone for the ambience and service quality of the business is the Unit/General Manager (GM) … It is my view that this is one of the most critical jobs of the HMUL – placing the *'right profile GM, in the right site'* … as the HMUL is the person most likely to understand the idiosyncrasies of the site (in terms of customer demographics, labour culture, site layout, transaction flows, lifecycle – growth, stable, declining/turnaround, relaunch, etc.) it is his/her job to put the appropriate person in and/or move on GMs who are inappropriate 'fits' ... How is this learnt? ... In part it is connected to the HMULs cognitive (thinking and problem-solving) ability and also 'emotional nous' ... In international situations unless managers abandon the false belief that keeping a high level of distance reinforces their authority, they will never get close enough to judge operational needs and capability matches ... in addition it goes without saying that having created capacity to do value-added activities, effective MULs spend a disproportionate amount of time (in comparison to their colleagues) building the benchstrength of their portfolio by personally interviewing, developing and tracking talent within their units (such as chefs, deputies, shift leaders, etc.) ...

The third characteristic is *courage* and *adaptability*: courage to 'do the right thing' rather than just 'doing it right' and adaptability, as in 'changing gears'. *Courage* is a commodity that is in short supply in some international contexts due to socio-historical reasons – taking risks outside prescribed rules and procedures was usually punished in the past! ... however, HMULs that have the courage to try new things (within an ethical framework) – without fear for the consequences of failure – that improve the customer experience are, in my mind, to be applauded ... also possessing the ability to '*change gears*' is important ... there are times when an MUL needs to act in a reflective and listening manner and other occasions when (s)he needs to act in a passionate, infectious, energising way ... this might be related to seasonality, trading, the launch of initiatives, etc. ... the point is this – HMULs that act in a one-dimensional manner and are not able to adapt their behaviour/style to situational circumstances will be less effective than those that do! ... again the concept of 'changing gears' is not well understood in some international IMUE situations where managers believe that their role is to act as dispassionate functionaries (i.e. transactional managers) for centrally-conceived policy implementation, rather than as cheerleaders and motivators (i.e. transformational local leaders).

Case Study 19 – Developing Area Management Expertise in Growth Markets

Mara Swan is EVP Global Strategy and Talent of ManpowerGroup (brands include Manpower, Experis and Right Management), the world leader in providing innovative workforce solutions (31,000 staff, 3,600 branches in 80 countries handling 400,000 associates on job assignments at any given point). An experienced senior international operator, Mara has executive board-level responsibility at ManpowerGroup for HR, Talent, CSR and Marketing.

Given the scale of our branch network across multiple territories and cultures it is necessary to bind the organisation together with a coherent set of values that emphasise what ManpowerGroup is all about – none more so than the aphorism that 'putting people in work is honourable work', which gives our employees a sense of meaning and fulfilment that leads to high levels of attachment to our brand and organisation. But what '*hard*' and '*soft*' skills do our field-based personnel require in developing/growth markets in order to ensure organisational success and how do we develop them at ManpowerGroup?

First, from a '*hard*'-skills perspective we look for high levels of branch and area manager *sector expertise* with regards to search, recruitment and selection techniques in developing markets. There are two ways that area managers acquire this: either through progression 'through the ranks' from consultant level (over 70 per cent in growth markets) or – in the case of new start-up markets – by training through what I term a 'reverse expatriate' manner – placing recruits in territories nearby that mimic the prevailing host market characteristics ... I am an absolute believer in employing local home country personnel rather than US or European expats whose presence might degrade perceptions of meritocratic progression ... In addition, '*hard*' skills obviously include '*business knowledge*' as to how to run client accounts, a great P&L and '*local knowledge*' of the language, employment law, labour market structures and client expectations ... Local language skills and labour law expertise are absolutely vital given the people business we are engaged in ...

Allied to these 'hard' technical skills, however, is a high degree of *judgement* ... At ManpowerGroup although we seek to orientate people through the brand we also have what we call '*fixed*' and '*flexible*' frameworks that act as 'boundaries' for permissible field-based activities ... The '*fixed*' framework set by the centre sets the business-line contribution levels and rules that *all* assignments must be preceded by candidate experience and 'legal' work permit checks ... '*Flexible*' frameworks allow 'host' country managers (i.e. regional and area level) to adapt their systems and approaches in accordance to local legal requirements, the business cycle position of each territory (HRM outsourcing in mature contexts to boost margins – volume recruitment in growth situations) and cultural traditions (the process of 'greeting' candidates varies from territory to territory according to local norms and customs) ... This 'flexibility' is also designed to encourage/empower field managers to be agile and act in an entrepreneurial manner ... This behaviour is viewed positively rather than penalised, substituting protective 'collective inertia' in some operational theatres with displays of individual initiative and endeavour ...

Second, from what I would term a '*soft*'-skills perspective we expect our area managers to display good *leadership* and *managerial skills* ... passionately motivating, teaching and coaching our branch managers to deliver outstanding candidate, associate and client service ... also fostering a high degree of inter-branch/brand collaboration and information sharing. This latter point is important as what we are trying to create at ManpowerGroup is a 'collaborative' organisational structure ... although country/line managers in developing markets have a direct *accountability* to their 'host' country structure (in terms of targets, business development, etc.) they also have *responsibility* to their various brands ... this requires quite a high level of *agility* and *flexibility* amongst our field-based personnel who inevitably make difficult trade-offs at certain times ...

How do we encourage/develop Area Managers to display these behaviours, given the competitive nature of the industry and cultural forces that might run counter to notions of participation, involvement and 'enlightened' leadership practice? ... The truth is we try to develop these 'soft' skills by employing people that have the right 'service-based' mindset in the first place (testing them out in entry-level consultant roles) ... also through constant communication from the top of the organisation regarding desired value-based behaviours (our CEO is extremely vocal – both through face-to-face and digital forums – regarding the standards and ethics required) ... and, most crucially, modelling and training in the 'basics' (I have coached motivational techniques to area managers in the past!) ... and our executive board is staffed with a wide range of nationalities which provides good exemplar behaviour....

7.2 Emotional and Environmental Intelligence

Given the importance of, first, the human dimension of IMUEs with their heavy operational reliance on labour, and second, the level of cross-cultural understanding required by both parties in IMUEs (i.e. home and host), it is unsurprising that the second major characteristic of field-based local leaders is what this book denominates as emotional and environmental intelligence (EEI). Generally EEI (usually termed EI) is defined within academic commentaries as an ability, skill or perceived ability to identify, assess and control the emotions of oneself, others and groups (Goleman 1998; Mayer et al. 2001, 2003). Goleman's (1998) 'mixed' or trait model conceives EI as a set of competencies and skills that shape leadership performance based around four principal items: self-awareness, self-management, social awareness and relationship management, all of which can be learned and developed in order to produce exceptional leadership performance. The reason why 'environmental' has been added to the normal EI nomenclature is derived from the evidence that has been garnered for this research combined with explicit academic acknowledgement that effective managers in international organisations require high levels of 'environmental awareness' (otherwise labelled cultural intelligence):

> ... cultural intelligence is related to emotional intelligence, but it picks up where emotional intelligence leaves off. A person with high emotional intelligence grasps what makes us human and at the same time what makes us different from one another. A person with high cultural intelligence can somehow tease out of a person's or group's behaviour those features that would be true of all people and all groups, those peculiar to this person or this group, and those that are neither universal nor idiosyncratic. The vast realm that lies between these two poles is culture. (Earley and Mosakowski 2004: 140)

Sources of cultural intelligence are derived from the head (cognitive learning strategies), body (physical actions and demeanour) and heart (high emotional motivation to engage).

7.2.1 SELF-AWARENESS AND HUMILITY

The combination of 'knowing oneself' and exercising a high degree of humility in IMUE service-led environments is an important characteristic of HMULs. Due to extant societal cultural norms and levels of conditioning, HMULs need to acquire a degree of self-knowledge and discipline with regards to how they react to certain situations, demonstrating a fair amount of personal humility in situations where staff and peers might be more used to overbearing, arrogant behaviour by their leadership cadre. In the academic literature *self-awareness* includes accurate self-reflection and assessment, whilst self-control is expressed through attributes such as emotional self-management, transparency, adaptability, initiative and optimism (Goleman 1998). By the same token, humility – to be seen to act in a 'grounded' manner – is a multi-faceted construct including behaviours such as openness, honesty and self-awareness. In many societies it has religious resonance, with Hinduism stressing the subjugation of personal ego in order to achieve propriety, Islam proposing that individuals should 'surrender' themselves to their maker and Taoism advancing the notion that humility (or a lack of arrogance) is a prime characteristic of enlightened people. Indeed Collins (2001) in his description of 'Level 5' leader types argues that effective leadership is characterised by humility and 'fierce resolve'.

   The requirement to achieve some level of self-awareness in order to act in a grounded and transparent manner was acknowledge during the course of the research:

> ... *recruitment systems should be aligned with the firm's* core values *(which in the case of Burberry were 'protect, explore, inspire'), which in turn are anchored in the company's purpose (made all the more powerful if it has a strong emotional connection). What does this mean? It requires local recruiters (HR, regionals, store managers, etc.) to, first, have high levels of self-awareness as to what is required to function effectively within the ambient organisational culture and then, second, locate and calibrate appropriate talent that voluntarily* buys into *and* fits *(through attitude, behaviour and disposition) these espoused values ... sometimes these values might transcend local ones ... but getting local colleagues to believe in and commit to the* why and how *is essential ... Upholding and reinforcing these values through constant messaging, communication and modelled behaviours is also key ... at Burberry we had transitioned our CEO quarterly webcasts down to monthly ones accompanied by real-time company-wide Facebook interaction. (Reg Sindall, EVP Group Resources, Burberry Plc [Case Study 10])*

However, issues – again – stem from the fact that because of extreme conditioning, it might be difficult to either recruit individuals with the right characteristics or 'mould' them once they have been recruited:

> *Similarly, in Asia the concept of 'leader' ... [is] framed by* 'content' *notions of expertise and positional primacy rather than facilitation/enabling, 'process notions' of telling and directing rather than delegating/empowering and 'emotional factors' such as aggressive power rather than emotional proximity. (Bob Dignen, York Associates [Case Study 12])*

... people are very conscious of their positions and what 'is' and 'isn't' their responsibility ... for instance, in one of our US sites if a manager sees any garbage or litter on the floor they will just pick it up ... in India, managers will get somebody else to do it! ... In this society the caste system *plays a major part in people's preconceptions of what 'they' and 'others' should do. (Robin Jarvis, AAI India [Case Study 14])*

Getting managers to reach a level of self-awareness where they can acknowledge and understand how negative patterns of managerial behaviour – based on 'culturally inherited' dispositions towards maintaining high levels of 'power distance', masculinity and uncertainty avoidance – have a deleterious effect 'down the line' upon service providers and customers is problematic. Previous sections discussed interventions such as training and modelling behaviours, but in the case of raising levels of self-awareness other tools are required (especially in extreme circumstances):

1. *Profiling and psychometrics* – One way in which self-awareness can be increased – particularly in relation to individuals' managerial styles and their effect on follower behaviour – is through the use of psychometric testing. Tests that are 'culturally valid' (i.e. questions are located in the idiom of the culture and language) will be of great value to managers who have hitherto been 'flying blind'. Three hundred and sixty degree profiling is also of assistance although it should be recognised that in some cultures the validity of this type of assessment can be contaminated by both managers and followers, giving – for self-protective reasons – unrealistically positive responses. However, getting managers to undertake personal assessments to understand the utility of adjusting their style to differing personalities and 'situational dispositions' can yield significant benefits – although organisations should be wary that managers not undertake such self-analysis for 'fashion' or 'fad'-based motivations:

   ... fertile ground for many western training consultancies; for instance in country x there are over 5,000 training providers peddling 'how to' managerial solutions. Courses such as situational leadership, personality profiling and psychometric testing are particularly popular as local managers want to understand the concepts of 'difference, adaptive style and performance outcomes'. The dangers inherent in this are the degree to which highly educated specialists in emerging markets take courses because they regard them as 'fashionable' or a 'nice to have' on the CV rather than as a practical tool for help! (Dr Nollaig Heffernan, Ecole Hotelier Lausanne [Case Study 15])

2. *One-to-one coaching and development* – Having located 'where they are' following a degree of self-analysis, it is prudent for organisations to have personal development programmes that include coaching and mentoring interventions. Ideally, subjects should be paired with coaches/mentors who are equipped (from both a professional and business perspective) to develop more effective behaviours. Constraints in IMUEs obviously relate to the lack of requisite manpower/skills to deliver such interventions. One means of getting around this is to send managers on developmental and/or educational courses with a high level of reflective content in relation to the art and science of management practice.

7.2.2 AWARENESS OF OTHERS AND RESPECT

Field-based operatives in IMUEs operate in a highly social context where it is necessary to exercise high levels of *social awareness* of – and concurrently *respect* for – others (staff, peers *and* customers) and extant networks. With regards to *awareness of others*, this would typically denominate, from a psychological perspective, a capacity to empathise with others through listening and seeking to understand *ally goals* and expectations. More significantly, perhaps, it also includes the ability, once insights have been processed, to control, guide and shape the behaviours of others in a transparent manner (Goleman 1998). Seeking to understand others in a respectful way signals to others that they have a level of esteem and 'worthiness'. Indeed, respect is an important ethical facet of many cultures, being one of five universal values shared by differing societies (Haidt and Graham 2007).

Why is awareness of others and respect a prime characteristic among HMULs in IMUEs? First, being charged with ensuring that their sites execute high levels of service during multiple transactions, they require 'sensitisation' to the needs of their customers:

> ... our success in building a multi-site portfolio has been built upon not ubiquity but micro-market differentiation ... important because with regard to customers who entrust us with their child's well-being and safety (a highly emotional transaction) addressing what they require cannot necessarily be prescribed by a process or system but has to be met through in-depth understanding of specific needs and aspirations ... [therefore it is important] to ensure our area and unit managers are sensitised and capable of 'tweaking' the offer to certain customer needs. (John Woodward, EVP KUE Inc. Singapore [Case Study 8])

Second, HMULs need to have good horizontal and vertical social networks within their organisation to ensure that they can learn from others (both in 'sense making' terms and acquiring knowledge and best-practice tips):

> For me it is clear that what successful organisations do is appoint managers who have a high level of social awareness and connectivity. What do I mean by this? Frankly, managers that can emotionally connect ... possessing the ability to network ... 'making sense' of the functional central/local linkages ... They also require cognitive thinking skills for problem-solving and prioritization ... but also (and most crucially) they require the ability to apply a cultural filter ... sifting through what has come down from 'on high' to make it locally relevant and impactful. (Professor Paul Turner, BCBS [Case Study 6])

Issues that IMUEs have in nurturing field-based local leaders that have high degrees of social awareness relate to the fast-changing nature of many growth markets, levels of 'mood management' within certain cultures and the endemic conflict that often pervades centre-subsidiary/partner relations:

> ... [emerging markets have an] expanding young, aspirational middle class who are quite different – from a consumptive point of view – compared to their parents ... their levels of expectation regarding service quality (reinforced by social media, travel and high disposable incomes) place far greater demands on multi-site operators ... this means that multi-site

operators must – in some instances – devise service delivery systems and consumer-friendly products that exceed standards in developed contexts ... These expectations ... demand 'local' leaders who are sensitised, empathetic and attuned to consumer micro-trends and can drive change quickly through an understanding of what strategic leadership approaches work best in which context ... the problem lies in finding the people who can do it or be trained to do it! (James Hyde, Senior Partner, Korn Ferry International [Case Study 2])

... two issues seemed to generate tension: culture and strategy ... In the case of culture the fact that Sodexo was a French-owned company ... compared to Anglo-American IMUE companies I have worked for there was a more 'ambiguous' approach to task-setting (more deliberating and discussion) and performance management. (Andy Vaughan, SSD, Sodexo [Case Study 3])

So how do IMUEs ensure that HMULs are emotionally attuned and respectful towards their staff, customers and organisational stakeholders? The empirical evidence from the expert respondents alighted upon three principal areas:

1. *'Intrinsic alignment'* – To some respondents during the course of this research, checking for the 'awareness of others' was an important component of the recruitment and selection exercise. Either individuals 'got' what the company stood for or had the 'intrinsic capacity' to do so:

   What stands out for me is the degree to which successful IMUEs measure what I call the 'intrinsic alignment' of new recruits ... thus, high-end premium apparel companies will relentlessly calibrate whether candidates 'get it' – what the organisation/brand stands for, its ethos and service delivery system requirements, etc. – and are sufficiently emotionally intelligent to meld their behaviours accordingly! ... These organisations will ask themselves whether hires in 'local' markets are prepared to act as brand ambassadors, *are capable of living the values and whether they* fit with the organisational culture? *(Nick Wylde, Stanton Chase International [Case Study 11])*

2. *Immersion and rotation* – Socialisation through significant immersion on joining the organisation and then 'rotation' around the organisation to observe and absorb 'the way things are done around here' is another way in which IMUEs can ensure their field-based local leaders become aware and make sense of their environment:

   HCMs (host country managers) have been sent on significant immersion programmes at the parent's centre, exposed to best-practice approaches through business school sponsorship or inducted into organisational 'ways of working' through 'home country' job placements and/or rotation. This has given them behavioural insight into leading-edge practice and/or the way in which 'things are done around here', affording instruction and insight into policies and practices that are deemed to represent the 'glue' of the organisation. (Professor Paul Turner, BCBS [Case Study 6])

3. *Social networking opportunities* – With regard to 'respecting the contribution of others' in the organisation certain IMUEs made sure that they laid on conferences and events where managers could mingle and interact. Previous reference has been made to

the importance of social capital and its role with regard to encouraging knowledge diffusion (see section 6.2.2); its propagation through the methods outlined below also contributes to higher degrees of mutual understanding and respect:

In addition these programmes were underpinned by constant endorsement through senior management making frequent international store visits, regular regional conferences and awards ceremonies, where store, call centre and HQ-level service excellence (i.e. politeness, knowledge and quality) was publically recognised and rewarded! ... such events also provided excellent networking opportunities across our international operations. (Reg Sindall, EVP Group Resources, Burberry Plc [Case Study 10]

Case Study 20 – Reflections on Locating and Developing Emotional Intelligence in IMUE Local Leaders in Developing Markets

Dr Nollaig Heffernan, Chartered Psychologist, teaches resilience, leadership and change-management to multi-site leaders in emerging markets (particularly the Middle Eastern Gulf States). Designer of the ILM 72 psychometric test, she teaches at the EHL (Ecole Hotelier Lausanne), is a visiting lecturer on the MSc in Multi-Unit Leadership at BCBS and is employed as a consultant and coach by many major international corporations. Dr Heffernan has assessed and coached numerous cohorts of emerging market multi-unit leaders with the aid of the MTQ48 personality profiling questionnaire.

On self-awareness and humility: While a high level of self-awareness is essential for all managers and leaders to optimise their performance, it is actually critical for developing resilience in middle managers such as HMULs. The role of the HMUL is highly pressured due to the expectations placed on it to respond to the demands of the centre as well as each unit the HMUL is accountable for. These pressures are further compounded by the often conflicting objectives of the foreign centre and culturally dissimilar host unit. Self-awareness allows the HMUL to understand his own strengths, preferences, limitations and stress-coping mechanisms, giving him the opportunity to leverage his existing skills and to improve on potentially restrictive weaknesses, enabling effective management in this often hostile organisational environment. The development of self-awareness is an ongoing process that requires much reflection and introspection on behalf of the individual. Self-report questionnaires, appraisals including 360-degree feedback, continuous professional development, using a reflective journal and coaching, etc., are all excellent tools for enhancing an individual's self-awareness and are routinely used by conscientious HMULs looking to develop themselves. Such a structured approach to self-awareness development paradoxically gives the HMUL the flexibility to react appropriately to unexpected events in the workplace because such strategic self-development creates a more rounded and adaptable individual.

A further outstanding characteristic of the effective HMUL is the presence of humility in their everyday approach to their work. The demonstration of such humility is evident in the HMULs belief that success is a collective process to which many parties have contributed, that feedback or rather constructive criticism is a pre-requisite for self-improvement and that an open and receptive attitude which includes the sharing of knowledge and information is a fundamental building block for effective communication and relationship management. In addition to these beliefs is the effective HMULs' ability to subordinate their personal goals to those of the organisation and team by constantly challenging how they can best serve rather than be served. This desire to serve is not politically motivated and is revealed as an equal concern for the welfare of those at the lower end as well as those at the top of the organisational ladder.

In reality it is often impossible to establish an individual's degree of humility or values in general without monitoring that individual on the job (see Respect below). It has become common practice however for many large organisations to use psychometrics to assess the alignment of an individual's attitudes/values with those of the organisation during the selection programme, i.e. before they have even been offered the job. This approach is inherently flawed. While many psychometrics use such techniques as balancing directionality or the inclusion of a Social Desirability scale, it is not very difficult to fake on these tests. Indeed it is often the organisation's insistence on publishing its values, usually on its own website, that results in such faking because applicants complete the value statements based on what the company has publicly declared about itself rather than revealing their true position in relation to the psychometric measure's statements.

A further complication relating to HMULs who demonstrate genuine humility is the real threat of the typical western individualist company's tendency to attribute unit, area or regional success to a single individual rather than the team and to reward that individual accordingly. Without strong self-awareness, self-discipline and self-regulation such biased attention can distort an individual's self-perception and behaviour and a once admired and respected manager can eventually become a symbol of all that is disliked about the foreign company's practices as other employees draw attention to how the individual has changed (e.g. no longer acts with humility) as a result of these practices. Taking the time to understand how the host country rewards and acknowledges high performance and views individual recognition, for example, would prevent the foreign company imposing practices that are counter-productive in other cultures.

On awareness of others and respect: An awareness of others is an extension of self-awareness known as social awareness which in turn becomes cultural awareness when it transcends national boundaries. Related to cultural awareness is the notion of cultural intelligence, an identifiable characteristic of the effective HMUL. The culturally intelligent and therefore effective HMUL creates alignment by looking for and working with the similarities between the parent company's values and attitudes and those of the host market rather than negatively highlighting the differences which inevitably leads to distrust, resistance, toxic relationships and ultimately mutual contemptuous disrespect of the respective foreign entities. The HMUL achieves this by understanding the positive aspects and limitations of his own and the foreign entity's cultural idiosyncrasies, promoting these positive aspects and neutralising the impact of less constructive culturally driven preferences.

In practices where the two cultures diverge, the effective HMUL operates within a paradigm of deep respect, taking time to understand, appreciate and even value the potential of these differences, viewing them as points of leverage to enhance managerial unit performance rather than resenting, ignoring and even fearing these disparities. These latter negative practices are often readily identifiable as deep-rooted issues in underperforming international companies where the 'us and them' mentality has festered unchecked, subconsciously becoming the local company norm. Such a mentality inevitably leads to operational failure and in worst-case scenarios to the necessity for withdrawal from the host market. This amalgamation rather than imposition of cultural values, therefore, greatly enhances the likelihood of success for international companies in emerging markets. In practice, the leveraging of cultural respect as a positive managerial characteristic epitomises situational leadership, in which the individual takes the time to understand the demands of the situation, e.g. cultural differences, and responds accordingly to the benefit of all stakeholders.

The effective HMUL also demonstrates respect at a more core or micro level. Many managers in a bid to satisfy senior management often neglect the needs of those they manage by disproportionately focusing upwards. This behaviour, although not necessarily intended to, can be perceived by those at lower organisational levels as a lack of respect for the 'ordinary' employee. Such a perceived lack of respect leads to the de-motivation and disengagement of employees leading in turn to resistance, conflict and, in extreme circumstances, sabotage. In contrast, effective HMULs demonstrate respect for their unit-level employees by taking the time to listen and communicate with them as actively as they do with the centre or senior management, by addressing their concerns as honestly as possible and by simply engaging with all employees as essential contributors to the overall functioning of the organisation rather than non-essential or replaceable cogs in an impersonal machine.

7.3 Energy and Ethics

Alongside the critical characteristics of expertise and EEI HMULs also require a high degree of *energy* and – given the dilemmas they face on the ground in some cultural contexts – a sound *ethical* predisposition. With regards to the former, given the aforementioned challenges and stresses of the role – derived from geographical, span of control and positional pressures – effective MULs require significant reserves of energy to overcome 'interference' in order to get the job done. To academic commentators energy is defined as 'the capacity to work' and is derived from 'four wellsprings in human beings; the body, emotions, mind and spirit', renewable and expandable 'through establishing specific rituals' (Schwartz 2007: 64). It was a notable feature of this research that during the analysis of expert respondent data effective HMULs demonstrated high reserves of energy or capacity to work (for instance see Case Study 18 above), the principal manifestations of which were *pace* coupled with *passion*.

With regards to ethics, HMULs in IMUEs will sometimes be placed in situations where they are faced with seemingly intractable decisions. Given their distance from the centre and the demands placed upon them to hit certain financial targets, should they cheat (i.e. bribe officials or falsify data/accounts) to get ahead? The field of business ethics (which, in the current climate, seems somewhat oxymoronic) has received considerable attention over the past few years in developed contexts, not least due to the dubious behaviours of bankers which contributed to the 2008 financial collapse in the 'west', which occurred in spite of previous attempts by policy-makers to instil legal codes of permitted behaviour (i.e. Sarbannes Oxley in the United States). IMUEs, like other corporate entities, all have CSR and compliance frameworks which define rights and obligations which should govern relations between themselves, their employees, customers, suppliers and local communities. In particular employees are prescribed ethical obligations to their organisations, i.e. reporting malfeasance through whistle-blowing or use of the grievance procedure. The issue in IMUEs is how – given the dispersed multi-site nature of the organisational entity – organisations are able to regulate behaviours effectively? In this respect, they are highly reliant on their field-based personnel to conform to their codes of ethics by displaying high degrees of probity through a possession of robust *moral* compasses. These dimensions of energy and ethics – namely, pace, passion and morals – will be discussed in turn.

7.3.1 PASSION AND PACE

IMUEs are 'people' businesses where MULs need to convey infectious enthusiasm and a 'can do' attitude that engages and motivates their staff, who – in turn – will enthuse their customers. Within the academic literature *passion* is typically conceived as personal commitment or positive energy. With regards to the former, high levels of personal commitment are thought to be achieved through job role 'fit', goal alignment and HRM practice interventions such as development, reward, communication and involvement. With regards to the latter, positive energy is conceptualised as helping people to perform at their best through techniques such as 'expressing appreciation to others' thereby fuelling 'positive emotions' (Schwartz 2007). Conveying passion within IMUEs is inextricably linked to *pace* and urgency. Given the service orientation of IMUEs where front-line staff are expected to respond immediately and sympathetically to customer demands, effective HMULs set the 'dynamic tone' by dispatching tasks and requests quickly and efficiently. The importance of pace is recognised by academic commentators, most notably by Belbin (2000 a, b), who argued that organisations and teams require 'completer finishers' (a prime requirement of field-based operatives in IMUEs) alongside other actors, in order to ensure that tasks are implemented on time, to specification.

Passionate commitment to servicing customer needs is a prime requirement of HMUL behaviour, no more so than in 'high-end' premium contexts (where – due to price – the customer expects a fair degree of intimacy) and/or 'highly emotional' environments such as early years child care:

Again I would stress that in this business it is important to liberate front-line staff so that they are passionate, flexible and responsive to service individual customer needs … this is a 'high emotion' business; you have to match the service to individual requirements to satisfy customers … after all, parents are entrusting us with their children! (John Woodward, EVP KUE Inc. [Case Study 8])

However, in order to set the pace for responsive customer service, HMULs must be well organised so that they can model and 'release capacity' to concentrate on inculcating desired sales-led service behaviours:

… [good area managers] 'get' operational excellence, can 'manage at a distance' and are well organised and professional (i.e. they prepare properly for on-site strategic, operational and personal development meetings) and understand the necessity of engaging 'hearts and minds' … I expect my MULs (as I do hopefully) to set the 'dynamic pace and tone' not just in word but in deed. (Paul Willcock, Managing Director, Genting [Case Study 9])

Issues relating to hiring and developing field-based operatives with the wherewithal to generate passion and pace are, once again, related to cultural impediments in some territories. Section 5.1.1.2 elucidated some of the issues that organisations face in developing and embedding a service ethos in some cultures that – for various reasons (i.e. socio-economic development, education, skills development, etc.) – have lacked a tradition of high standards of customer order fulfilment. Indeed, many expert respondents for this research commented on how difficult it was to hire local talent and staff who 'got' the concepts of service and change. This was connected to pace and the 'longer-term' temporal perspectives that are characteristic of some developing markets:

Inevitably clashes do occur between 'home' central policy-makers and these 'local' leaders … for instance, 'process driven/outcome-led' Anglo-American managers might struggle to understand the need for a more 'highly diffuse' approach towards 'getting things done' in certain markets … in short-termist cultures where there might be a focus on 'delivering the quarterly plan', there might be frustration relating to the patient, long-termist approach adopted by some 'local' leaders … Also, in management practice terms it might be perceived by 'developed' managers that 'local' multi-site leaders do not necessarily follow the 'rational' managerial best-practice manual, relying instead on more 'intuitive', 'unscientific' approaches in cultures that are derived from a more small-family-business, entrepreneurial mindset. (James Hyde, Senior Partner, Korn Ferry International [Case Study 2])

In addition, given certain cultural predispositions to 'avoid uncertainty', the rhythm of the business can be slowed down if field-based operatives feel that they have to do everything in order to avoid sanctions or punishment:

For instance, in some cultures where a high level of literal interpretation applies international MUEs must be careful not to overload those 'on the ground' with rules and procedures, as operatives will feel that they have 'to do everything'. This may result in them doing the wrong things, at the most inappropriate times, for what they believe to be all the right reasons. (Professor Paul Turner, BCBS [Case Study 6])

Also, due to the immense wealth of some growth regions, there might be an absence of urgency and pace because individuals, with a low incentive to behave professionally, act in a 'lackadaisical' manner:

> *... in the Middle East ... due to huge wealth reserves in some states, [there is a reported] huge tolerance for individual and team underperformance, temporal imprecision and a more relaxed attitude towards detail and implementation. (Bob Dignen, York Associates [Case Study 12])*

How do IMUEs *develop* the key characteristics of passion and pace amongst their field-based operatives? To be sure, some of the development interventions outlined above, such as behavioural modelling, immersion and training are appropriate in setting out the requisite 'tone' and 'tempo'. In addition, however, IMUEs would do well to ensure 'executional speed' through keeping things simple and utilising 'cultural bridges' such as TCNs who are well-versed in acting as transference mechanisms between cultures:

1. *Simplicity* – In order to generate pace, IMUEs who concentrated on keeping things simple for field-based operatives – especially with regards to service level requirements – stood a greater chance of success than others that confused and complicated matters through unnecessary complexity:

    > *The service delivery system at Burberry was called the 'Burberry Experience' which all employees were made conversant with, whatever their level, position, function or location ... interestingly this programme ... which was easily understandable and digestible ... had been developed through empirical analysis of the behaviours of the best sales associates globally and then packaged as a consistent approach to drive intentional, passionate and* purposeful *behaviours. (Reg Sindall, EVP Group Resources, Burberry Plc [Case Study 10])*

2. *TCN 'cultural bridges'* – The use of 'third country nationals' (TCNs) to interpret and transmit initiatives was also deemed necessary by some respondents for resolving issues relating to transferability. TCNs who can understand the original intentions of the policy-makers and the cultural idiosyncrasies of the 'recipients', moulding practices for optimal impact, can be effective in certain circumstances:

    > *IMUEs (such as one I dealt with recently) will have designated senior HR/Operational/Marketing personnel who focus upon driving service improvement ... increasingly these are Third Country National (TCN) 'global' appointments – appointees with a high level of cultural intelligence ... Thus, whilst the central principles of the organisation's service delivery system remain constant, sensitive allowance is granted in relation to the way it is trained out, communicated and explained by 'local leaders' in certain cultures (due to differing preferred learning styles, etc.). (Nick Wylde, MD Stanton Chase International [Case Study 11]*

7.3.2 MORALS AND VALUES

The foundation of ethical behaviour is sound *morals*, namely, the ability to act 'properly' in a 'good' way. Essentially individual morality is derived from ethical 'social mores' enshrined in organisational, religious and cultural *values*. Often its practice depends on 'in-group' or 'out-group' membership. 'Good' moral behaviour will be exchanged between clan members of an 'in-group' whilst 'bad' behaviour – i.e. discrimination and territorialism – occurs towards 'out-group' members. This is particularly the case in homogenous societies that display excessive nationalism and patriotism, using 'in-group' protectionism as a form of moral turpitude. The question posed by academics and commentators alike is the degree to which organisations can ensure high standards of morality in cultural contexts where they are perceived as 'outsiders'. More succinctly, how can they ensure their organisational values are accepted by 'insiders' who, first, might be conditioned to operate according to a contrary set of values and, second, might fundamentally reject 'outsider' influences?

The necessity to ensure field-based operatives act in a 'good' way is self-evident, not only from an organisational 'reputational' point of view but also as a form of best practice in service-based IMUEs with a high reliance upon human capital. It is also regarded as an important universal facet of leadership that cuts across all cultures (House et al. 2004: 7). Indeed – as in the case of demonstrating respect and humility (see sections 7.2.1 and 7.2.2 above) – moral rectitude appeals across most cultures such as the Middle East:

> ... values such as 'treat people with respect', 'act with integrity', are already embedded as part of the clan cultures and rituals within the Middle East Region. 'In-country' managerial behaviours to 'insiders' are remarkably similar to those that have been put forward by western management gurus over the past ten years – most notably 'servant leadership'. Notions of serving other members of the clan in order to gain loyalty and trust are important tenets of local custom. (Nollaig Heffernan, Ecole Hotelier Lausanne [Case Study 7])

The main issue is the degree to which – as stated above – 'insiders' of societies (and clans within these contexts) define their own moral standards and the degree to which they might converge or diverge with those of 'outsiders' (such as foreign companies). What might be termed as 'institutionalised corruption' in developed markets is a tacit form of 'social mores' in some developing contexts:

> As regards trust, one of the main issues is that the word is rather 'light' in Chinese translation, being subsumed by a far more powerful adjective 'guanxi' which means 'connection', 'ties' or 'relationship' ... no trust can exist unless 'guanxi' is established first ... what are the implications of this? ... it means that 'ties' must be built through acts such as gifting and exchange ... In a broader context this has caused difficulties for IMUEs who have refused to allow their local managers to build 'guanxi' through gifting with powerful local officials (i.e. the city MUM with the city mayor) at key calendar events ... this not only threatens to 'hold back' business growth in certain regions (particularly during the recent slowdown and rising rents, wages, product costs, etc.) but is extremely embarrassing for local managers who feel that they have 'lost face' by not showing sufficient respect ... in some cases this is a major reason why local managers might leave and work for local firms. (Lisa Qixun Siebers, NBS [Case Study 13])

Inevitably local managers will feel conflicted when called upon to enact organisational values in situations that – because of local cultural traditionsaffectations – limit their 'room for manoeuvre'. Indeed, according to some respondents national values will always – when push comes to shove – transcend organisational ones:

... when choices arise between job/company and country values, the latter will usually always win out, a situation that companies attempt to ignore, overturn or countermand at their peril ... As these emerging nations become more self-confident the treatment of 'outsiders' might change as part of a progressive change process – but an understanding of 'insider' mentality is important with regards to the permeability of country values systems. (Nollaig Heffernan, Ecole Hotelier Lausanne [Case Study 7])

How do IMUEs overcome these issues when they attempt to introduce or impose their values and moral 'codes of conduct' amongst their highly dispersed field-based operatives? The previous section alluded to ensuring 'intrinsic alignment' (i.e. selecting people with values that converge with those of the organisation) but this, in itself, might not be sufficient given the 'hard-wired' nature of certain cultural value systems. Thus, in addition to some of the other interventions already mentioned (modelling, behavioural adjustment, etc.), two further measures can be taken; namely, benefit upselling and the reinforcement of a coherent logic:

1. *Selling the upsides* – Some commentators stress the need for internationalising organisations to take a 'best of each' approach to value-setting. Another option is for companies to demonstrate that adopting certain 'ways of work'-based values, for instance, can actually result in beneficial personal outcomes for individuals:

   ... from an organisational perspective it is imperative that companies sell the upsides of the values they are attempting to inculcate throughout their international operations. One of the main problems I encounter during my training sessions with highly intelligent and motivated multi-site managers in the Middle East is that due to their 'high context' needs to maintain relationships and family ties outside of work, at times their inability to delegate (due to notions of hierarchical managerial primacy) ... causes them stress and anxiety that they are being restricted from sustaining their external networks ... However, by taking a value such as 'taking responsibility', or 'displaying a can-do attitude' – one which is deployed by most companies – and showing them that this allows them to delegate purposively to subordinates that are bound by the same values, shows the benefit of adoption; in this case de-stressing them by facilitating a 'spreading of the load' that, in turn, allows them to devote more physical and 'mental' time and/or connection with their families. (Nollaig Heffernan, Ecole Hotelier Lausanne [Case Study 7])

2. *Reinforcing a 'coherent logic'* – In addition, by showing that the adoption of certain values has been performance-enhancing in a number of contexts, organisations also stand a far greater chance of buy-in if they build their value systems around their brand and/or organisational positioning:

   How do IMUEs overcome some of these cross-cultural barriers and – indeed – what do local leaders do themselves to engender team-working that ultimately results in positive sales-led service within multi-unit businesses? Some IMUEs will design and communicate a 'coherent logic' in the way in which they address certain customer groups ... IKEA is frequently cited as having been successful in that regard, engendering cross-border coherence through shared values and behaviours backed up by solid systems (i.e. IT, supply chain, SOPs, etc.). (Bob Dignen, York Associates [Case Study 12])

Case Study 21 – Expert Reflections Upon Ethics in IMUEs

1. Reg Sindall, Group HRD (Bass Plc and GUS Plc) and EVP Group Resources, Burberry Plc (1994–2012)

I think – along with one of the CEOs I once had the pleasure of working with – that in addition to IQ (intelligence quotient) and EQ (emotional quotient), *MQ (moral quotient)* is an absolutely critical component of any IMUE's DNA. In Burberry, MQ was enshrined in the values as honesty and integrity, and courage … that is: the *integrity and honesty* to know when something isn't right, combined with the *courage* to speak up … in three-dimensional cultures this might be an issue … the important thing to do in MUEs is to ensure that corporate values *transcend* (certain) cultural values and – where people are faced with seemingly intractable dilemmas – they can speak up courageously without any fear of retribution … Where this works is when people are *selected* for the right values in the first place and are not *purely* motivated by self-interested financial gain.

2. Dr Lisa Qixun Siebers, one of the leading authorities on IMUE expansion in China and Africa

IMUEs operating in China are stuck on the horns of a dilemma! … should they engage in what might be speciously called 'gifting' (i.e. bribery and corruption) with powerful local officials (i.e. the City Mayor, politicians, regulatory authorities – police, environmental health, etc.) in order to secure the best sites, supply chain access and 'light intervention'/protection *or* stick rigidly to 'western' notions of propriety? … In a way I regard this as an interesting question because the notion that all of the IMUEs operating in China are 'squeaky clean' in their own domains smacks somewhat of hypocrisy! … Frankly, at times, some companies who claim 'sea green incorruptibility' at home are being somewhat disingenuous … How ethical is their supply chain, to what extent do they exploit labour, how do they treat wider stakeholders, how robust are their procedures for checking 'kick backs' with suppliers, etc.?! … Can they claim absolute honesty, transparency and morality regarding all aspects of their trading?! … Frankly, at times IMUEs take a rather haughty imperialist tone when discussing business practices in China when they would do well to consider the ones that prevail in their home territories! …

However, I accept that it is a matter of *moral relativism* … the fact is that in China, due to its socio-historical 'roots of *civilisation*' – the acceptance of political 'grip' exercised by a strong 'elite' – doing business is fraught with moral conundrums on a day-to-day basis … Although there is (limited) evidence that this is changing, it still means that *local managers have to tread a careful line* between what their IMUE CSR policy might say, and what they might have to do in local markets to 'get ahead' … the fact is that at present, if they fail to engage in what their corporate centre might label '*malpractice*', but is locally seen as '*normal practice*', then others will profit in their place – particularly during the recent economic slowdown which has been coupled with rising rents, increasing 'human resources' costs and severe competition ... Sometimes IMUEs such as *x* (a large Northern European retailer) have been caught out by Central Government for 'going too far' locally (according to one report, allegedly closing their Shaoxing store in October 2012 'by demobilising local staff through unethical methods – staff stealing the union seal, using the signature stamp as a means to force early termination of contracts') ... but it remains a major problem for IMUEs; do you desist or privately sanction/turn a blind eye to what would be deemed unethical business practice elsewhere? ... how do you monitor it and what sanctions do you apply when you find it ?

3. *Bob Dignen, Director, York Associates – experts in international leadership development*

To my mind at the current time there are two main dimensions to ethics within IMUEs ... The first relates to *macro-CSR* issues such as the 'green agenda', sustainability and operating in a manner in international territories that respects all local stakeholders (i.e. communities, suppliers, customers, etc.) ... The second relates to *micro-people issues* – the way in which local staff in IMUEs are treated ... there is no doubt in my mind that as global economic pressures have intensified over the past five years, middle managers (and by implication local leaders in IMUEs) have become 'squeezed' and 'overloaded' as the pressure is ratcheted up for international investments to deliver decent rates of ROI/ROCE ... in part this has been driven by shareholder pressure but also by a 'super cadre' of leadership who, fearing for their positions, no doubt, have expected people to perform well with less 'hard' and 'soft' resources ... what has been the consequence of this? ... in my view it has meant that in some areas a culture has emerged which places *accuracy of performance reporting at risk*, e.g. 'over-stating/reporting of results' (sales/profit), the non-disclosure of serious problems/malfunctions/system conflicts, etc. In some situations, local leaders are seemingly driven to adopt a 'survival strategy', reporting change initiatives and projects as on track or successes when more accurate analysis would potentially reveal a very different picture. Whilst the ethics of such behaviour might be regarded as questionable, its manifestation as a form of 'behavioural defence mechanism' against overambitious targets underpinned by ludicrously low resources – a toxic organisation – is understandable.

7.4 Chapter Summary

This chapter has synthesised what the respondents to this research exercise deemed to be the most important personal characteristics pertaining to HMULs and the way in which they could be developed. Most respondents had been apprised of 'developed' market MUL competencies through receipt of a draft/first edition copy of Edger (2012). The empirical observations that they made about what the salient differences were and the construct changes that needed to be made have been triangulated and incorporated into the framework presented above. The significant additions – that might aid IMUEs during their considerations of high performance competency matrices – are *courage* (under the banner of expertise), *humility*, *respect* and conceptualisations of 'environment' (under EI) and *ethics* (combined with energy in this book). A number of expert respondents have subsequently read drafts of this chapter and validated their inclusion. Why? The insertion of *courage* is supported due to the fact that at times HMULs will have to step outside societal/ cultural patterns of behaviour in order to, for instance, drive output-led performance in diffuse, relational cultures and/or 'speak up' in collectivist contexts where traditionally 'clan' members are bound by codes of passivity in order to save 'face'. *Humility* and *respect* are included in the EI cluster because respondents recognised that in contexts where 'self-protective' leadership styles predominated, such 'contra' behaviours generated higher levels of followership. The concept of *'environment'* being attached to the EI construct stems from the need for HMULs to be 'culturally intelligent' in terms of processing their wider internal/external environments which are more ambiguous and complex than those encountered by 'developed' market MULs. Finally, *ethics* is included due to an explicit need for IMUEs to ensure that their highly dispersed operations are operating legally; HMULs are instrumental in fulfilling a checking role to ensure that 'corners' are *not* being cut, safeguarding the health and safety interests of customers. But how easy is it for IMUEs to change behaviours and develop all of the personal characteristics outlined above? Some of the developmental solutions will be reprised in the next chapter, suffice to say that changing ingrained attitudes and pre-dispositions is extremely difficult. One further thought that might be added to the constructs and interventions outlined above is the notion that – as in a developed context – HMULs might be able to perform *cognitive dissonance* or operate according to *multiple identities*. That is to say that the way they condition themselves to act 'within the corporation' might be at odds with the way they act outside of the workplace. The final chapter will now bring all the themes of this book together, assess its contribution and make suggestions for further research.

8 *Conclusion*

This project was prompted by the desire to enquire more deeply into how service-based IMUEs are evolving their approaches to internationalising their operations within developing and growth markets. Having reached/encountered high levels of market penetration/saturation within developed market contexts, how have they expanded their 'frontiers of operations' in unfamiliar and challenging environments? In addition, given the problems that have been noted by several commentators relating to the scarcity of 'local talent' (ATKearney 2012, CIPD 2012), how have they *co-opted and developed* 'host' country management (most importantly HMULs) to expedite their plans and objectives? The exploration of these questions is important not only to practitioners considering growth market investments but also academics who have – to date – focused more exclusively on understanding, first, path dependencies relating to MNCs rather than IMUEs and, second, the impact and efficacy of expatriates and culturally adept 'geo-leaders' rather than HCMs ('host country managers').

To be sure, the opportunities that still exist for IMUEs in emerging markets remain significant as service-based consumption is driven upwards through 'economic enfranchisement' over the next 20 to 30 years – potentially to current developed economy levels (GSAM 2012, Sorrell 2012). However, as the Introduction to this book highlighted), there are a number of 'macro' and 'micro' challenges faced by MUEs seeking to internationalise. From a 'macro' *external environmental* perspective IMUEs have been hampered by economic disruption in their 'home' markets, which has restricted their access to 'expansion capital', and by fast-paced developments in emerging markets, including emergent (and imitative) local competition and smart technology adoption allied to national business system/cultural idiosyncrasies of nascent markets (i.e. laws, legal system, infrastructure, customs, tastes and preferences). From a 'micro' *internal organisational* point of view, IMUEs are faced with a number of challenges in some territories – not least a scarcity of local skilled 'emotional labour' and span of control/ distance issues that threaten consistency and quality, the complexities of customising products/services to conform to local preferences, ever-present 'centre versus subsidiary' tensions over strategy and operational tactics and evolving format, product, channel and contract arrangements in response to competitive and commercial exigencies.

Responses to these challenges were highlighted in Chapters 2 and 3, where 'home' parent and 'host' subsidiary/partner performance factors were elucidated by both the academic literature (with regards to the former) and practitioner insight (in respect of the latter). This book then concentrated upon extrapolating the activities, behaviours, characteristics and development of a key 'host country' managerial cohort within IMUEs; namely HMULs. Thus, Chapters 4 to 7 were framed by what the academic literature has had to say about various aspects of growth/developing market managerial behaviour and, more importantly, what the expert panel for this book regarded as being of empirical significance. As the summaries to each chapter stated, what emerged from these accounts seemed to be, at face value, complex and contradictory. Indeed, the key 'unifying theme' that presented itself from the literature and data was, in itself, hardly unitary. In fact, the *answers to the questions posed by this enquiry insinuated a host of paradoxes and conundrums.* That is to say, the choices faced by MUEs wishing to successfully internationalise and co-opt local talent *are not binary* but multi-faceted *dualisms.* In short, IMUEs – in order to optimise their chances of success – must effectively manage the conundrums they are confronted with or, to put it in the words of Reg Sindall, EVP Burberry Plc, 'effectively play three-dimensional chess'. This concluding chapter will firstly outline the various main 'thematic dimensions' of this book, and then consider its contributions, gaps and suggested areas for further research.

8.1 Key Theme – The Conundrums and Dualisms of IMUEs

The stand-out feature of this investigation are the conundrums faced by MUEs as they attempt to internationalise. Within the academic literature researchers have attempted to establish which contigual path in relation to product, policies and practices is adopted by MNCs, wrestling with notions of *'home'* versus *'host', universal* versus *contextual, integrated* versus *diffuse, convergence* versus *divergence* and *prescriptive* versus *adaptive.* Contingent variables affecting these choices have included institutional/cultural 'country of origin'/'host country' factors, globalising forces/'dominance' effects, industry type, and intra-organisational dispositions (i.e. strategy, culture, power, architecture, 'contracts', expertise, etc.). With regards to this research the same tensions were visible, albeit specific conundrums applied to IMUEs due to their business models' heavy reliance on service providers in dispersed, remote locations providing a consistent level of service quality.

In essence there are a number of questions and choices faced by IMUEs to which answers and solutions will vary according to a number of factors. This means that decision-makers must be agile, possessing the ability to both process information and respond according to the 'way things are' rather than 'how they want them to be'. Thus 'uniformity' must be juxtaposed against 'best fit'. Where tradeoffs are made they should be judged in terms of economic optimisation (i.e. minimising the effects of institutional and cultural non-conformance). As the summaries to each chapter demonstrated the choices confronting IMUEs were not optional or mutually exclusive but – to one degree or another – combined. That is to say, as one respondent put it elegantly, IMUEs must be able 'to jog and chew gum'. Choosing an 'either/or' approach is not sensible; IMUEs must – at times – attempt to juggle two seemingly irreconcilable and oppositional activities in order to ensure success. Thus, this section will now consider the *'duality'* of approaches required by IMUEs, derived from the narratives from the empirical evidence.

8.1.1 CALIBRATION AND COGNISANCE

Chapter 2 ('Internationalisation Performance Factors') considered the academic literature relating to the performance factors which affect internationalising organisations. Two dominant narratives were derived from the plethora of this body of work – *calibration* and *cognisance*; namely, firms were more likely to be successful if they *rationally* and dispassionately calibrated 'growth market' economic trends *combined* with a deep *emotional* understanding and cognisance of the idiosyncrasies of the market they were analysing/addressing. Companies that took a scientific approach without any recourse to deep contemplation of nuanced differences (closing down psychic distance) were likely to fail. On the other hand those organisation that believe that – due to prior experience – their ability to 'read' cultures has led to success in the past should also methodically calculate the costs and likely paybacks of entering markets that are (possibly) more dynamic and mature than they had originally estimated. Thus, the choice is not binary – organisations must simultaneously calibrate and be cognisant.

But combining art with science, measurement with intuition/perception – in order to minimise business risk – is a highly complex process. The strategic decision-making capability of key personnel in IMUEs can be informed by inquisitive mindsets (disaggregating both quantitative and qualitative data) and prior experiential knowledge (combining explicit and tacit insights). Indeed, it is opportune if policy-makers calibrate, and are cognisant of, the effect of overlaying their business model and 'modus operandi' in unfamiliar environments, perhaps taking a 'deliberately naïve' approach, as John Woodward stated in Case Study 8:

> ... *the central insight I would offer is that our success has been built not upon replicating 'sameness' but* 'seeing the differences' ... *I call it being 'deliberately naive' – approaching a market with no pre-conceptions. (John Woodward, EVP KUE Inc. Singapore)*

Nevertheless, the whole 'raison d'être' of standardised forms of IMUEs – due to reasons of economic efficiency – is repetition and replication. Thus, some commonalities must prevail whilst allowances are made for local adaptation.

8.1.2 CONGRUENCE AND CUSTOMISATION

The end of Chapter 2 (see 2.3.4 and 2.3.5) detailed how the mode of market entry and type of intra-firm architecture chosen by internationalising organisations had a major influence on whether or not 'loose' or 'tight' forms of control prevailed between the parent and its subsidiary/partner. In Chapter 3 ('Activities and Issues'), other considerations such as funding, expertise, adaptive capability and access/reference to power resources (i.e. inimitable local tacit knowledge) were also highlighted as mediating factors. It was also shown that at various times strategic and operational tensions between the two parties arose, not least due to the centre's need to assert some form of conformance and regularity (to achieve desired outputs) and the subsidiary/partner's requirement for a degree of autonomy to 'fit' the product, concept and/or service delivery mechanism to achieve local salience. The reality – as highlighted by the Case Studies and associated empirical data – is that this is not a binary choice; IMUEs both *enforce congruence* and *permit customisation* – albeit to varying degrees according to product and service mix – simultaneously.

In terms of *congruence*, respondents during the course of this research highlighted the transmission of standard operating blueprints, back of house systems and generic KPIs from 'home' to 'host' operations. Also, universal value systems were deployed as 'soft' binding mechanisms, with moves from country management to globally coordinated brand/sector structures providing better 'line of sight' and shared best practice:

> *In Rosinter we have just changed the operational architecture to focus more around* single *rather than* multi-brand sites, *which in turn creates a sense of purpose, identity and (most importantly)* autonomous know-how *(i.e. how to slightly adapt the format and product sales mix to add value in distinctive micro-markets). (Kevin Todd, CEO Rosinter Restaurants, Russia [Case Study 5])*

> *... rather than dividing the business up by region and/or country, the company has gone down the route of dividing the business internationally by six or seven specific sectors ... Global sector directors are now hard-lined into direct reports in each territory, with the view being taken that technical expertise needs to be shared 'within sector' ... my sense is, actually, that this is a local business (due to local labour laws) and in-country operators will still need to retain a lot of autonomy. (Andy Vaughan, Senior Strategy Director, Sodexo [Case Study 3])*

Combined with with this requirement for congruence is an implicit need for local adaptation and *customisation* – but to what elements and by how much? What emerges from the research is that with regards to *goods and service mix*, higher degrees of customisation are required for '*pure services*' due to extant 'host' institutional forces. As Figure 8.1 below illustrates, those IMUEs in the business of providing 'pure services' – local recruitment solutions (ManpowerGroup), early years education (KUE, Inc.), 'hygiene solutions' (Rentokil-Initial) and 'on-site service solutions' (Sodexo) – were prone to customise and localise their propositions *more* due to the need for local legal and environmental conformance (employment, buildings, health and safety, climate, etc.). Where the mix between tangible goods and intangible services became more intertwined, a greater degree of standardisation became permissible for companies, hence the positioning – based on the accounts of respondents – of the rest of the IMUE offers:

Whilst the position of various multi-unit goods and services in Figure 8.1 can be disputed, the evidence garnered for this research demonstrated that for companies providing 'pure services' or products where service constituted an integral part of the overall offer, IMUEs had no option other than to adapt and customise their propositions to a far greater extent than those with a heavier reliance on tangible goods. For instance, as Mara Swan acknowledged in Case Study 19, whilst ManpowerGroup had a strict set of 'fixed' criteria governing certain aspects of its operation (outputs and compliance), a 'flexible' operating framework allowed local discretion and autonomy at a local level:

> *At ManpowerGroup [we have] 'fixed' and 'flexible' frameworks that act as 'boundaries' for permissible field-based activities ... The 'fixed' framework set by the centre sets the business-line contribution levels and rules that all assignments must be preceded by candidate experience and 'legal' work permit checks ... 'Flexible' frameworks allow 'host' country managers (i.e. regional and area level) to adapt their systems and approaches in accordance to local legal*

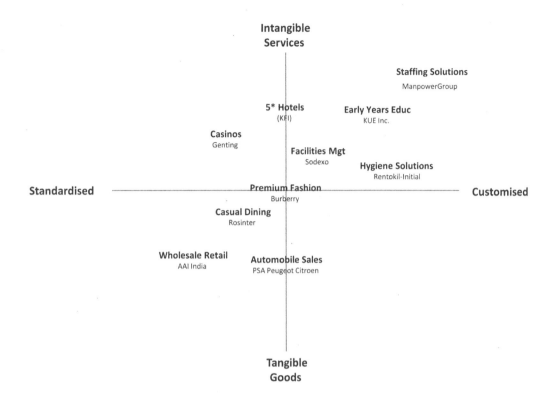

Figure 8.1   Goods/service mix and standardisation/customisation dependencies

requirements, the business cycle position of each territory (HRM outsourcing in mature contexts to boost margins – volume recruitment in growth situations) and cultural affectations (the process of 'greeting' candidates varies from territory to territory according to local norms and customs) … This 'flexibility' is also designed to encourage/empower field managers to be agile and act in an entrepreneurial manner. (Mara Swan, EVP Strategy and Talent, ManpowerGroup)

Mara Swan's reference to local field-based managers fulfilling a critical role – whether with regards to enforcing congruence or customising policies and practices to local requirements – leads us on to the next dualism, that of how IMUEs actually facilitate control through the line to ensure optimal outcomes.

8.1.3 COORDINATION AND CONSENT

At the conclusion of Chapter 3 ('Activities and Issues') the generic practices of field-based area managers or HMULs were elucidated, detailing the degree to which they were expected to expedite a number of key tasks on behalf of the organisation. Chapter 4 ('Ensuring Control') then sought to unpack one of the key dimensions of the role – that of exerting *managerial 'grip'* on behalf of the IMUE. But how did they achieve this? Academic research suggests that internationalising organisations achieve conformance through *bureaucratic control* and *values transference* (Jaeger 1983, Ouchi 1981). Empirical data collected from respondents endorsed these observations – IMUEs viewed HMULs as key linkages in performing control-related activities through bureaucratic means (blueprint execution and output prioritisation) and values (acting as transmissional and 'confessional' conduits).

However, the narrative captured from respondents suggested that whilst such activities and practices were important from a *co-ordination* perspective, they could only be effective if field-based management *consented* themselves. 'Home' notions of structure and agency might run counter to 'host' concepts of 'managerialism', with extant organisational values contradicting those of the local culture – gifting to officials in China being a prime example:

> ... should [area/city managers] engage in what might be speciously called 'gifting' (i.e. bribery and corruption) with powerful local officials (i.e. the city mayor, politicians, regulatory authorities – police, environmental health, etc.) in order to secure the best sites, supply chain access and 'light intervention'/protection or stick rigidly to 'western' notions of propriety? (Dr Lisa Qixun Siebers, NBS, Author 'Retail Internationalisation in China' [Case Study 21])

So how did IMUEs solve this conundrum – achieving consent and buy-in to managerial 'co-ordinated' ways of working and values systems that might seem alien to the recipients? Also, how did HMULs achieve these outcomes amongst their direct reports and teams?

With regards to *values* (see Chapter 7), interventions suggested by respondents included:

- Ensure that 'value systems' have a 'coherent logic';
- Select people according to their 'intrinsic alignment';
- Immersion through on-the-job/corporate training, rotation or 'reverse expat' training
- Modelling from 'exemplars' (i.e. corporate, expats, best-practice HMULs, etc.);
- Value 'benefit' selling – demonstrate the upside to recipients.

Whilst practitioners interviewed for this research stressed the necessity and importance of doing all of the above in order to inculcate the right value-driven behaviours, doubts persisted amongst some respondents that organisations could actually ensure that organisational values transcended cultural ones, given the impervious nature of certain norms and customs. Indeed, whilst selecting for values *sounds* intellectually compelling, some questioned whether or not such an approach would ever be successful:

> ... it is not very difficult to fake on these tests. Indeed it is often the organisation's insistence on publishing its values, usually on its own website, that results in such faking because applicants complete the value statements based on what the company has publicly declared about itself rather than revealing their true position. (Dr Nollaig Heffernan, Ecole Hoteliere Lausanne [Case Study 20])

Hence the importance that many respondents attached to entry-level immersion and ongoing reinforcement of 'good practice' by exemplars, from the top to the bottom of the organisation. In addition, the fact that many societies were undergoing 'value shifts' (i.e. increasing emancipation and self-expression) through rising incomes (permitting travel and greater autonomy), foreign education, social media, etc. also means that gaps that previously existed between 'developed' and 'developing' market values might be narrowing (Inglehart et al. 2010), making the task of values transmission for IMUEs easier in the longer term.

Whilst gaining consent for 'ideological' forms of control – that might run counter to extant cultural norms – is problematic, so too is the process of gaining consent for certain types of prescribed *bureaucratic co-ordination*. In *polychromic, diffuse* societies – or indeed contexts like certain parts of the Middle East where respondents reported that too much wealth had 'affected' managerial behaviour – 'loose' dispositions to budgets, deadlines and targets may prevail *in spite* of extrinsic KPI incentivisation. In these environments significant management training is required to embed basic skills such as objective setting, prioritisation, delegation, time management, performance management, appraisals, auditing/checking up, etc. Also, in cultural contexts where high levels of *power distance* predominated, leading to self-protective leadership styles (i.e. tell rather than coach, threaten/punish rather than motivate, etc.) and high *uncertainty avoidance* behaviours by followers (i.e. constant checking with higher authorities and only doing what has been instructed), IMUEs had to concentrate their efforts towards building the 'softer' leadership capability of their HMULs – the subject which will now be discussed below.

8.1.4 CAPABILITY AND COMPATIBILITY

As outlined in Chapter 5 ('Generating Commitment'), alongside asserting managerial control to provide assurance on certain outcomes (i.e. standards, safety, quality and systems adherence), IMUEs require their field-based HMULs to *motivate* and engage their teams to provide 'point of purchase' service levels which exceed local customer expectations; for instance, by displaying high levels of product knowledge to gain consumer trust (Furrer et al. 2000). At the beginning of the chapter reference was made to how internationalising firms have approached the recruitment and conditioning of service providers in different cultural contexts and the leadership style preferences that might elicit optimal outcomes. In addition, the international HRM literature was discussed, with an extrapolation of 'universal' and 'contextual' perspectives (the former being heavily influenced by US-based nomothetic social science, the latter by European idiographic methodological approaches). The overarching narrative, however – when combined with empirical evidence from respondents – was that in order to raise the leadership *capability* of local field-based personnel, organisational HRM practices required a high degree of *compatibility* with both the practical aspects of the job itself and the leadership predispositions of the target cohort.

With regards to practical dimensions, 'local know-how' was a key capability component. In the main this was exemplified by:

- *local language skills* (or bilingual local/English in hospitality and retail in traveller/ tourist destinations);
- *employee relations familiarity* (especially dealing with local unions);
- *local regulatory contacts* (with key officials and authorities);
- *local 'operational' knowledge and insight* (i.e. competitor, supply chain, labour market, contractors, site availability, etc.).

This local technical expertise (developed through grounded socialisation and experience), however, required melding with behavioural and cognitive capabilities to lead and motivate teams. Chapter 5 elucidated what respondents had agreed effective HMULs did; namely, framing a local vision for their portfolios, attracting and developing talent, displaying 'teamship', generating trust through open communications, etc. However, finding and developing local leaders to act in this way was problematic, not least because of deep-rooted cultural barriers in some areas:

> *Similarly, in Asia the concept of 'leader' or 'manager' is reportedly framed by* 'content' *notions of expertise and positional primacy rather than facilitation/enabling,* 'process notions' *of telling and directing rather than delegating/empowering and* 'emotional factors' *such as aggressive power rather than emotional proximity. (Bob Dignen, York Associates – International Leadership Specialists, author,* Communicating Internationally in English *[Case Study 12])*

So how do IMUEs develop local leadership capabilities in such (potentially) unreceptive environments? Solutions were advanced by respondents throughout the body of this work and summarised in Chapter 7. The key point, however, is that IMUE HRM interventions designed to raise the capabilities of local leaders had to be *compatible* and sympathetic to context (see references to values transmission in 8.1.3 above). Overlaying unitarist, individualistic HRM policies and practices in hierarchical, collectivist contexts does not provide any guarantee of success. But what are the practices that are universally agreed upon as providing a sound means for *facilitating* the local leadership activities of HMULs in their quest to motivate/engage service providers? IMUE interventions that were thought by respondents to be of *particular significance* included:

- *Avenues for meritocratic progression* (especially in youthful labour markets – signalling that 'know-how' is more important than 'who you know' to progress)
- *'Fit for purpose' service-based training and development*:
  - *Content* that is rooted in the idiom of the culture;
  - *Delivery processes* that are adapted to preferred learning styles (i.e. action-based learning/small-group learning in some Asian cultures);
  - *Accreditation* to enhance its meaning and status.
- *'Hygiene' employment practices that encourage retention*:
  - *Pay and benefits* (competitive rates of pay, holiday, sickness/absence entitlements, etc.);
  - *Working conditions* (good physical environment, 'fair' hours of work, etc.);
  - *Performance-related pay* (either individually or collectively based, to reward discretionary effort).

Local and regional HR personnel can assist in the design and implementation of the above, as well as ensuring that HMULs with the right local leadership characteristics are appointed in the first place. This is becoming easier for IMUEs as 'developed' market business approaches and philosophies are diffused by HCNs that have been exposed to such 'ways of working' by studying or working abroad, or through IMUEs themselves, hastening *'isometric convergence'* through the dissemination of western leadership discourse:

... there is some evidence that some elements of leadership/managerial practices are changing and that IMUEs are actually affecting the behaviours and policies of local companies ... Why? ... First, local nationals that have either been educated at western institutions or worked in developed contexts are far more comfortable with so-called 'best-practice' HRM techniques such as open communications and fostering trust through good leadership practice (i.e. putting a high premium on training and development, talent building, performance-related reward, etc.); these managers are able to model behaviours that can be imitated at workplace level ... Second, the 'flexible' managerial approaches used by companies such as Tesco, Carrefour and B&Q are being diffused into the wider system as managers leave and join local companies ... Take meritocratic progression based on performance and know-how rather than status and authority; this concept is certainly gaining traction in certain companies, particularly those in extremely competitive sectors. (Dr Lisa Qixun Siebers, NBS, author, 'Retail Internationalisation in China' [Case Study 13])

8.1.5 CAPACITY AND COLLABORATION

In Chapter 6 ('Implementing Change'), issues pertaining to effecting 'top-down' change in IMUEs were discussed alongside considerations relating to intra/inter-organisational knowledge diffusion. The two dominant themes that emerged (endorsed by respondent accounts elsewhere in the book) were that change/knowledge diffusion was highly contingent on the 'installed *capacity*' of organisational actors (i.e. their abilities and motivations) which, in turn, had an impact on levels of 'middle-down-up' *collaboration*. It was acknowledged by many respondents, however, that inculcating a continuous improvement philosophy in growth market subsidiaries might be fraught with difficulty on a number of accounts, not least lack of basic managerial skills, behavioural aversion to cross-company working and lack of resources:

The problem that we have in some Asian Pacific markets is that people are used to operating to servant-master principles ... this is an extreme issue when you are trying to operate a matrix structure ... Area managers who are used to 'serving' only one person are incapable of collaborating across brands and territories. (Anon Respondent, IMUE Senior Executive)

... as global economic pressures have intensified over the past five years, middle managers (and by implication local leaders in IMUEs) have become 'squeezed' and 'overloaded' as the pressure is ratcheted up for international investments to deliver decent rates of ROI/ROCE ... In some situations, local leaders are seemingly driven to adopt a 'survival strategy', reporting change initiatives and projects as on track or successes when more accurate analysis would potentially reveal a very different picture. (Bob Dignen, York Associates – International Leadership Specialists, author, Communicating Internationally in English *[Case Study 21])*

So how do IMUEs create capacity (i.e. abilities and motivation) within their organisations for change and collaborative knowledge diffusion? From an academic standpoint, change and information/insight sharing is facilitated through increasing individual/team capacity by addressing the issues: lack of trust (solved through face-to-face communications), different cultures (education, team-building), languages/frames of reference (job rotation), lack of time (creating temporal and physical space), status/power (collapse hierarchies), limited recipient absorptive capacity (educate employees for flexibility), knowledge hoarding (make ideas more important than status), error intolerance (remove sanctions and retribution) (Davenport and Prusak 2000: 97). Indeed, best-practice HRM (training, performance appraisal, merit-based promotion, performance-based compensation, open communications) is believed to play a major part in increasing the abilities and motivation of subsidiary actors in international organisations to absorb and transmit change (Minbaeva et al. 2003).

Indeed, many of these interventions were raised by respondents as being important during the course of this research (see 8.1.3 and 8.1.4 above), with emphasis being accorded to the following practices as having a significant impact upon 'installed capacity' and collaboration in IMUEs:

- *Organisational design/architecture* (i.e. switching to single brand structures to create more effective 'communities of practice');
- *'Reinforcement' communications* (i.e. face-to-face CEO 'town hall' briefings to adjust 'mindsets and buy-in');
- *Frequent rotation* (i.e. movement of personnel to facilitate 'on-the-job' tacit knowledge capture);
- *Cross-company meetings and 'celebratory' events* (i.e. to increase knowledge transference through 'relational' social capital);
- *'Flight path controllers'* (i.e. appointment of 'middle-men' to minimise change overload and capture 'best practice').

At a local, rather than organisational level, the need for capacity and collaboration was acknowledged – particularly in 'pure service' environments (see Figure 8.1 above):

> ... we expect our area managers to display good leadership and managerial skills ... passionately motivating, teaching and coaching our branch managers to deliver outstanding candidate, associate and client service ... also fostering a high degree of inter-branch/brand collaboration and information sharing. This latter point is important as what we are trying to create at ManpowerGroup is a 'collaborative' organisational structure ... this requires quite a high level of agility and flexibility amongst our field-based personnel. (Mara Swan, EVP Global Strategy and Talent, ManpowerGroup [Case Study 19])

The means by which respondents reported that HMULs created capacity throughout their districts to foster collaborative 'knowledge sharing' and – indeed – engaged in it (horizontally and vertically) themselves were highlighted in the following ways:

- *Behaviour modification* (i.e. adjusting mindsets through 'benefit upselling', removing sanctions for failure, rewarding/recognising ingenuity, etc.);
- *District architecture* (i.e. appointment of 'subject champions', creation of geographical 'clusters', 'families', 'hub and spokes' designed around 'houses of excellence' to encourage collaboration, sharing and mutually beneficial 'hidden value' exchange, etc.);
- *Transmission vehicles* (i.e. people 'site swaps/placements', district meetings 'topped or tailed' by social events, spontaneous interactions, use of smart communications technology, etc.);

- *Wider organisational diffusion* (i.e. through participation on work groups, projects and improvement initiatives, social network interaction, information/insight exchanges at regional meetings, etc.).

8.2 Contributions

This research has been a modest attempt to add to the body of knowledge on the internationalisation of MUEs into emerging markets and the manner in which they develop a key cohort, namely, their field-based area managers (HMULs). Whilst there is a large literature relating to MNC and retail internationalisation, enquiry relating to broader service-based multi-unit entities has been lacking. More significantly there has been almost no attempt to understand in *specific* terms (in spite of the HCN literature) how IMUEs seek to locate, develop and retain their key field-based area managers in growth markets. Previous commentary in this area (see 1.5.2) has concentrated almost exclusively upon examining this cohort within developed market contexts, almost exclusively within US fast food or casual dining contexts (Umbreit 1989, Mone and Umbreit 1989, Umbreit and Smith 1991, Ryan 1992, Muller and Campbell 1995, DiPietro et al. 2007, Rivera et al. 2008). A previous study that incorporated some international case studies (Edger 2012) led the author to conclude that the skill sets and behaviours of HMULs in growth territories – due to societal conditioning, local context and extreme distance – were not the same as their 'western counterparts' and that generic (mainly US-informed) approaches were not sufficient to provide IMUEs any route map for success.

The author contends that, in spite of the multiple flaws of this study, this research partially addresses the request of practitioners and commentators to provide solutions to field-based 'talent pool' shortages within developing markets.

Its main contributions can be said to fall in three areas:

- *Integrated model* – The book is constructed around an international multi-unit leadership framework which provides the reader with the following benefits:
  - An appreciation of the overall *context* in which IMUEs function and operate;
  - An understanding of the pertinent *linkages and connections* relating to the subject in question;
  - *Theoretical constructs* (i.e. institutional and power resource) that help explain dynamic interactions.
- *Growing importance of host country management* – The 21 case studies in this book provide valuable up-to-date accounts on how IMUEs are strategising at the current time, coupled with deep insights into the importance they attach to developing 'host-grown' local leadership cadres. The accounts of the IMUE experts (practitioners, academics and consultants) on how international service-based organisations are tackling the selection, development and engagement of growth market HMULs are, in themselves, significant contributions but they also emphasise the growing importance of this cohort – particularly as IMUEs continue to expand their operations in these territories. There was a universal view among the respondents that, to date, this cohort has been poorly researched and not properly understood. This book provides readers with a better understanding of:

- The *complexities and ambiguities* faced by IMUEs trying to co-opt and develop field-based leadership in developing markets;
- *Specific solutions, techniques and interventions* that might – in certain contexts – raise the operational performance and financial contribution of this cohort.

- *Hybridisation* – The research for this book established that IMUEs had to take adaptive approaches to growth markets whilst retaining some semblance of uniformity. That is to say, given institutional/cultural differences and economic/political relativities, IMUEs had to carefully plot their market entry/growth strategies, adopting a hybrid perspective. Often this took the form of exporting standard operational platforms and values combined with customisation in product/service mix and local policies and practices. Indeed, the sections above outlined the *duality* of approaches required by IMUEs which might help students and practitioners better understand how service-based organisations tackle the conundrums they face in this area. Of particular note are the following tentative observations:
  - *'Pure service'*-based IMUEs (i.e. recruitment, facilities management and early years education) are more likely to customise their 'customer facing' operations due to *institutional* and national business pressures.
  - Whilst movement to *'single- brand'* channels in IMUEs (i.e. hotels, casual dining, 'on-site solutions' and car dealerships) might suggest that withdrawing from multi-brand country management structures is an attempt to dilute 'local focus', it is in fact an attempt to simultaneously achieve greater central coherence (reducing 'home' versus 'host' *power resource* struggles) *and* local insight, flexibility and responsiveness.
  - Given the *management and leadership activities* that developing market HMULs are expected to expedite and their extant context, socialisation and behavioural conditioning, IMUEs must deploy sophisticated forms of development that are cognisant of the *sociological* and *psychological* predispositions of the subjects in question.

8.3 Further Research

This research has triangulated evidence from a number of respondents that hold privileged access to data and insights within IMUEs that are expanding their operations in developing markets. Most of the respondents have had *direct* responsibility for developing HMULs or have been contracted to do so. Prior to interview all respondents had been in receipt of draft copies of my first book (Edger 2012), which reflected on the activities, behaviours and characteristics of MULs in developed market MUEs, and had time to contrast this account and their own developing market perceptions/experiences. When interviewed they were asked a number of questions; principally, *what* HMULs actually did (or were expected to do) and *how* their organisations – or the entities that they provided training/consultancy services to – co-opted, *developed* and retained 'host' country area management talent to ensure optimal outcomes. The output from this endeavour has produced a book which has attempted to capture the essence of these narratives, drawing out major themes, observations and (hopefully) contributions. Given that a work of this particular nature – *in this domain* – has not been attempted before, the author apologises for its multiple and manifest imperfections, not least the fact that he has – due to issues of access –

drawn evidence from the 'developers' rather than the 'recipients' (i.e. HMULs). Thus, the accounts of those that *do* the developing have not been cross-checked or correlated against the accounts of those that are in receipt of it. This raises questions – in spite of the best ontological efforts of the author – of perceptual bias, data contamination and error. It is therefore proposed that further studies (if they can obtain unfettered access) conduct in-depth, cross-national research into the HMUL cohort itself. Indeed – with my publisher's blessing – this might be the subject of my next book.

8.4 Summary

The main point of enquiry of this book has been to establish the context, substance and dynamics of HMUL 'local leader' development within growth and emerging markets. Its pertinence is highlighted by the growing recognition amongst practitioners and commentators that 'local talent' deficits are inhibiting their expansion plans in these territories. This work, based on significant empirical research derived from experts directly involved in HMUL development, does not argue that properly trained and well-orientated field-based personnel are the sole contingent variable contributing to IMUE success. Indeed, given the challenges IMUEs face (i.e. home market disruption, local competition, rapid technological change, etc.), performance factors such as strategy, experience, intra-firm architecture at 'home country' level *and* levels of funding, local knowledge/expertise and *adaptability* at 'host' subsidiary/partner level, can be counted as more important precursors to success. Nevertheless, strategy and tactics count for nothing in IMUEs unless plans are implemented effectively through the line.

HMULs are 'where the rubber hits the road'. As this study has shown they have a significant local role to play in ensuring that standards, systems and sales-led service activities are expedited at unit level. They achieve this through exerting effective managerial *control* (through blueprint execution and effective values transmission), driving *committed* and motivated behaviours (through 'leading from the middle'), overseeing the successful implementation of *change* and diffusion of knowledge. The personal characteristics required to do this include high levels of managerial expertise (including local knowledge, judgement, courage and adaptability), environmental emotional intelligence (including self-awareness/humility and awareness of others/ respect), energy and ethics. However, due to a number of issues in emerging markets – not least those relating to institutional/cultural factors – certain aptitudes, cognitive capabilities and behaviours might be lacking. This book contends that IMUEs therefore need to spend a lot of time and resources puzzling over the right development solutions that will optimise performance in any given developing market context. Hybrid interventions might be the answer – given the insights of the book – but IMUEs will at least stand a chance of success if they ask which *standardised* approaches are permissible and/or which *customised* solutions are essential? This is the non-trivial conundrum faced by IMUEs across a range of issues – addressing it successfully might contribute to effective international multi-unit leadership.

Bibliography

Abbott, K. 2006. 'A Review of Employment Relations Theories and Their Application'. *Problems and Perspectives in Management* 1, 187–99.

Agarwal, S. 1994. 'Socio-cultural distance and the choice of joint ventures: a contingency perspective'. *Journal of International Marketing* 2(2), 63–80.

Albrecht, K. and Zemke, R. 1995. *Service America! Doing Business in the New Economy*. New York: Warner Books.

Alexander, N. 1990. 'Retailers and international markets: motives for expansion'. *International Marketing Review* 7(4), 75–85.

———. 1997. *International Retailing*. Oxford: Blackwell.

Alexander, N. and Myers, H. 2000. 'The retail internationalisation process'. *International Marketing Review* 17(4/5), 334–53.

Ali, A. and Al-Kazemi, A. 2006. 'Human Resource Management in Kuwait'. In *Managing Human Resources in the Middle East*, eds P. Budwhar and K. Mellahi. London: Routledge, 79–96.

Almond, P., Edwards, T., Colling, T., Ferner, A., Gunnigle, P., Muller-Camen, M., Quintanilla, J. and Wachter, H. 2005. 'Unravelling Home and Host Country Effects: An Investigation of the HR Policies of an American Multinational in Four European Countries'. *Industrial Relations* 44(2), 276–305.

Alvesson, M. and Karreman, D. 2004. 'Interfaces of control: Technocratic and socio-ideological control in a global management consultancy firm'. *Accounting, Organizations and Society* 29, 423–44.

Anthony, R.N. and Govindarajan, V. 2004. *Management control systems*. New York: McGraw-Hill.

Argote, L. 1999. *Organizational Learning: Creating, retaining and transferring knowledge*. Norwell MA: Kluwer Academic.

Arrow, K. 1962. 'Economic welfare and the allocation of resources for invention'. In *The Rate and Direction of Invention Activity: Economic and Social Factors – A Report of the National Bureau of Economic Research*, ed. K. Arrow. Princeton NJ: Princeton University Press, 609–25.

Arthur, W. and Bennett, W. 1995. 'The international assignee: the relative importance of factors perceived to contribute to success'. *Personnel Psychology* 48(2), 99–114.

Ashkanasy, N., Wilderom, C. and Peterson, M. (eds). 2000. *Handbook of Organizational Culture and Climate*. Thousand Oaks, CA: Sage.

Asma, S. 2012. *Against Fairness*. Chicago: Chicago University Press.

ATKearney. 2012. *Global Retail Expansion: Keeps on Moving*. New York: ATKearney Inc.

Autry, J. 2001. *The Servant Leader*. New York: Three Rivers Press.

Bach, S. and Sisson, K. 2000. *Personnel Management*. Oxford: Blackwell.

Barker, J.R. 2005. 'Toward a philosophical orientation on control'. *Organization* 12(5), 787–91.

Barley, S.R. and Kunda, G. 1992. 'Design and devotion: Surges of rational and normative ideologies of control in managerial discourse'. *Administrative Science Quarterly* 37(3), 363–99.

Barney, J. 1991. 'Firm resources and sustained competitive advantage'. *Journal of Management* 17(1), 99–120.

Bartlett, C. and Goshal, S. 1989. *Managing across Borders*. Boston, MA: Harvard Business School.

Batrus Hollweg International [BHI]. 2005a (April 7). 'Tackling the multi-unit manager challenge', Part 1. *Peak Performance Update*. http:/www.batrushollweg.com/files/4-7-05.newsletter.MUM1.pdf.

——. 2005b (April 24). 'Tackling the multi-unit manager challenge', Part 2. *Peak Performance Update*. http:/www.batrushollweg.com/files/4-24-05.newsletter.MUM_2.pdf.

Beck, B. and Moore, L. 1995. 'Linking the Host Culture to Organizational Variables'. In *Organizational Culture*, ed. P. Frost. Beverly Hills: Sage.

Beckerman, W. 1956. 'Distance and the pattern of intra-European trade'. *Review of Economics and Statistics* 28, 31–40.

Belbin, R.M. 2000a. *Team Roles at Work*. New York: Butterworth-Heinemann.

——. 2000b. *Beyond the Team*. New York: Butterworth-Heinemann.

Benson, J. and Ugolini, L. 2003. *A Nation of Shopkeepers*. New York: Tauris.

Birkinshaw, J. 2000. *Entrepreneurship in the Global Firm: Enterprise and Renewal*. London: Sage.

Birkinshaw, J. and Bresman, H. 2000. 'Managing the Post-Acquisition Integration Process: How the Human Integration and Task Integration Processes Interact to Foster Value Creation'. *Journal of Management Studies* 37, 395–425.

Birkinshaw, J. and Fry, N. 1998. 'Subsidiary Initiatives to Develop New Markets'. *Sloan Management Review* 39(3), 51–62.

Birkinshaw, J. and Hood, N. 1998. 'Multinational Subsidiary Evolution'. *Academy of Management Review*, 23(4), 773–94.

Birnberg, J.G. and Snodgrass, C. 1988. 'Culture and control: A field study'. *Accounting, Organizations and Society* 13, 447–64.

Blake, R.R. and Mouton, J.S. 1985. *The Managerial Grid III*. Houston: Gulf Publishing.

Bland, B. 2013. 'Fast Food Chains Battle to Eat into Indonesia'. *Financial Times*, 8/9 (June) – 19.

Bligh, M. and Riggio, R. (eds). 2013. *Exploring Distance in Leader-Follower Relationships: When Near is Far and Far is Near*. New York: Routledge.

Bower, J. 2001. 'Not all M&As Are Alike and that Matters'. *Harvard Business Review* 79(3), 93–101.

Boyacigiller, N. 1990. 'The role of expatriates in the management of interdependence, complexity and risk in multinational corporations'. *Journal of International Business Studies* 21(3), 357–81.

Branine, M. 1996. 'Observations on training and management development in the People's Republic of China'. *Personnel Review* 25(1), 25–35.

——. 2005. 'Cross-Cultural training of managers: an evaluation of a management development programme for Chinese managers'. *Journal of Management Development* 24(5/6), 459–61.

Bresman, H., Birkinshaw, J. and Nobel, R. 1999. 'Knowledge transfer in international acquisitions'. *Journal of International Business Studies* 30(3), 439–62.

Brewster, C. 1999. 'The Value of Different Paradigms in HRM'. In *Strategic Human Resource Management*, eds R. Schuler and S. Jackson. Oxford: Blackwell.

——. 2002. 'Human Resources in Multinational Companies'. In *The Blackwell Handbook of Cross Cultural Management*. Oxford: Blackwell.

Brezezicki, M. 2008. *Examining the competencies required to be a successful multi-unit manager*. Unpublished PhD dissertation, North Central University.

Broad, G. 1994. 'The Managerial Limits to Japanisation: A Manufacturing Case Study'. *Human Resource Management Journal* 4(3), 52–69.

Brumby, M. 2012. 'Accor Announces Major Restructuring of Management'. *Langton Capital Briefing*, 7 (December), 1.

Burns, J.M. 1978. *Leadership*. NY: Harper & Row.

Butler, S. 2011. 'Stores in Scramble for Smartphone Salvation'. *The Times*, 31 May, 38.

Carnall, C. 2007. *Managing Change in Organisations* (5th edn). Harlow: Pearson.

Carraher, S., Sullivan, S. and Crocitto, M. 2008. 'Mentoring across global boundaries: an empirical examination of home and host country mentors on expatriate careers'. *Journal of International Business Studies* 39(8), 1310–26.

Cartwright, S. and Cooper, C. 1993. 'The Role of Cultural Compatibility in Successful Organizational Marriage'. *Academy of Management Executive* 7, 57–70.

———. 1996. *Managing Mergers, Acquisitions and Strategic Alliances: Integrating People and Cultures.* Oxford: Butterworth-Heinemann.

Cavusgil, S. and Zou, S. 1994. 'Marketing strategy-performance relationship: an investigation of the empirical link in export market ventures'. *Journal of Marketing* 58(1), 1–21.

Chalos, P. and O'Connor, N.G. 2004. 'Determinants of the use of various control mechanisms in US Chinese joint ventures'. *Accounting, Organizations and Society* 29, 591–608.

Chan, P., Finnegan, C. and Sternquist, B. 2011. 'Country and firm level factors in international expansion'. *European Journal of Marketing* 45(6), 1005–22.

Chang, E. and Taylor, M.S. 1999. 'Control in multinational corporations (MNCs): The case of Korean manufacturing subsidiaries'. *Journal of Management* 25(4), 541–65.

Chang, M-H. and Harrington, J. 2000. 'Centralization vs. Decentralisation in a Multi-Unit Organization: A Computational Model of a Retail Chain as a Multi-Agent Adaptive System'. *Management Science* 46(11), 1427–40.

Chase, W.E. and Simon, H.A. 1973. 'Perception in Chess'. *Cognitive Psychology* 4, 55–81.

Chatman, J. and Jehn, K. 1994. 'Assessing the Relationship between Industry Characteristics and Organizational Culture: How Different Can You Be?' *Academy of Management Journal* June, 522–53.

Chhabra, S. 1996. 'Marketing adaptations by American multinational corporations in South America'. *Journal of Global Marketing* 9(4), 57–74.

Chilkoti, A. and Jopson, B. 2013. 'Walmart's India Chief in Sudden Departure'. Financial Times, 27 (June) – 17.

Christensen, C.M. and Overdorf, M. 2000. 'Meeting the Challenge of Disruptive Change'. *Harvard Business Review* March–April, 67–76.

CIPD (Chartered Institute of Personnel and Development). 2012. *Learning, talent and innovation in Asia.* Available from cipd.co.uk/sop [accessed 15 November 2012].

Clark, A. 2012. 'Are Koreans ready to break their family ties?' *The Times*, 12 December, 51.

Clark, I. and Almond, P. 2004. 'Dynamism and Embeddedness: Towards a Lower Road? British Subsidiaries of American Multinationals'. *International Journal of HRM* 35(6), 536–56.

Clover, C. 2012. 'Kremlin Tightens the Screws'. *Investing in Russia*, Financial Times Special Report, *Financial Times*, 19 October, 1.

Coe, N.M. and Wrigley, N. 2007. 'Host economy impacts on transnational retail: the research agenda'. *Journal of Economic Geography* 7, 341–71.

Cohen, W. and Levinthal, D. 1990. 'Absorptive Capacity: A new perspective on learning and innovation'. *Administrative Science Quarterly* 35, 128–52.

Collins, J. 2001. 'Level 5 Leadership: The triumph of humility and fierce resolve'. *Harvard Business Review* July, 66–76.

Conner, K. and Prahalad, C. 1996. 'A Resource Based Theory of The Firm: Knowledge vs Opportunism'. *Organization Science* 7, 477–501.

Cropanzano, R. and Mitchell, M.S. 2005. 'Social exchange theory: an interdisciplinary review'. *Journal of Management* 31, 874–900.

Daley, L., Jiambalvo, J., Sundem, G. and Kondo, Y. 1985. 'Attitudes toward financial control systems in the United States and Japan'. *Journal of International Business Studies* Fall, 91–109.

Davenport, T. and Prusak, L. 2000. *Working Knowledge: How Organizations Manage What They Know*. Boston, MA: Harvard Business School Press.

Dawson, J. 1993. *The internationalisation of retailing*. Department of Business Studies, University of Edinburgh, Working Paper, 93(2).

———. 1994. 'Internationalization of retailing operations'. *Journal of Marketing Management* 10, 267–82.

———. 2007. 'Scoping and conceptualizing retailer internationalisation'. *Journal of Economic Geography* 7, 373–97.

Dawson, J. and Mukoyama, M. 2006. 'Retail internationalisation as a process'. In *Strategic Issues in International Retailing*, eds J. Dawson, R. Larke and M. Mukoyama. New York: Routledge, 31–50.

De Vries, M. and Florent-Treacy, E. 2002. 'Global leadership from A to Z: creating high commitment organizations'. *Organizational Dynamics* 30(4), 295–309.

De Vries, M., Korotov, K.R. and Florent-Treacy, E. 2007. *Coach or Couch: The Psychology of Making Better Leaders*. Paris: INSEAD Business Press.

Delery, J. and Doty, D. 1996. 'Modes of Theorising in Strategic Human Resource Management: Tests of Universalistic, Contingency and Configurational Performance Predictions'. *Academy of Management Journal* 39(4), 802–35.

DiPietro, R.B., Murphy, K.S., Rivera, M. and Muller, C.C. 2007. 'Multi-unit management key success factors in the casual dining restaurant industry: a case study'. *International Journal of Contemporary Hospitality Management* 19(7), 524–36.

Doherty, A. and Alexander, N. 2004. 'Relationship development in international retail franchising: case study evidence from the UK fashion sector'. *European Journal of Marketing* 83(9/10), 1215–35.

Donnelon, A. 1996. *Team Talk*. Boston, MA: Harvard Business School Press.

Dowling, P.J., Schuler, R.S. and Welch, D.E. 1994. *International dimensions of human resource management* (2nd edn). Belmont, CA: Wadsworth.

Earley, C. and Mosakowski, E. 2004. 'Cultural Intelligence'. *Harvard Business Review* October, 139–46.

Easterby-Smith, M., Malina, D. and Yuan, L. 1995. 'How culture-sensitive is HRM? A comparative analysis of practice in Chinese and UK companies'. *International Journal of Human Resource Management* 6(1), 31–59.

Ebrahimi, H. 2013. 'Pret's Appetising Refinancing Deal'. *The Sunday Telegraph*, 10 February, B3.

Edger, C. 2012. *Effective Multi-Unit Leadership: Local Leadership in Multi-Site Situations*. Aldershot: Gower.

Edstrom, A. and Galbraith, J.R. 1977. 'Transfer of managers as a coordination and control strategy in multinational corporations'. *Administrative Science Quarterly* 22, 248–63.

Edwards, T. and Kuruvilla, S. 2005. 'International HRM: National Business Systems, Organisational Politics and the International Division of Labour in MNCs'. *International Journal of Human Resource Management* 16(1), 1–21.

Egelhoff, W.G. 1984. 'Patterns of control in US, UK, and European multinational corporations'. *Journal of International Business Studies* 15, 73–83.

Eisenhardt, K. 1985. 'Control: Organizational and economic approaches'. *Management Science* 31, 134–49.

———. 1989. 'Building Theories from Case Study Research'. *Academy of Management Review* 14(4), 532–50.

Ericsson, K.A. 2000. *Expert Performance and Deliberate Practice*. Available at http://www.psy.fsu.edu/faculty/ericsson/ericsson.exp.perf.html [accessed 21 June 2011].

Etgar, M. and Rachman-Moore, D. 2008. 'International expansion and retail sales: an empirical study'. *International Journal of Retail and Distribution Management* 36(4), 241–59.

Etzioni, A. 1980. 'Compliance Structures'. In *A Sociological Reader on Complex Organizations* (3rd edn), eds A. Etzioni and E. Lehmon. New York: Rinehart and Winston, 87–100.

Evans, J., Bridson, K., Byrom, J. and Medway, D. 2008. 'Revisiting retail internationalisation'. *International Journal of Retail and Distribution Management* 36(4), 260–80.

Evans, J., Treadgold, A. and Mavondo, F. 2000. 'Psychic distance and the performance of international retailers'. *International Marketing Review* 17(4/5), 373–91.

Ezzamel, M. and Willmott, H. 1998. 'Accounting for teamwork: A critical study of group-based systems of organizational control'. *Administrative Science Quarterly* 43(2), 358.

Faulkener, D., Pitkethky, R. and Child, J. 2002. 'International Mergers and Acquisitions in the UK 1985–94: A Comparison of National HRM Practices'. *International Journal of HRM* 13(1), 106–22.

Fayol, H. 1916. 'Administration industrielle et generale'. *Bulletin de la Societe de l'Industrie Minerale* 10, 5–164.

Felsted, A. 2012. 'Food Retailing Analysis – All Lined Up'. *Financial Times*, 6 January, 9.

Ferner, A. 1997. 'Country-of-Origin Effect and HRM in Multinational Companies'. *Human Resource Management Journal* 7(1), 19–37.

———. 2003. 'Foreign Multinationals and Industrial Relations in Britain'. In *Industrial Relations*, ed. P. Edwards. Oxford: Blackwell.

Ferner, A., Almond, P. and Colling, T. 2005. 'Institutional Theory and the Cross-National Transfer of Employment Policy: The Case of Workforce Diversity in US Multinationals'. *Journal of International Business Studies* 36, 304–21.

Ferner, A. and Edwards, P. 1995. 'Power and the Diffusion of Organisational Change within Multinational Enterprises'. *European Journal of Industrial Relations* 1(2), 229–57.

Fiedler, F.E. 1967. *A Theory of Leadership Effectiveness*. New York: McGraw-Hill.

Fineman, S. and Sturdy, A. 1999. 'The emotions of control: A qualitative exploration of environmental regulation'. *Human Relations* 52(5), 631–63.

Fitzsimmons, J.A. and Fitzsimmons, M.J. 2006. *Service Management* (5th edn). New York: McGraw-Hill.

Florkowski, G. and Schuler, R. 1994. 'Auditing Human Resource Management in the Global Environment'. *International Journal of Human Resource Management* 5(4), 143–62.

Foa, U.G. and Foa, E.B. 1980. 'Resource theory: Interpersonal behavior as exchange'. In *Social exchange: Advances in theory and research*, eds K. Gergen, M. Greenberg and R. Willis. NY: Plenum.

Forsgren, M. 1990. 'Managing the International Multi-Centre Firm'. *European Management Journal* 8(2), 261–77.

French, R. 2010. *Cross-Cultural Management in Work Organisations* (2nd edn). London: CIPD.

FT Analysis. 2012a. 'The Family Fortunes of Beijing's New Few'. *Financial Times*, 11 July, 10.

———. 2012b. 'IKEA: Against the Grain'. *Financial Times*, 14 November, 11.

Furrer, O., Liu, B. and Sudharshan, D. 2000. 'The relationships between culture and service quality perceptions: Basis for cross-cultural market segmentation and resource allocation'. *Journal of Service Research* 2(4), 355–71.

Garvin, D.A. and Levesque, L.C. 2008. 'The Multi-Unit Enterprise'. *Harvard Business Review* June, 1–11.

Gelfand, M., Nishii, L. and Raver, J. 2006. 'On the nature and importance of cultural tightness-looseness'. *Journal of Applied Psychology* 91(6), 1225–44.

Gielens, K. and Dekimpe, M. 2001. 'Do international entry decisions of retail chains matter in the long run?' *International Journal of Research in Marketing* 18, 235–59.

Gladwell, M. 2008. *Outliers: The Story of Success*. New York: Little, Brown and Co.

Goh, S. 2002. 'Managing effective knowledge transfer: an integrative framework and some practice implications'. *Journal of Knowledge Management* 6(1), 23–30.

Goldman, A.I. 1999. *Knowledge in a Social World*. Oxford: Oxford University Press.

Goleman, D. 1996. *Emotional Intelligence*. New York: Bloomsbury.

———. 1998. *Working with Emotional Intelligence*. New York: Bantam Books.

Green, S.G. and Welsh, M.A. 1988. 'Cybernetics and dependence: Reframing the control concept'. *Academy of Management Journal* 13(2), 287.

GSAM (Goldman Sachs Asset Management). 2012. *The Rise of Growth Markets*. Available at http://www.goldmansachs.com/our-thinking/focus-on/growth-markets/dataviz/index.html [accessed 20 June 2012].

Gupta, A.K. and Govindarajan, V. 1991. 'Knowledge flows and the structure of control within multinational corporations'. *Academy of Management Review* 16(4), 768–92.

———. 2000. 'Knowledge flows within multinational corporations'. *Strategic Management Journal* 21(7), 473–96.

———. 2002. 'Cultivating a global mindset'. *The Academy of Management Executive* 16(1), 116–26.

Haidt, J. and Graham, J. 2007. 'When Morality Opposes Justice'. *Social Justice Research* 20(1), 98–116.

Haleblian, J. and Finkelstein, S. 1999. 'The Influence of Organizational Acquisition Experience on Acquisition Performance: A Behavioural Learning Perspective'. *Administrative Science Quarterly* 44, 29–56.

Hall, E. 1976. *Beyond Culture*. New York: Anchor Press/Doubleday.

Hall, P. and Soskice, D. (eds). 2001. *Varieties of Capitalism: The Institutional Foundations of Comparative Advantage*. Oxford: Oxford University Press.

Hamilton, R. and Kashlak, R. 1999. 'National influences on multinational corporation control system selection'. *International Management Review* 39(2), 167–89.

Harrison, G. and McKinnon, J. 1999. 'Cross-cultural research in management control systems design: A review of the current state'. *Accounting, Organizations and Society* 24, 483–506.

Harrison, R. 1972. 'How to Describe Your Organization's Culture'. *Harvard Business Review* May–June, 119–28.

Harry, W. 2007. 'Employment creation and localization: the crucial human resource issue for the GCC'. *International Journal of Human Resource Management*, 18(1), 132–46.

Harzing, A. 1999. *Managing the Multinationals – An International Study of Control Mechanisms*. Cheltenham: Edward Elgar.

Harzing, A. and Sorge, A. 2003. 'The relative impact of country of origin and universal contingencies in internationalization strategies and corporate control in multinational enterprises: Worldwide and European perspectives'. *Organization Studies* 24(2), 187.

Hatfield, E., Capioppo, J. and Rapson, R. 1994. *Emotional Contagion*. Cambridge, UK: Cambridge University Press.

Hawkes, S. 2013. 'Supermarket Giants Rue Lost Decade of Investment'. *Daily Telegraph*, 11 August, B1.

Helfat, C., Finkelstein, S., Mitchell, W., Peteraf, M., Singh, H., Teece, D. and Winter, S. 2007. *Dynamic Capabilities: Understanding Change in Organizations*. Oxford: Blackwell.

Hemphill, J.K. 1950. 'Relations between the size of the group and the behavior of "superior" leaders'. *The Journal of Social Psychology* 32, 11–22.

Hendry, J. 1999. 'Cultural theory and contemporary management organization'. *Human Relations* 52(5), 557–77.

Hersey, P. and Blanchard, K.H. 1993. *Management of Organizational Behavior: Utilizing Human Resources* (6th edn). New York: Prentice-Hall.

Hille, K. 2012. 'Wang takes responsibility for stopping rot in public office'. *Financial Times*, 12 December, 4.

Hirokawa, R. and Miyahara, A. 1986. 'A comparison of influence strategies utilized by managers in American and Japanese organizations'. *Communication Quarterly* 34(3), 250–65.

Hochschild, A. 1983. *The Managed Heart: Commercialization of Human Feeling*. Berkeley, CA: University of California.

Hocking, J.B., Brown, M. and Harzing, A. 2004. 'A knowledge transfer perspective of strategic assignment purposes and their path-dependent outcomes'. *International Journal of Human Resource Management* 15(3), 565–86.

Hofstede, G. 1978. 'The poverty of management control philosophy'. *Academy of Management Review* 3(3), 450–61.

———. 1980. *Culture's Consequences: International Differences in Work-Related Values*. Beverley Hills, CA: Sage.

———. 1991. *Cultures and Organisations*. London: McGraw Hill.

———. 1993. 'Cultural Constraints in Management Theories'. *Academy of Management Executive* 7(1), 81–93.

Hofstede, G., Hofstede, G.J. and Minkov, M. 2010. *Cultures and Organisations* (3rd edn). New York: McGraw-Hill.

Hough, J. 1986. *Power and authority and their consequences in franchise organisations: a study of the relationship between franchisors and their franchisees*. Unpublished PhD thesis, Polytechnic of Central London.

House, R.J. 1971. 'A Path-Goal Theory of Leadership Effectiveness'. *Administrative Science Quarterly* 16, 321–38.

House, R., Hanges, P., Javidan, M., Dorfman, P. and Gupta, V. 2004. *Culture, Leadership and Organization: The GLOBE Study of 62 Societies*. Thousand Oaks, CA: Sage.

Hume, M. 2011. 'The Secrets of Zara's Success'. *Daily Telegraph*, 22 June, 23.

Huselid, M. 1995. 'The Impact of HRM Policies on Turnover, Productivity and Corporate Financial Performance'. *Academy of Management Journal* 38, 635–72.

Inglehart, R. and Welzel, C. 2005. *Modernization, Cultural Change and Democracy*. Cambridge: Cambridge University Press.

Inglehart, R., Basanez, M., Catterburg, G., Diez-Medrano, J., Moreno, A., Norris, P., Siemienska, R. and Zuasnabar, I. 2010. *Changing Human Beliefs and Values: A cross-cultural sourcebook based on the world values surveys and European values studies*. Mexico: siglo xxi editores.

Jacoby, S. 1997. *Modern Manors: Welfare Capitalism Since the New Deal*. Princeton: Princeton University Press.

Jaeger, A. 1983. 'The transfer of organizational culture overseas: An approach to control in the multinational corporation'. *Journal of International Business Studies* 14(2), 91–114.

Janis, I. 1972. *Victims of Groupthink*. Boston: Houghton Mifflin.

Janson, J., Simsek, Z. and Cao, Q. 2012. 'Ambidexterity and Performance in Multi-Unit Contexts: Cross-level Moderating Effects of Structural and Resource Attributes'. Strategic Management Journal 33: 1286–1303.

Johnson, M. and Felsted, A. 2011. 'Inditex Keeps its Finger on the Pulse'. *Financial Times*, 23 May, 13.

Johnston, R. 2001. *Service Excellence = Reputation = Profit*. Colchester: Institute of Customer Service.

Johnston, R. and Clark, G. 2008. *Services Operations Management – Improving Service Delivery*. London: Pearson.

Jones, P. and Inkinci, Y. 2001. *An analysis of multi-unit management in UK restaurant chains*. Proceedings from the 2001 CAUTHE National Research Conference, Queensland, Australia: Council for Australian University Tourism & Hospitality Education.

Jones, S. 2012. *BRICS and Beyond: Executive Lessons on Emerging Markets*. Chichester: John Wiley.

Jonsson, A. and Elg, U. 2006. 'Knowledge and knowledge-sharing in retail internationalisation: IKEA's entry into Russia'. *International Review of Retail, Distribution and Consumer Research* 16(2), 239–56.

Judge, T.A., Bono, J.E., Ilies, R. and Gerhardt, M.W. 2002. 'Personality and leadership: A qualitative and quantitative review'. *Journal of Applied Psychology* 87(4), 765–80.

Kavanagh, M. and Ashkanasy, N. 2006. 'The Impact of Leadership and Change Management Strategy on Organizational Culture and Individual Acceptance of Change during a Merger'. *British Journal of Management* 17, 83–105.

Kazmin, A. 2012. 'McDonald's Offers India's Pilgrims Vegetarian Outlets'. *Financial Times*, 5 September, 16.

Keely, G. 2012. 'How 50 ideas a day can keep the Customer satisfied'. *The Times*, 14 April, 48.

Kerin, R.A. and Varadarajan, P.R. 1992. 'First-mover advantage: a synthesis, conceptual framework, and research propositions'. *The Journal of Marketing* 56, 33–52.

Kim, W. and Mauborgne, R. 2000. 'Making Global Strategies Work'. In *Transnational Management: Text, Cases and Readings in Cross Border Management*, eds C. Bartlett and S. Ghoshal. New York: McGraw-Hill International.

Kirkpatrick, S.A. and Locke, E.A. 1991. 'Leadership: Do Traits Really Matter?' *Academy of Management Executive* May, 48–60.

Kluckhohn, F. and Strodtbeck, F. 1961. *Variations in Value Orientations*. New York: Peterson.

Kobrin, S.J. 1988. 'Expatriate reduction and strategic control in American multinational companies'. *Human Resources Management* 27, 63–75.

Kolb, D. 1984. *Experimental Learning: Experience as the Source of Learning and Development*. London: Prentice Hall.

Konrad, A.M., Kashlak, R., Yoshioka, I., Waryszak, R. and Toren, N. 2001. 'What do managers like to do?' *Group and Organization Management* 26(4), 401–33.

Kotter, J. and Heskett, J. 1992. *Corporate Culture and Performance*. New York: The Free Press.

Kotter, J.P. and Cohen, D.S. 2002. *The Heart of Change*. Boston, MA: Harvard Business School Press.

Kottler, P. 2000. *Marketing Management* (10th edn). New York: Prentice-Hall.

Kreder, M. and Zeller, M. 1988. 'Control in German and U.S. Companies'. *Management International Review* June, 58–66.

Kristensen, P. and Zeitlin, J. 2001. 'The Making of a Global Firm: Local Pathways to Multinational Enterprise'. In *The Multinational Firm: Organising Across Institutional and National Divides*, eds G. Morgan, P. Kristensen, and R. Whitley. Oxford: OUP, 163–81.

Lane, H., Maznevski, M., DiStefano, J. and Dietz, J. 2009. *International Management Behaviour: Leading with a Global Mindset* (6th edn). Chichester: John Wiley.

Lashley, C. 1997. *Empowering Service Excellence: Beyond the Quick Fix*. London: Cassell.

———. 1999. 'Employee empowerment in services: a framework for analysis'. *Personnel Review* 28(3), 169–91.

Laurent, A. 1986. 'The cross-cultural puzzle of international human resource management'. *Human Resource Management*, 25(1) 91–102.

Leahy, J. 2012. 'Brazil Capital Markets: First Signs of Return to Growth'. *Financial Times*, 3 October, 2.

Leahy, T. 2012. *Management in 10 Words*. London: Random House.

Legge, K. 2005. *Human Resource Management: Rhetorics and Realities* (Anniversary edn). Basingstoke: Palgrave Macmillan.

Lewin, K. 1951. *Field Theory in Social Science*. New York: Harper and Row.

Lovelock, C. and Yip, G. 1996. 'Developing global strategies for service businesses'. *California Management Review* 38(2), 64–86.

Lubatkin, M., Schweiger, D. and Weber, Y. 1999. 'Top Management Turnover in Related M&As: An Additional Test of the Theory of Relative Standing'. *Journal of Management* 25(1), 55–73.

Lukes, S. 1975. *Power: A Radical View*. London and Basingstoke: Macmillan.

Mahajan, A. 2009. *Importance of Host Country Nationals in International Management: Looking at the other side of the coin*. PhD dissertation, New Mexico State University. Ann Arbor, MI: UMI Dissertations Publishing.

Mallaby, S. 2013. 'Africa hooked on growth after 12 years of progress'. *Financial Times*, 2 (January) – 9.

Marr, J. and Reynard, C. 2010. *Investing in Emerging Markets*. Chichester: John Wiley.

Martenson, R. 1987. 'Is standardisation of marketing feasible in culture-bound industries? A European case study'. *International Marketing Review* 4 (Autumn), 7–17.

Martinez, Z. and Ricks, D. 1991. 'Multinational Parent Companies' Influence Over Human Resource Decisions of Affiliates: US Firms in Mexico'. *Journal of International Business Studies* 20(3), 465–88.

Massey, M. 2005. *What You Are is Where You Were When!* Cambridge, MA: Enterprise.

Mathias, P. 1967. *Retailing Revolution: A History of Multiple Retailing in the Food Trades Based upon the Allied Suppliers Group of Companies*. London: Europa Publications.

Mayer, J.D., Salovey, P., Caruso, D.R. and Sitarenios, G. 2001. 'Emotional Intelligence as Standard Intelligence'. *Emotion* 1, 232–42.

———. 2003. 'Measuring Emotional Intelligence with the MSCEIT V2.0 Edition'. *Emotion* 3, 97–105.

Mead, R. and Andrews, T. 2009. *International Management* (4th edn). Chichester: John Wiley.

Menon, T. and Pfeffer, J. 2003. 'Valuing Internal versus External Knowledge'. *Management Science* 49(4), 497–513.

Meyer, J. and Rowan, B. 1977. 'Institutionalized Organisations: Formal Structure as Myth and Ceremony'. *American Journal of Sociology* 83, 340–63.

Miles, M. and Huberman, A. 1994. *Qualitative Data Analysis*. Thousand Oaks, CA: Sage.

Minbaeva, D., Pederson, T., Bjorkman, I., Fry, C. and Park, H. 2003. 'MNC knowledge transfer, subsidiary absorptive capacity, and HRM'. *Journal of International Business Studies* 34, 586–99.

Mintzberg, H. 2009. *Managing*. London: Pearson.

Mone, M.A. and Umbreit, W.T. 1989. 'Making the transition from single-unit to multi-unit fast-service management: what are the requisite skills and educational needs?' *Journal of Hospitality and Tourism Research* 13(3), 319–31.

Moore, C.M., Birtwistle, G. and Hurt, S. 2004. 'Channel power, conflict and conflict resolution in international fashion retailing'. *European Journal of Marketing* 38(7), 749–69.

Morarjee, R. 2012. 'Eastern Premise: Is Learning Through Doing The Best Way To Navigate Business In Russia'. *FT Business Education Report, Financial Times*, 20 October, 37–9.

Morgan, G., Kelly, B., Sharpe, D. and Whitley, R. 2003. 'Global Managers and Japanese Multinationals: Internationalisation and Management in Japanese Financial Institutions'. *International Journal of Human Resource Management* 14(3), 389–407.

Muller, C.C. and Campbell, D.F. 1995. 'The attributes and attitudes of multi-unit managers in a national quick-service restaurant firm'. *Journal of Hospitality and Tourism Research* 19(2), 3–18.

Muller, M., 1998. 'Human Resources and Industrial Relations Practices of UK and US Multinationals in Germany'. *International Journal of HRM* 9(4), 732–49.

Muniz-Martinez, N. 1998. 'The internationalisation of European retailers in America: the US experience'. *International Journal of Retail and Distribution Management* 26(1), 29–37.

Nelson, R. and Winter, S. 1982. *An Evolutionary Theory of Economic Change*. Cambridge, MA: Harvard University Press.

Newman, K. and Nollen, S. 1996. 'Culture and Congruence: The Fit Between Management Practices and National Culture'. *Journal of International Business Studies* 27(4), 753–78.

Nonaka, I. and Konno, N. 1998. 'The Concept of Ba: Building a foundation for knowledge creation'. *California Management Review* 40(3), 40–54.

Nonaka, I. and Takeuchi, H. 1995. *The Knowledge Creating Company*. New York: Oxford University Press.

———. 2011. 'The Wise Leader'. *Harvard Business Review* May, 58–67.

Nonaka, I., Toyama, R. and Konno, N. 2000. 'SECI, Ba and Leadership: A Unifying Model of Dynamic Knowledge Creation'. In *New Perspectives on Knowledge-Based Firm and Organization*, eds D. Teece and I. Nonaka. New York: Oxford University Press.

Oliver, C. 1991. 'Strategic Responses to Institutional Processes'. *Academy of Management Review* 16(1), 145–79.

Olsen, M.D., Tse, E.C. and West, J.J. 1992. *Strategic Management in the Hospitality Industry*. NY: Van Nostrand Reinhold.

O'Neill, J. 2011. *The Growth Map*. London: Portfolio Penguin.

O'Reilly, C., Chatman, J. and Caldwell, D. 1991. 'People and Organisational Culture: A Profile Comparison Approach to Assessing Person-Organisation Fit'. *Academy of Management Journal* September, 487–516.

O'Reilly, C. and Tushman, M. 2004. 'The Ambidextrous Organisation', *Harvard Business Review* April, 74–81.

Ortiz, L. 1998. 'Union Response to Teamwork: Differences at National and Workplace Level'. *Industrial Relations Journal* 29(1), 42–57.

Ouchi, W. 1977. 'The relationship between organizational structure and organizational control'. *Administrative Science Quarterly* 22(1), 95.

———. 1978. 'The transmission of control through organizational hierarchy'. *Academy of Management Journal* 21(2), 173.

———. 1979. 'A conceptual framework for the design of organizational control mechanisms'. *Management Science* 25(9), 833.

———. 1980. 'Markets, Bureaucracies and Clans'. *Administrative Science Quarterly* March, 129–41.

———. 1981. *Theory Z: How American Business Can Meet the Japanese Challenge*. Reading, MA: Addison-Wesley.

Ouchi, W. and Jaeger, A. 1978. 'Type Z Organization: Stability in the Midst of Mobility'. *Academy of Management Review* April, 305–14.

Patel, C. 2003. 'Some cross-cultural evidence on whistle-blowing as an internal control mechanism'. *Journal of International Accounting Research* 2, 69–96.

Pelle, S. 2007. *Understanding Emerging Markets*. Thousand Oaks, CA: Sage.

Perlmutter, H. 1969. 'The Tortuous Evolution of the Multinational Firm'. *Columbia Journal World of Business* January, 9–18.

Peters, T. and Waterman, R. 1992. *In Search of Excellence: Lessons from America's Best-Run Companies*. New York: Harper & Row.

Pfeffer, J. 1998. *The Human Equation: Building Profits by Putting People First*. Boston, MA: Harvard Business School Press.

Pfeffer, J. and Cohen, Y. 1984. 'Determinants of Internal Labor Markets in Organizations'. *Administrative Science Quarterly* 29, 550–72.

Pfeffer, J. and Fong, C.T. 2005. 'Building organization theory from first principles: The self-enhancement motive and understanding power and influence'. *Organization Science* 16, 372–88.

Pfeffer, J. and Salancik, G. 1978. *The External Control of Organizations: a Resource Dependence Perspective.* New York: Harper and Row.

Phatak, A.V. 1997. *International management: Concepts and cases.* Cincinnati: Southwestern Publishing Co.

Polanyi, M. 1957. *The Tacit Dimension.* New York: Doubleday.

———. 1962. *Personal Knowledge.* New York: Harper.

Pooripakdee, S. 2003. *The effect of the type of control used by American and Japanese firms on the effectiveness of their subsidiaries in Thailand.* Proceedings of the 4th International Conference on Co-operation and Competition, Vaxjo, Sweden.

Posner, B.Z. and Butterfield, D.A. 1979. 'Personal correlates of organizational control'. *Journal of Psychology* 102(2), 299–306.

Powell, W. and DiMaggio, P. (eds). 1991. *The New Institutionalism in Organisational Analysis.* Chicago: University of Chicago Press.

Quelch, J. and Jocz, K. 2012. *All Business is Local: Why Place Matters More than Ever in a Global, Virtual World.* London: Portfolio Penguin.

Quinn, B. 1999. 'The temporal context of UK retailers' motives for international expansion'. *The Services Industry Journal* 19, 101–16.

Quinn, B. and Doherty, A. 2000. 'Power and control in international retail franchising – evidence from theory and practice'. *International Marketing Review* 17(4/5), 354–72.

Reichheld, F. and Markey, R. 2011. *The Ultimate Question 2.0: How Net Promoter Companies Thrive in a Customer Driven World.* Boston, MA: HBR Press.

Reynolds, D. 2000. 'An exploratory investigation into behaviorally based success characteristics of foodservice managers'. *Journal of Hospitality and Tourism Research* 24(1), 92–103.

Ritzer, G. 1993. *The McDonaldization of Society.* Thousand Oaks, CA: Sage.

Rivera, M., Di Pietro, R.B., Murphy, K.S and Muller, C.C. 2008. 'Multi-unit managers: training needs and competencies for casual dining restaurants'. *International Journal of Contemporary Hospitality Management* 20(6), 616–30.

Robertson, D. 2012. 'Bosses still offered bribes in Indonesia'. *The Times,* 19 December, 40.

Rugman, A.M. 1981. *Inside the Multinationals: The economics of internal markets.* New York: Columbia Press.

Rugman, A.M. and Hodgetts, R.M. 2003. *International Business.* London: Pearson.

Ryan, W.E. 1992. *Identification and comparison of management skills required for single and multi-unit management in independently operated college and university food services.* Unpublished PhD dissertation, Oklahoma State University, Stillwater.

Salmon, W.J. and Tordjman, A. 1989. 'The Internationalisation of retailing'. *International Journal of Retailing* 4(2), 3–16.

Sandberg, J. 2000. 'Understanding human competence at work: An interpretative approach'. *Academy of Management Journal* 43(1), 9–25.

Scarborough, J. 1998. 'Comparing Chinese and Western cultural roots: why "east is east" and ...' *Business Horizons* November–December, 15–24.

Schaffer, A. and Hyuk, J. 2005. 'Consider Cost and Strategy when Choosing between Expatriate and Host-National Managers'. *Journal of Business and Management* 11(1), 59–71.

Schein, E. 1985. *Organizational Culture and Leadership: A Dynamic Review.* San Francisco: Jossey-Bass.

Schneider, S. and Barsoux, J.-L. 2003. *Managing Across Cultures*. London: FT Prentice Hall.

Schuler, R., Jackson, S. and Luo, Y. 2004. *Managing Human Resources in Cross-Border Alliances*. London: Routledge.

Schwartz, I. 2007. 'Manage Your Energy, Not Your Time'. *Harvard Business Review* October, 63–73.

Schwartz, S. 1994. 'Are there universal aspects of the structure and contents of human values?' *Journal of Social Issues* 50(4), 19–45.

———. 1999. 'A theory of cultural values and some implications for work'. *Applied Psychology: An International Review* 48(1), 23–47.

Schweiger, D. 2002. *M&A Integration: A Framework for Executives and Managers*. New York: McGraw-Hill.

Schyns, B. 2013. 'The Role of Distance in Leader-Member Exchange'. In *Exploring Distance in Leader-Follower Relationships: When Near is Far and Far is Near*, eds M. Bligh and R. Riggio. New York: Routledge, 136–54.

Scott, W. 1995. *Institutions and Organisations*. Thousand Oaks, CA: Sage.

Scullion, H. 2005. 'International HRM: an Introduction'. In *International Human Resource Management: A critical text*, eds H. Scullion and M. Linehan. Basingstoke: Palgrave Macmillan, 3–21.

Senge, P. 2005. *The Fifth Discipline: The Art and Practice of the Learning Organisation*. London: Random House.

Sewell, G. 1998. 'The discipline of teams: The control of team-based industrial work through electronic and peer surveillance'. *Administrative Science Quarterly* 43(2), 397.

Sharma, R. 2012. *Breakout Nations: In Pursuit of the Next Economic Miracles*. New York: W.W. Norton.

Simon, H.A. 1969. *The Sciences of the Artificial*. Cambridge, MA: MIT Press.

Skinner, B.F. 1976. *About Behaviorism*. New York: Vintage Bodis.

Slack, N., Chambers, S., Johnston, R. and Betts, A. 2009. *Operations and Process Management – Principles and Practice for Strategic Intent*. London: Pearson.

Smith, C. and Meiksins, P. 1995. 'Systems, Society and Dominance in Cross-National Organisational Analysis'. *Work, Employment and Society* 9(2), 241–67.

Snow, C., Canney Davidson, S., Hambrick, D. and Snell, S. 1993. 'Transnational Teams – A Learning Resource Guide'. *Transnational Teams Resources Guide*, ICEDR Report.

Sohn, J. 1994. 'Social knowledge as a control system: A proposition and evidence from the Japanese FDI behavior'. *Journal of International Business Studies* 25(2), 295–324.

Sorrell, M. 2012. 'Amid the Gloom There Are Some Bright Sparks'. *The Sunday Telegraph*, 9 December, B4.

Sparrow, P. and Hiltrop, J. 1997. 'Redefining the field of European human resource management: a battle between national mindsets and the forces of business transition'. *Human Resource Management* 36(2), 1–19.

Streeck, W. 1992. *Social Institutions and Economic Performance: Studies of Industrial Relations in Advanced Capitalist Economies*. London: Sage.

Tannenbaum, A.S. 1968. *Control in Organizations*. New York: McGraw-Hill.

Tannenbaum, A.S., Kavcic, B., Rosner, M. and Vianello, M. 1974. *Hierarchy in organizations*. San Francisco: Jossey-Bass.

Tayeb, M. 1988. *Organizations and National Culture*. London: Sage.

Taylor, F.A. 1916. *The Principles of Scientific Management*. New York: Harper.

Taylor, S., Beechloer, S. and Napier, N. 1996. 'Toward an Integrative Model of Strategic International Human Resource Management'. *Academy of Management Review* 21(4), 959–85.

Tharenou, P. and Harvey, M. 2006. 'Examining the overseas staffing options utilized by Australian headquartered multi-national corporations'. *The International Journal of Human Resource Management* 17(6), 1095–114.

Thomas, N. 'The Asian Tiger Battle'. *The Sunday Telegraph*, 9 December, B6.

Tichy, N.M. and Bennis, W.G. 2007. 'Making Judgement Calls'. *Harvard Business Review* October, 94–102.

Toh, S.M. and DeNisi, A.S. 2003. 'Host country national reactions to expatriate pay policies: a model and implications'. *Academy of Management Review* 28(4), 606–21.

Tolich, M., Kenney, M. and Biggart, N. 1999. 'Managing the managers: Japanese management strategies in the US'. *Journal of Management Studies* 36(5), 587–607.

Treadgold, A. 1991. 'Dixons and Laura Ashley: different routes to international growth'. *International Journal of Retail and Distribution Management* 19(4), 13–19.

Treasurer, B. and Shriver, L. 2011. *Courageous Leadership: A Program for Using Courage to Transform the Workplace*. San Francisco, CA: Pfeiffer.

Trompenaars, F. 1993. *Riding the Waves of Culture*. London: Nicholas Brearley.

Tung, R. 2008. 'The cross cultural research imperative: the need to balance cross-national and intra-national diversity'. *Journal of International Business Studies* 39(1), 41–6.

Tung, R. and Lazarova, M. 2006. 'Brain drain versus brain gain: an exploratory study of ex-host country nationals in Central and Eastern Europe'. *International Journal of Human Resource Management* 17(11), 1853–72.

Ueno, S. and Sekaran, U. 1992. 'The influence of culture on budget control practices in the USA and Japan: An empirical study'. *Journal of International Business Studies* 23(4), 659–74.

Umbreit, W.T. 1989. 'Multi-unit management: managing at a distance'. *Cornell Hotel and Restaurant Administration Quarterly* 30(1), 52–9.

Umbreit, W.T. and Smith, D.I. 1991. 'A study of the opinions and practices of successful multi-unit fast service restaurant managers'. *The Hospitality Research Journal* 14, 451–8.

Vahlne, J.-E. and Wiedersheim-Paul, F. 1973. 'Economic distance: model and empirical investigation'. In *Export and Foreign Establishments*, eds E. Hornell, J.-E. Vahlne and F. Wiedersheim-Paul. Uppsala: Almqvist & Wiksell, 81–159.

Van Looy, B., Gemmel, P. and Van Dierdonck, R. 2003. *Services Management: An Integrated Approach*. London: Prentice Hall.

Vance, C. and Paik, Y. 2005. 'Forms of host-country learning for enhanced MNC absorptive capacity'. *Journal of Managerial Psychology* 20(7), 590–606.

Very, P., Lubatkin, M., Calori, R. and Veiga, J. 1997. 'Relative Standing and the Performance of Recently Acquired European Firms'. *Strategic Management Journal* 18(8), 593–614.

Vida, I., Reardon, J. and Fairhurst, A. 2000. 'Determinants of international retail involvement: The case of large U.S. retail chains'. *Journal of International Marketing* 8(4), 37–60.

Volberda, H., Baden-Fuller, C. and van den Bosch, F. 2001. 'Mastering Strategic Renewal: Mobilising Renewal Journeys in Multi-Unit Firms'. *Long Range Planning* 34, 159–78.

Volkmar, J. 2003. 'Context and Control in Foreign Subsidiaries: Making a Case for the Host Country National Manager'. *Journal of Leadership and Organisational Studies* 10(1), 93–105.

Vroom, V.H. and Yetton, P.W. 1973. *Leadership and Decision-Making*. Pittsburgh: University of Pittsburgh Press.

Waldmeir, P. 'School of Etiquette Plots New Cultural Revolution'. *Financial Times*, 23 December, 5.

Wallop, H. 2012. 'Kingfisher CEO Ian Cheshire Reveals His Plans To Turn The Company Into A Global Retailer'. *The Sunday Telegraph*, 16 October, B9.

Wallop, H. and Ruddick, G. 2012. 'End of the Race for Space'. *Sunday Telegraph*, 29 January, B7.

Walsh, D. 2012. 'Starbucks Fires Two Shots in Coffee Bar Wars'. *The Times*, 2 March, 51.

Warner, M. 2000. 'The Asia-Pacific HRM Model Revisited'. *International Journal of HRM* 11(2), 171–82.

Weber, Y. and Schweiger, D. 1992. 'Top Manager Culture Conflict in Mergers and Acquisitions: A Lesson from Anthropology'. *International Journal of Conflict Management* 3(4), 1–17.

Weinstein, M. and Kochan, T. 1995. 'The Limits of Diffusion: Recent Developments in Industrial Relations and Human Resource Practices in the United States'. In *Employment Relations In a Changing World Economy*, eds R. Locke, T. Kochan and M. Piore. Cambridge, MA: MIT Press.

Welzel, C., Inglehart, R. and Klingemann, H. 2003. 'The Theory of Human Development: A Cross-Cultural Analysis'. *European Journal of Political Research* 42(3), 341–79.

White, A. 1995. *Cross-border Retailing: Leaders, Losers and Prospects*. London: Pearson Professional.

Whitley, R. 1999. *Divergent Capitalisms: The Social Structuring and Change of Business Systems*. Oxford: Oxford University Press.

Wigley, S. and Moore, C. 2007. 'The operationalization of international fashion retailer success'. *Journal of Fashion Marketing and Management* 11(2), 281–96.

Wild, J. 2012. 'Chinese Brand Seeks to Cash In on London Fashion Image'. *Financial Times*, 13 October, 2.

Winter, S. 1987. 'Knowledge and Competence as Strategic Assets', in *The Competitive Challenge*, ed. D. Teece. Cambridge, MA: Ballinger.

Worm, V. 2001. 'HRD for localisation: European MNCs in China'. In *Advances in HRM in Asia*, eds J. Kidd and F. Richter. Basingstoke: Palgrave.

Wright, P. and McMahan, G. 1992. 'Theoretical Perspectives for Strategic Human Resource Management'. *Journal of Management* 18(2), 295–320.

YahooFinance. 2012. 'Tata Chief lashes out at "venal" Indian business climate'. *Yahoo Finance*. Available from http://uk.finance.yahoo.com [accessed 7 December 2012].

Yukl, G. and Tracey, J.B. 1992. 'Consequences of influence tactics used with subordinates, peers, and the boss'. *Journal of Applied Psychology* 77, 525–35.

Yukl, G., Fu, P.P. and McDonald, R. 2003. 'Cross-cultural differences in perceived effectiveness of influence tactics for initiating or resisting change'. *Applied Psychology: An International Review* 52(1), 68–82.

Zucker, L. 1977. 'The Role of Institutionalization in Cultural Persistence'. *American Sociology Review* 42, 726–43.

Index

Page numbers in *italics* indicate figures.